Endorsements

This book is full of practical financial and life advice, for defining and achieving happiness and success. Concise and clearly written, it makes financial concepts understandable. Travis puts a twist on what readers think they already understand. As an Executive Coach, I consider myself financially literate, yet I found his approach challenging me to reassess some of my financial beliefs. For example, his discussion of mortgage down payments, illuminates the important difference between the amortization of a mortgage, versus the compounding, over time, of an investment. That is just one of his nuggets of financial wisdom. I will recommend this book to my young adult daughters, and also to executives and entrepreneurs I coach.

          – Dr. Mark Cook, PhD, Solution Focused Consultants LLC

The Fortune of Youth is a welcome addition to the tools needed for financial literacy. The book is easy to use, at any stage of life. It provides guidance and example situations that arise for everyone. From finding the first job, to estate planning and conclusion of life, everyone can find a chapter that describes the current situation and problem. That chapter has new or forgotten resources of help to maintain the wealth earned over time. It will become a reference resource for wealth planning.

          – Dr. James R. Scott, PhD

Travis speaks the language of finance that even I can understand. In his book you will discover the endless struggle for financial independence IS ATTAINABLE. Travis has a writing style that easily explains complex financial issues. This is one of the best financial books I've read and I'm confident it will help countless people.

          – Tim Hobart, CEO – H&H Health Associates

The Fortune of Youth is a confluence of thoughtfulness and actionable guidance for folks who are in the early innings of their financial lives to established career men and women who may want to understand their finances better.

Travis clearly enjoys using his own personal, financial, and professional life experiences, in creating an easy-to-understand, yet powerful guide that, I am sure readers will have more than a few "aha" moments when reading this book."

          – Christopher Beste, CFP®

THE
Fortune
OF
youth

Create Wealth, Happiness,
and Success Early in Life

Travis W. Freeman, CFP®

The Fortune of Youth
Create Wealth, Happiness, and Success Early in Life
Travis W. Freeman, CFP®
PlanWell Publishing

Published by PlanWell Publishing St. Louis, MO
Copyright ©2024 Travis W. Freeman, CFP®
All rights reserved.

Editor: Kyle Veltrop

Cover and Interior design: Davis Creative Publishing

Library of Congress Cataloging-in-Publication Data

(Provided by Cassidy Cataloguing Services, Inc.).

Names: Freeman, Travis W., author.

Title: The fortune of youth : create wealth, happiness, and success early in life / Travis W. Freeman.

Description: St. Louis, MO : PlanWell Publishing, [2024]

Identifiers: ISBN: 979-8-9902325-0-1 (paperback) | 979-8-9902325-1-8 (ebook) | LCCN: 2024904986

Subjects: LCSH: Wealth. | Young adults--Finance, Personal. | Finance, Personal. | Success. | Happiness. | BISAC: BUSINESS & ECONOMICS / Finance / Wealth Management. | BUSINESS & ECONOMICS / Personal Finance / General. | BUSINESS & ECONOMICS / Personal Success.

Classification: LCC: HG179 .F74 2024 | DDC: 332.024--dc23

Dedication

To my wife and our two boys,
who support me and cheer me on
in business and life.
You're my everything.

DISCLAIMER

The opinions voiced in this material are for general information only and are not intended to provide specific advice or recommendations for any individual. Please speak with a qualified tax, financial, or legal professional before making any changes to your personal situation. Past performance is not an indication of future results. Investing involves risk. Any illustration or mention of future growth is made for educational purposes only and should not be construed as an offer or promise.

The opinions expressed in this book are solely from the author and do not reflect the opinions of the author's business associates, boards, board members, or other associated organizations or individuals.

Certain names and details have been changed to protect the identities of individuals mentioned in this book.

Table of Contents

Foreword

Drilling, filling, and billing. That's how a 63-year-old dentist described his average day to me as we spoke about his financial goals. He had a gray beard, tired eyes, and spoke with stoicism throughout our meeting. I was a young financial planner at the time and was excited about this conversation. It was our first interaction, and he was in the market for someone like me to help him. He had a nice office with multiple staff. It was the kind of dental practice I could see myself using personally. As we finished our pleasantries and began discussing details, he explained he would like to retire in the next few years. He had worked for decades and was ready to slow down. While discussing his financial goals, he told me about his home, which was nice and matched the kind a typical doctor might own. He told me about travel goals and the vehicles he and his wife normally buy. He told me about all the activities he would rather be spending his time on than working. "I'm tired of drilling, filling, and billing," he said.

I then asked about his retirement savings. He had a group retirement plan for himself and his employees. His personal balance in the retirement plan was surprisingly low. I thought to myself it might be because the retirement plan is a new benefit in his practice. I asked about his investments outside of work. He had very little. Surprised, I asked him what his practice might be worth if he sold it. That's when he told me about his business debts. He then told me about his personal debts. That's when it hit me. This gentleman was in the market for someone like me because he was desperate. He knew he didn't have much saved for retirement and was looking for ways to solve an unsolvable math problem. When I say he didn't have much saved for retirement, he had less than $100,000 saved. His annual income was significantly more. If he sold his practice and retired, he would run out of money in a few years.

Instead of saving when he was younger, he and his wife bought nice homes, nice cars, and nice vacations. They paid for expensive schools for their children. They gave nice gifts to family members. They lived on the edge. Now, at 63, he was faced with a reality he didn't want to acknowledge. Even selling his beloved practice wouldn't provide much after paying off debts. He and his wife were essentially broke. I collected all the information I could and later provided him with a plan for retirement. It wasn't remotely close to what he envisioned, but it was the medicine he knew was best for him. I felt badly because he so direly wanted to retire. There was just no way to make it happen if they continued living the same lifestyle. I wished I could go back in time and help him make better financial choices when he was younger. Based on his income and all the wonderful opportunities he had over his lifetime, he could have been worth many millions of dollars by that age.

You may not realize it, but you were born with wealth. This dentist was born with it, too. A child today with the benefit of good health is naturally born with the most precious of commodities in this world. Not only are most children blessed with this precious commodity, they're born with plenty of it. While some people are born into affluent families, the treasure I'm talking about isn't money. I'm talking about being born with the precious commodity of time. With a life expectancy of 80 years, you would be born with more than 42 million minutes of time. Time allows us to shape our lives in myriad ways as we decide each day how we'll spend it. Some people are born into poverty and create generational wealth over their lifetimes. Some do very little with their time. Time is the precious commodity that allows people to become independently wealthy over their lifespan. While financial success has no limit, time does. If you want financial independence during your lifetime, your precious time should be dedicated to strategies that support your goal.

While winning a large lottery jackpot can make someone wealthy in an instant, roughly 99.999 percent of lottery players will never win the coveted grand prize. For most people, wealth comes with taking action over time. Think of it like driving three hours to another town for an important meeting. At 60 miles per hour, you need at least three hours to make it in time. If you leave with only two and a half hours to spare, you'll be forced to drive 72 miles per hour, risking a speeding ticket or an accident. If you leave with only two hours to spare, you'll be forced to drive 90 miles per hour, putting yourself and others at unacceptable risk. For some who never save for their retirement and find themselves reaching age 60, it's no surprise why they turn to lottery drawings to make up for lost time.

If you're reading this book, you're obviously not a newborn. Depending on your age, if you're healthy, you may still have millions of minutes left to live. If you're 48 years old and expect to live into your 90s, I still consider you young given the amount of time left ahead of you. If you're 28, you certainly have plenty of time. This book will help you spend those precious minutes wisely so you may achieve your own version of financial independence. The path may seem difficult, and you may doubt yourself along the way. There will be challenges, both personally and professionally. There will be times when your willpower is tested. However, if you remain focused on your goals, you'll be pleased with the results. You're about to learn how to live like a multimillionaire so you can become a multimillionaire.

The Fortune of Youth is about what it takes to reach your desired level of financial success while you still have time. The younger you are, the easier it becomes to reach your goals. Regardless of your age, though, you can apply these principles to begin taking the same journey I and many others have already forged. You may assume financially successful people inherited their wealth or were handed profitable businesses from their parents. Although that certainly happens, this book is about creating financial independence *independently*. Given my professional background as a CERTIFIED FINANCIAL PLANNER™, I've seen many others make this same journey, using the same strategies to become wealthy. Many of my clients came from modest beginnings and used these tactics to grow their own first-generation wealth. Some accumulated millions of dollars over their lifetimes by saving well and being smart with their money. Some started businesses and now have estates worth over $100 million. Wealth doesn't have to come from inheritance.

If you come from modest beginnings, you may relate to my story. As a child, I watched my family go through a very difficult divorce and custody battle. We were an average middle-class family at the time. A few years later, my brother and I were living with our mother and using food stamps to buy groceries. If you've ever had powdered milk, trust me, it doesn't taste like the real thing, even on your cereal. The government-paid lunches at school tasted just like anyone else's food, but I was terrified others would find out and tease us for being on a program for "poor people." Those difficult years didn't last forever, but they were eye-opening. Even as a child, I quickly realized how powerful money can be. It's almost a force, in and of itself. If used wisely, it can lead to a happy, healthy life. If used unwisely, it can lead to health issues, stress, and misery.

Once I entered college, I immediately declared my major — finance. I was an average student with average grades, but I was constantly looking for a challenge — a chance to prove myself. This led me to starting my career at age 19 and working at three financial services companies while balancing my schoolwork. I also worked my way up to the role of president of two organizations on campus. After graduation, I was eager to help people with the knowledge I had gained, both personally and professionally. I met with people from all walks of life and all backgrounds. The people I met were young, old, gay, straight, black, white, brown, modest, greedy, selfless, poor, and wealthy. Because I was a young financial professional with no network of rich family members or neighbors to call on, I met with anyone willing to speak with me. I met with hundreds of people in my first few years.

It didn't take long to notice a pattern with the people I had met. The most successful typically weren't born into wealth. They lived their lives a certain way, focused their time a certain way, and had similar habits. They were living like multimillionaires. They were living that way even *before* they became multimillionaires. Their success wasn't by accident or luck. Their success happened with intention.

If you have a goal of becoming a professional athlete and you're serious about your goal, you'll probably need to begin a rigorous training routine, eating a certain diet, and focusing on competitions. Think about an athlete you highly respect. Was this person born with these abilities or did he or she work hard to become that type of athlete today? Olympic athletes don't find their abilities overnight. They *live* like athletes to *become* athletes. Becoming financially successful is no different. You must first live the part. The recipe for financial independence is one part mindset, one part habit, and a dash of knowledge. Throughout this book, I'll show you the principles that are essential to financial independence. Not only have I personally used these principles in my own life, I've witnessed countless others use them as well. Luckily, it's easier than becoming a professional athlete.

Reaching financial independence is something anyone can do, but it may come easier for some. There are indeed external factors that can affect your journey. For example, there are more millionaires in the United States than any other country in the world by far[1]. Statistically speaking, if you want to become wealthy, you may have better luck in the U.S. than any other country on the planet. Living in a country with a weak economy or limited freedoms would make your journey much more difficult. If you do live in the U.S. or a country with similar opportunities, consider yourself fortunate as you begin your journey.

You may also believe there are other factors standing in your way. Many people assume becoming wealthy requires a hefty six-figure income or a PhD. While earning $200,000 a year certainly makes this journey easier than earning $60,000 a year, it's not required. Where you went to school doesn't matter. How much you know about investments doesn't matter. As you read this book, forget about what you think is required to reach your definition of financial success. We'll be discussing real-life examples of average people from all walks of life that have been able to grow their net worth to seven figures and beyond. I'll share the principles of how to live like a multimillionaire, while also sharing some of the most important knowledge I have as a CERTIFIED FINANCIAL PLANNER™.

This journey will take time, but you'll learn how time can be used as your best asset. This journey is also a privilege. Becoming wealthy is not something everyone is able to do. Some people are bound to a hospital bed due to their health. Some face addictions they can't overcome. Some were born in a country stricken with poverty and corruption. As you embrace the principles in this book, remember that you are fortunate.

If you're new to the concepts in this book, you'll find plenty of information that can help you. If you're an avid reader of finance and business books, you may already know some of it. Also, some of these topics may not apply to your situation. You may not have credit card debt, but because many people do, it's an important topic to cover. You might live in Europe as I give examples of U.S. tax rules. My goal in writing this book is to offer everyone at least one idea they can use to improve their lives. It may be on investing, starting a business, or tax planning. It may be on career goals, estate planning, or retirement. I've included plenty of information while also keeping this book relatively short, so I hope you find concepts that can help you.

You might also read a chapter on a familiar topic but learn to look at it from a different perspective. You might be a strong believer in passive index investing. I'm a fan of index investing, but not for every asset class. You might feel strongly about being debt free. I'm a fan of paying down debt, but not all debts are created equal. You might believe everyone needs life insurance because everyone is expected to die one day. Life insurance is important, but some people don't need it. Whether you learn to view a financial strategy from a different perspective or learn a new strategy altogether, I hope you finish this book with at least one idea that may benefit you and your family for years to come. Enjoy.

Chapter 1

Your Why

In this chapter:
- Finding your purpose
- Six layers of "why"
- Strengthening your foundation

Before we delve into financial strategies and wealth-building concepts, it's important to discuss "why" you want to become wealthy. Remember, the term "wealth" means something different to everyone, so I'm asking why you want to reach your definition of wealthy. The answers may seem obvious, but obvious answers may hide the real reason you wish to grow your wealth. If your reasons for building wealth come from a place of deep, heartfelt desire, you're likely willing to make the difficult decisions needed to become financially independent. If becoming wealthy were easy, everyone would do it. Usually, the choices people make keep them from reaching their goals. Even in situations where people have advantages and opportunities most people don't have, some make choices that squander those opportunities. Being grounded in reason helps someone stay focused and make the right choices.

You may recognize some of the greatest names in professional football, such as Joe Montana, Tom Brady, and Jerry Rice. These gentlemen worked extremely hard to reach their goals. There is another football player that worked hard to reach his goals that you may not remember though. His name is Inky Johnson. Inky grew up in a poor neighborhood in Atlanta, sharing a home with 13 other people. He typically slept on the floor but had the chance to share a bed about once per week. Six people would sleep in the bed at once.

He was interested in football at a young age and decided to begin practicing with his cousins. They would race between light poles without shoes. A local coach discovered him and enrolled him in organized sports. After practice, the other children would go home. Johnson, however, had to wait for his mother to finish her fast-food job to pick him up. It would often be around 10:00 p.m. Once she arrived to pick him up, he would often ask her to point the headlights of her car to the field so he could practice more. He knew she was tired, but he told her he would make it to the NFL so they would never have to live in poverty again.

His hard work and dedication brought him to play football for the University of Tennessee. In his junior year, one of his coaches let him know he was a projected top-30 draft pick for the NFL. His coach explained all he needed to do was play well for the next 10 games and he would be a guaranteed millionaire. He called his mother and grandmother to share the news. He let them know they were on their way to having the life they wanted and wouldn't have to miss another meal again.

That season, in 2006, his football career ended after sustaining a severe injury on the field. He had emergency surgery that saved his life, but he lost the use of his right arm and hand. He would never play competitively again and wouldn't be able to reach his NFL goals.

While some people would find themselves defeated by this tragic event, Inky didn't stop. Part of his body was paralyzed, but not his spirit, his drive, or his mentality. He was the same man that at age 7 was driven to practice his skills when everyone else had gone home. He was the same player who wanted to reach the very top. He knew it was about the process, not the product. Inky Johnson knew his "why." Today, he's a successful businessman, motivational speaker, husband, father, and philanthropist.

When your "why" is clearly defined, it grounds you and drives you. It becomes your foundation and your purpose. This is the reason we're focusing on "why" before financial strategies. I'll soon ask you to discover your "why" and will even share my personal example. Even if you've been through a "why" exercise before, this step is important. Early in my career, I was asked to find my "why." It was a helpful exercise, but I didn't dig deep enough to find what was truly driving me. My discovery came later when I worked with a coach who challenged me and asked me difficult questions. She wasn't afraid to rattle me a bit because she was committed to helping me thoroughly discover what drives me.

At the time, I was satisfied with my financial situation, but still wanted to take my life, my finances, and my career to the next level. I wanted more, but why? I was asked to answer this question *six* times, digging deeper each time to peel away layers of truth to discover the deepest reason for my goals. Below is what I experienced:

1. Why do I want to take my life to the next level? I want my wife and children to be proud of what I've accomplished.
2. Why is that important to you? I want them to know success can come from hard work and dedication.
3. Why? So they can create opportunities I didn't have early in life.
4. Why? Financial success offers financial independence.
5. Why is that important to you? Financial independence gives someone security.
6. Why is that important to you? I don't feel financially secure yet.

Here I was, a 30-something financial planner and businessman who made more money than most doctors and I didn't feel financially secure. Chills went through my body when I came to this realization. It was a humbling moment. I was saving 25 percent of my income for retirement, saving aggressively for college for our kids, had plenty of cash in the bank, lived well within my means, had a seven-figure net worth, and I still didn't feel secure. Most people may find this strange. It likely has something to do with my upbringing, but ultimately, I discovered I wanted to have enough wealth to be 100 percent secure. I wanted to be able to give money to charity without worrying about my retirement assets. I wanted to be able to buy or start a business if the opportunity presented itself without worrying how it may affect my future. I desired the freedom to spend my time on whatever I wanted. Above all, I didn't want to have to *depend* on anyone. We all depend on people every day, but I didn't want it to be a *requirement* for my finances. I wanted my own definition of financial security. Reaching this milestone could happen tomorrow if I change my goals, but I have lofty goals for a reason. I also enjoy challenges and find work to be therapeutic.

Finding my true "why" required digging deep, answering difficult questions, and making myself completely vulnerable. Everything suddenly felt clear and calm. What seemed like an obvious answer to why I save aggressively, take risks, and work hard was now clearly defined and became the unshakable bedrock of my decisions in life. While this exercise was years ago, my "why" remains about the same today. Rather than hiding it or being embarrassed by it, I embrace it and share this story as a way to help others find theirs.

Your "why" may be identical to mine. It may also be completely different. No matter what drives you, it must come from within. You may think your "why" is to make your father proud because he didn't believe in you as a child. That's certainly a deep, motivating reason for many goals in life. What happens when your father tells you he's proud of you? Will you consider your goals in life accomplished? What if he dies prematurely? Your "why" is likely deeper than any one person or thing. It's internal, not external. When our children bring us a project from school and ask my wife and me if we're proud of them, we ask them if they're proud of *themselves*. If they remain driven *internally*, they're much more likely to continue working on these projects with pride.

Establishing your "why" before diving into the nuts and bolts of financial planning will help ground you and motivate you. Becoming financially successful is difficult. Rarely do people find an elevator to reach the level of success they desire. We often see these examples in the news though. They're lottery winners, technology entrepreneurs, and people who were in the right place at the right time. In reality, financial success is achieved by climbing the stairs. It's hard work, which makes establishing your "why" critically important. It's the fuel you'll need to continue climbing and to let you know when you've reached the top.

What does reaching the top mean? With my personal example of having complete financial security, it means reaching a level of wealth where my wife and I can live the lifestyle we desire, even if we live until age 100. It means managing that wealth wisely and in a way that offers both growth potential and some element of protection. While it's hard to predict how long we'll live, what inflation may be in the future, and how markets may perform, this amount of wealth is easily measured by making conservative assumptions. It's an amount we've calculated and continue to monitor year after year as we work toward the goal. Once we reach "the top" and achieve this goal, does that mean my "why" goes away? I can't predict what will be on my mind in the future, but it's likely my "why" will still be focused on absolute security. It's likely to shift from reaching this goal to maintaining it.

While money can bring someone a feeling of security, we've all been taught that money doesn't bring happiness. That statement is mostly true. Basic financial security, such as having enough cash in the bank to buy groceries for the next six weeks and survive a car repair, *can* bring happiness. My personal goal of financial security and complete financial freedom is far from the definition of *basic* financial security. Living paycheck to paycheck and constantly worrying about the unexpected means living with perpetual anxiety. That doesn't sound like happiness. If additional discretionary income gives some-one the freedom to build an emergency fund, buy a dependable car, and live in a safe area, then money does bring some level of happiness.

In a 2010 study from Princeton University, after surveying more than 450,000 people, happiness was found to increase with additional amounts of annual income[2]. However, happiness essentially lev-eled off at annual incomes of $75,000 at the time. Someone making $100,000 or $250,000 per year may have more income and financial freedom but not necessarily more happiness. According to the study, the relationship between money and happiness is correlated, but only to a point. One additional dollar of income may equal one additional unit of happiness when below an income level set by societal factors, but one additional dollar of income above that level doesn't necessarily mean one additional unit of happiness. For my fellow statistics nerds, the marginal returns of happiness diminish.

Imagine someone who started a business and struggled financially in the first two years. Let's assume this person made less than $30,000 per year in the first two years. Then the business began to grow, along with their income. Within five years, let's assume they were making $100,000 per year. According to the Princeton study, this person's happiness likely increased with their income, not to mention the growth and success of their business. Let's now assume, however, that this person began spending significantly more money as their income grew. They traded in their Honda for a Mercedes. They moved from a small apartment to a large home. They began buying custom-made clothing and joined a country club. As their income grew to $200,000 and then $300,000, so did their lifestyle. Add a lake house, a boat, international travel, and a Ferrari. As their collection of material goods grew, so did their debt. They accumulated two large auto loans, a boat loan, and two mortgages.

This businessperson whose income continues to grow may feel happier than they did in the early years of their business, but growing and spending uncontrollably may bring the return of stresses felt years ago when income was much lower. Collecting more material things in life is not bad behavior in and of itself. On the contrary, people are free to earn a living and spend the fruits of their labor as they see fit. When someone wants to become wealthy with the idea that these material goods will bring them happiness, they typically don't find it. In fact, they continue to upgrade their lifestyle to buy more expensive items in hopes that happiness will be found at the next level. It's an unsustainable path often fueled with significant debt.

Growing your wealth and income will likely lead to buying nicer material goods over time. However, thinking through what drives you, what you find fulfilling in life, and what makes you happy, will help you find balance in your financial decisions as you grow. Wanting to become wealthy simply for wealth's sake can be dangerous. Wanting to become wealthy for reasons that satisfy your "why" in life and enjoying new material goods along the way is more sustainable. Money is a powerful force and you'll be working to bring more of it into your life.

In Chapter 8, we'll discuss how to create a financial plan. The financial planning process is important after you've established your "why" because it can help you calculate a very important number. Your financial plan will help you determine how much money is "enough." This might mean how much income you need to live a certain lifestyle. Then, you might save more as your income grows faster than your lifestyle. Having "enough" may also mean a certain amount of wealth. Only once you have a formal financial plan can you realistically determine how much is enough. If you live a simple life, your number will be lower than someone who enjoys a more expensive lifestyle. If you enjoy the finer things in life, more power to you. Your version of "enough" will be higher. We all, however, have that threshold that's enough. If you can't envision having enough or your lifestyle expands with every financial success, you may never find fulfillment. Just as Icarus flew too close to the sun in the story of Greek mythology, wanting to go ever higher and higher without knowing when is enough can end in ruin.

As you complete this exercise to find your "why," fight any temptations of guilt or shame around money you may experience. Not everyone experiences these feelings regarding wealth, but many do. I find some people reach a certain age and are ashamed they don't have more money saved for retirement. I've met people of equal age and wealth who feel guilt from the wealth they *do* have at that point in their lives. This means two people who are 50 with the *same* amount of wealth may experience two completely different feelings about their financial situation. How can one feel shame while the other feels guilt? Money can evoke strong emotions about our past and present.

You shouldn't feel shame or guilt about your past or present financial situation, nor should you feel these emotions about where you want to be financially in the future. I once struggled with guilt regarding my financial situation. I was driving cars and enjoying luxuries most of my extended family members had never experienced. I wanted badly to tell them I was still living within my means and saving 20–30 percent of my income for the future, but that idea triggered my guilt even more. Most of us want to fit in with those around us, and if we begin living much differently than others in our social circles, it can lead to these feelings of guilt.

Imagine if one of your friends created an invention that was purchased by Microsoft for tens of millions of dollars. It would likely be in the news. People would be congratulating your friend on social media. Your friend may even move to Silicon Valley to work on another venture. Would you be jealous? Would you envy your friend? Would you be resentful that they became wealthy and you didn't? If this is a true friend of yours, I'm guessing you would be happy for them. As you dream of becoming independently wealthy over time and begin to see your progress toward this goal, remember this. Your true friends and family will be happy for you. Your guilt would be a manifestation of your mind and your mind alone. Shake it off and allow yourself to be comfortable with the idea of financial success.

Before you begin your journey to financial independence, establish your own "why." Ask yourself this question six times, going deeper at each level. Just as any strong building first requires a strong foundation, your "why" will serve as your base upon which you will build your goals, your career, and your nest egg. For those of you that find vulnerability difficult, no one is looking. You don't have to share this with anyone. You don't have to write a book about it. If you feel it's an exercise you can skip, I encourage you to try it anyway before investing time in the chapters to come. Ask yourself, "why not?" After finding your "why," the following chapters will help you make wise financial decisions, learn about the finance industry from an insider's perspective, and establish a plan for becoming wealthy.

Chapter 2

Rethinking the Basics

In this chapter:
- Compounding is queen
- Buying your dream home
- Good debt vs. bad debt

Years ago, I was presenting an educational training program to a group of employees. Their employer arranged for me to present a program called Financial Boot Camp that taught them various financial planning strategies. The purpose was to help their workforce make wise financial decisions, which in turn would help the employees feel more confident about money, decrease financial stress, and increase productivity at work. After the training, one of the employees approached me and said, "I knew most of what you talked about today, but you made me think about it completely differently." He went on to say some of my tips even flew in the face of conventional wisdom. This is common feedback from my corporate training programs, and you may have the same experience in this chapter. This is one of the reasons I was motivated to write this book.

Some of the topics covered in this chapter will provide new information, while others may be a healthy review of information you already know. You may also find a new perspective on a classic financial strategy. For example, brushing your teeth after meals is a wise strategy for tooth and gum health. However, when I learned that brushing right after eating something acidic, like fruits or hot sauce, can hurt tooth enamel, I gained a new perspective on a strategy I thought I knew quite well since I was a kid. My dentist never mentioned this in all the years I went in for cleanings.

The following sections of financial planning topics are a mix of time-tested strategies, mixed with a modern approach and my own experience as a financial planner and business owner. Misinformation is rampant online with millions of articles grasping for your attention. In later chapters, I'll cover entrepreneurship, intrapreneurship, passive income, career planning, and more. Some of these topics, such as business ownership, can lead to significant wealth over time. However, a business owner needs to know solid strategies with home ownership, insurance, debt, and investing for the best chance of success. This chapter is comprehensive and includes strategies used by my clients and within my own family. Where my strategies fly in the face of conventional wisdom, it may be time to rethink what's considered conventional.

Appreciate Appreciation

I once met someone who worked at a Lamborghini dealership. For those of you not familiar with Lamborghini, they make exotic cars that any auto enthusiast would drool over. You could buy a small home for the same price as an average Lamborghini. While speaking with this gentleman about how neat it must be to surround himself with beautiful cars all day, he explained that buying one isn't that hard. While many car dealerships offer five-year loans to help customers buy cars, this special dealership offered 11-year loans. He was proud of this fact, but I was floored. Why would anyone borrow so much money, and for so long, to acquire an exotic car that would cost them even more money through insurance, fuel, maintenance, and more?

Americans love to spend money on material things. Don't get me wrong. I have a smartphone, a nice car, and a home larger than I truly need, but I also live within my means by saving well and staying out of debt. Spending hard-earned money on material objects isn't necessarily a negative. It's also one of the reasons the U.S. economy is among the strongest in the world. Consumer spending accounts for approximately 70 percent of America's gross domestic product, or the measure of all goods produced and services rendered in a given country over a given period of time[3]. Consumer spending has grown for the European Union, United Kingdom, India, Brazil, and many others, too. This wasn't always the case. Consumerism began booming in the 1980s.

In 1975, the average American family saved approximately 13.4 percent of household disposable income[4]. This average savings rate means the rest, net of taxes, was being spent on anything from food to cars. By 1980, the average savings rate had fallen to 11.1 percent. Five years later, it dropped to 9.2 percent. By 1990 it was 8.4 percent. In five more years, it was 7.1 percent. By the year 2000, the average American family was only saving approximately 4.8 percent of disposable income. Splurging on the newest gadgets and household goods became a way of life. After all, if your friends all have new handbags or fancy electronics, doesn't it feel better to fit in and buy one for yourself, too? No matter the decade, for most people, it generally feels good to have nice things.

Free-market economies reward those who find financial success through taking risks and working hard. If you're fortunate enough to find financial success, you might spend some of your money on luxury items. However, if you don't have much disposable income, the next best thing to being rich is feeling rich. This was one of the primary drivers of consumerism in the U.S. in the 1980s. This trend even became part of popular culture. Look no further than Madonna's hit song "Material Girl," which was released in 1984. During her music video, she flaunts designer sunglasses, a red convertible, cash, pearls, dresses, furs, and diamonds. She encapsulates the trend of consumerism in that music video and many followed suit for decades to come. I can think of countless music videos where cash is thrown in the air, expensive champagne is sprayed, or exotic cars are shown off — all in an effort to show the world how wonderful it is to have nice things.

If someone is saving well toward their goals and paying off credit card balances each month, they're following two of the most important contributors to building wealth. If someone is on their way to reaching their goals and staying away from bad debts, they can generally spend the rest of their money on whatever they would like. However, many people don't save enough of their income each year. The allure of having nice things is one of those reasons. If someone drastically changes their lifestyle by cutting out nonessential spending, they can likely increase their savings rate. Saving for goals becomes easier as someone makes more income, but as someone makes more income, they generally increase their standard of living and their spending.

If you're interested in stretching your money and increasing your wealth, you should limit your spending on assets that depreciate. If your goal is to grow your wealth over time, your focus will be on saving well and investing your money into assets that can appreciate, such as stocks, private businesses, real estate, and more. At the same time, you'll want to avoid assets that deteriorate wealth and depreciate instead of grow wealth.

Generally, all purchases fall into one of three buckets — consumables, appreciators, and depreciators. Consumables are purchases like food or haircuts — expenses that are necessary and consumed in the short term. Instead of coaching you on why you shouldn't eat expensive caviar for lunch every day, let's focus more on appreciators and depreciators. The best example I have for depreciators is vehicles.

You may have heard the saying, "New cars depreciate as soon as you drive them off the lot." There's truth to this phrase. In fact, as a general rule, new cars will lose approximately 15–25 percent of their value in the first year. Then, for the next four years, they generally lose about 10 percent of their value each year. This means in the first five years of ownership, a new car worth $50,000 may depreciate by roughly $27,000 to $32,000. Your hard-earned money may disappear every year on that vehicle purchase. How many hours of your life did you work to make that money? In a way, you're watching hours, days, weeks, and months of your life "depreciate" with that car's value. If someone makes $35 per hour and their car depreciates by $32,000, that depreciation will cost them 914 hours of work. That deprecation cost them 114 workdays of their life. If you worked seven days a week, that's equal to roughly four months of your life spent on depreciation.

When you begin looking at your spending as how much of your life it takes to pay for certain items, you may change your perspective. For most people, time spent working is exchanged for a paycheck. Whether you earn a salary, an hourly wage, or a commission, you likely exchange your time for compensation. You're trading part of your limited time on earth — your life — for money. Time is a limited resource, but money technically isn't. You can't create more time, but you can create more money. If your time is always exchanged for money and you spend it on consumables and depreciators, your money will be limited to your time. If you spend your limited resource of time to make money and spend part of that money on appreciators, such as investments, now you can make more money outside of your limitations of time. Spending money on assets that depreciate is a great way to have fun but destroys your wealth over time.

With the car example, aside from depreciation, below are more expenses you might incur that further drive home the point about destroying your wealth:

- Sales tax
- Property tax
- Maintenance (tires, oil changes, batteries, brakes, wiper blades, etc.)
- Repairs (engine trouble, alternators, electrical issues, etc.)
- Interest charges, if using a loan
- Fuel (gas, diesel, electricity, etc.)

On average, Americans drive their cars for about six years before trading them in for another[5]. This also happens to be about the same time when many auto loans are paid off. Think about how much money is spent over someone's lifetime on depreciating, costly vehicles. With that said, vehicles are also a part of life. If you're a car enthusiast, they may also be a hobby. Many people need vehicles to make it to work, buy groceries, and visit family. Instead of doing away with vehicles altogether, I recommend buying a reasonable car for your level of income and driving it for 10 years or more.

Over my lifetime, I've never purchased a new vehicle. I've always bought them used. When I traded in my last car, I had driven it for 11 years. When I bought my next car, I bought one that was about two years old. I let someone else take the brunt of the depreciation, while I enjoyed a nice upgrade from my last car and paid cash. I realize driving cars this long doesn't work in all situations, but, if possible, you'll be enjoying less depreciation and more hard-earned income to put toward wealth-building assets.

Because many people still need a depreciating vehicle to travel, let's talk about my strategy for buying them with cash instead of using loans. Many people find themselves in a never-ending cycle of auto loan debt when they buy a car on a five- or seven-year loan and trade in the car for another as soon as the loan is paid off. Financing a car may not seem like a terrible strategy if interest rates are low, but you can't count on rates being low year after year. Interest rates are largely a factor of economics and beyond your control. If interest rates increase and you don't have enough cash to buy a car outright, you may be forced to borrow at higher interest rates when your car needs to be replaced. This can create a vicious cycle of debt that works against financial independence.

If you rely on loans to finance vehicle purchases, consider using a three-year loan the next time you buy a vehicle. Five- and seven-year loans have become popular choices over the years, but I would stay away from them. By using a three-year loan, your monthly payments will be higher than a five- or seven-year loan. This means you may force yourself to buy a car that's a little less expensive, such as a used car versus a new one. Let's assume your monthly payment for the three-year auto loan is $500. After three years, your auto loan will be paid off. You'll then have an additional $500 of cashflow each month. Instead of spending those dollars on improving your lifestyle, save the $500 into a brand-new bank account. The only reason for this new bank account is to save for your next car. Set up an automatic transfer of $500 per month to this account, just as if you were still making your car payment. Assuming you drive your car for another seven years after you paid it off, you'll have about $42,000 saved up for your next one. This means you might be able to buy your next car with cash instead of relying on financing.

If you're already buying vehicles with cash, that's great. If not, this strategy requires discipline. You may be tempted to use this money in your new vehicle bank account because it's readily available. However, promise yourself that you will only touch it if it's being used for the next car. If you follow this strategy, you may never need to borrow money for vehicles purchases again in your life. It's a liberating feeling to know it doesn't matter how high interest rates may climb in the future. You'll be paying cash. It's also a great feeling to know it doesn't matter what your credit score may be. You'll be paying cash. This strategy may not help with how much vehicles depreciate, but it can save you significantly over your lifetime by avoiding debt.

Although cars are notorious for depreciation, other assets that depreciate include computers, electronics, toys, and clothing. For these types of purchases, you'll need to determine how much you want to reasonably spend, knowing you typically won't receive much money back once you're done with them, if any at all. Televisions are a great example of a purchase that you might live without for a while. My wife and I waited years to upgrade our televisions to the newest, fancy models. Most of our friends had new TVs that functioned more like computers. It wasn't a matter of affording them. Our old television worked just fine. We used our money for more important matters, like saving for college. This is a simple example of using self-discipline to pick between depreciating assets or appreciating assets.

This discipline can be very difficult to maintain. In the U.S., companies that sell discretionary products or services, which aren't essential needs, spend hundreds of billions of dollars on advertising each year. They have entire departments of people who analyze data on how to increase sales and entice you to make a purchase. Some of these companies have teamed up with psychologists to learn how to push the limits of sales using unique strategies. In his book Influence:

The Psychology of Persuasion, Dr. Robert Cialdini teaches people how to use human nature to persuade someone to make a certain decision.

One principle he teaches is on the concept of genuine scarcity. Most people are hardwired to place value on items that are scarce. Cialdini quotes a study by scientist Stephen Worchel. Worchel gave a group of people two jars of cookies. One jar was filled with 10 cookies and the other only held two. The subjects sampled a cookie from each jar and were asked to rate how well they liked them. Despite the cookies being exactly the same between each jar, the average person preferred the cookies from the jar with limited supply. This is one of many examples of how we're hardwired to place higher value on something that's become scarce. Some call it FOMO, or fear of missing out, but it's grounded in psychology. Just as animals are hardwired to have certain instincts from birth, humans are hardwired with similar inclinations from birth.

Companies that sell anything from electronics to hotel rooms will use these strategies to trigger your subconscious into taking action. You may visit a discount hotel website and notice a box showing how many people are also looking at the same hotel room. You may notice a countdown clock that appears to show you'll lose out on the purchase if you don't finish checking out in time. Commercials that say, "Limited Supply" or "Flash Sale" are examples of incorporating the psychology of persuasion into traditional marketing. If you're faced with a discretionary purchase you don't truly need, you must fight your instincts and remember that this is all creative marketing. For what it's worth, I really like Cialdini's book and recommend reading it.

As you consider how you spend your money, remember that you're spending your life. You can choose to spend your money on assets that appreciate and support your financial goals or depreciate and hurt your financial goals. The chapters to follow will focus more on your options for appreciators. Only you can determine what's worthy of your time and your treasure.

Speaking of being worthy of your time and money, if you like what you're hearing throughout this book, please share your experience. These concepts and strategies can have a significant impact on someone's life. Business books live or die by reviews because people are busy and reviews are the quickest way to determine if it's worth someone's time and money. By leaving a review, you could be helping hundreds of people create wealth and give to their communities over time. If you've already left an honest review, I thank you.

Compounding Is Queen

Did you have any obsessions when you were a kid? Maybe it was skateboarding, a celebrity crush, or a video game you couldn't stop playing. For me, when I was about 12, I was obsessed with a Super Nintendo game. It's all I wanted to do from sunup to sundown. I didn't just want to beat the game, I wanted to master it. For those of you who were never into video games, mastering a game means figuring out every secret, beating every level, and completing every challenge. Mastering a game is more than just winning at it. Luckily, my obsession didn't stop me from completing my homework, but I was constantly thinking about the game.

Eventually, my obsession evolved into something that still consumes the way I think today. It's a healthy obsession and one I encourage you to think about, if not obsess about, as you make financial decisions. My obsession is with compound interest. It's one of the most important lessons in this book. Compounding is something that amazed even Albert Einstein. He was reportedly quoted as calling compound interest the "eighth wonder of the world."

In concept, compounding is like a snowball rolling down a hill. A child can create a small snowball and throw it down a steep hill. As that snowball rolls, it picks up more snow. As it grows, the surface area of the snowball grows and can pick up even more snow. Not only does the snowball grow, it grows at an increasing pace. If you look at a graph of how compounding works, it would look like an airplane taking off from the ground. At first, the plane moves slowly along the ground. Next, it continues picking up pace and begins pointing upward. Then, it increases elevation at an increasing rate. Imagine that this plane can continue doing this well into the stratosphere. This is the power of compounding. Fortunately, like the snowball, even a child can do it.

For compounding to work, time is needed. Compounding can't exist without time. For this reason, my obsession over compounding includes obsessing over how I spend my time. There's truth to the phrase, "time is money." That snowball needs time to roll down the hill. The more time it has to roll, the larger the snowball can become. Below is a simple example. This chart assumes two people invest their money in the same type of investment with the same growth rate of 7 percent. They both start with nothing and save the same amount of money each year. The only difference is how long they allow compounding to work for them.

Saving $2,000 per year			Saving $2,000 per year		
Age	John Early	John Late	Age	John Early	John Late
25	$2,140		46	$104,872	$4,430
26	$4,430		47	$114,353	$6,880
27	$6,880		48	$124,498	$9,501
28	$9,501		49	$135,353	$12,307
29	$12,307		50	$146,968	$15,308
30	$15,308		51	$159,395	$18,520
31	$18,520		52	$172,693	$21,956
32	$21,956		53	$186,922	$25,633
33	$25,633		54	$202,146	$29,567
34	$29,567		55	$218,436	$33,777
35	$33,777		56	$235,867	$38,281
36	$38,281		57	$254,518	$43,101
37	$43,101		58	$274,474	$48,258
38	$48,258		59	$295,827	$53,776
39	$53,776		60	$318,675	$59,680
40	$59,680		61	$343,122	$65,998
41	$65,998		62	$369,281	$72,758
42	$72,758		63	$397,270	$79,991
43	$79,991		64	$427,219	$87,730
44	$87,730		65	$459,264	$96,011
45	$96,011	$2,140			

Assumes $2,000 saved annually and compounded at 7 percent per year. Hypothetical return for illustrative purposes only.

As you can see from the chart, if someone decides to begin investing at age 25 instead of starting at 45, they have a significant advantage. The difference amounts to more than $363,000. The 25-year-old, who I've dubbed as John Early, only saved $80,000 over his lifetime. Because of compounding, it amounted to roughly $460,000 by age 65.

Think about that for a moment. John Early only saved $80,000 and turned it into nearly $460,000. Unfortunately for the other guy, who I've dubbed John Late, his $2,000 per year only turned into $96,000. That's a significant difference. John Late was late to the game when it came to saving and investing, which cost him hundreds of thousands of dollars in this example.

What if John Late decided to hustle and save twice as much as John Early to make up for lost time? If John Late saved $4,000 per year instead of $2,000, he would still be well behind John Early. At age 65, John Late would only have $192,000. That's still over $260,000 short of catching up to John Early, who only saved $2,000 per year. So how much money would John Late need to save each year to catch up with John Early? He would need to save $9,600 annually. That's almost five times the amount John Early saved each year. The following chart proves the point.

Age	Saving $2K per year John Early	Saving $4K per year John Late	Age	Saving $2K per year John Early	Saving $4K per year John Late
25	$2,140		46	$104,872	$8,860
26	$4,430		47	$114,353	$13,760
27	$6,880		48	$124,498	$19,003
28	$9,501		49	$135,353	$24,613
29	$12,307		50	$146,968	$30,616
30	$15,308		51	$159,395	$37,039
31	$18,520		52	$172,693	$43,912
32	$21,956		53	$186,922	$51,266
33	$25,633		54	$202,146	$59,134
34	$29,567		55	$218,436	$67,554
35	$33,777		56	$235,867	$76,563
36	$38,281		57	$254,518	$86,202
37	$43,101		58	$274,474	$96,516
38	$48,258		59	$295,827	$107,552
39	$53,776		60	$318,675	$119,361
40	$59,680		61	$343,122	$131,996
41	$65,998		62	$369,281	$145,516
42	$72,758		63	$397,270	$159,982
43	$79,991		64	$427,219	$175,461
44	$87,730		65	$459,264	$192,023
45	$96,011	$4,280			

Assumes $2,000 saved annually by John Early and $4,000 saved annually by John Late and compounded at 7 percent per year. Hypothetical return for illustrative purposes only.

Regardless of your age, you can see why I'm obsessed with compounding. Time is such a significant factor in growing wealth that it pains me to see people wait until their 40s or 50s to begin investing. I see the lost potential of compounding and what someone may need to do to catch up. The same concept applies to saving for a child's college. Waiting until a child is 10 to begin saving for college means a decade of compounding opportunity was lost. It's never too late to begin saving for goals such as college, but it will take significantly more work to save the same amount over eight years when there was a runway of 18 years from birth.

The examples I used for John Early and John Late assume an annual growth rate of 7 percent on their dollars. To achieve any rate of return, you have to put your money to work. That may include using conservative investments like money markets or aggressive investments like stocks or private business interests. Each will have different levels of risk and potential return. No matter what rate of return you assume, the magic of compounding still applies. We'll discuss investing in a later chapter, but the key is to at least put your money to work somewhere. Burying your money in the backyard is fine, but it won't support you long term. You need some type of growth. If cash is king, compounding is queen. This royal duo should be used together to reach your long-term goals.

Throughout this book, I'll reference the powers of time and compounding. If you like what you just read, you'll love the compounding career information in Chapter 9. As you learn more from these lessons, think about how time can affect your decisions in the years to come and how your financial decisions can mean exponential differences later in life. If you don't use your time to your advantage, you'll miss out on significant compounding opportunities.

The Dream Home

The largest home in the U.S. covers more than 135,000 square feet[6]. For those of you on the metric system, that's more than 12,500 square meters. The home is located in Asheville, N.C., and was originally built for George Washington Vanderbilt. It rests on more than 6,900 acres of land and boasts 35 bedrooms, 43 bathrooms, 65 fireplaces, and three kitchens. Some may call this a dream home. I assume most people would call it excessive, but the structure was built thanks to the opportunities created by the Vanderbilt family. Whether you agree with it or not, their wealth allowed them the freedom to build this mansion.

What's interesting about homes is they often hold us back from creating more wealth. They can actually *keep us* from achieving our financial dreams. You may have been taught that home ownership is an important part of creating wealth, but that's not entirely correct. Although you may not yearn for a home larger than a hospital, I'm going to show you how you can own your dream home.

I've seen families that live in homes of all sizes and prices. While each case is a little different, here's a typical example of a couple I might meet in their mid-30s who want to prepare a comprehensive financial plan. Let's call them Tom and Sally. Tom and Sally were making good money for their ages, had two young children, and lived in a nice home. They had just purchased this home the year prior. While we discussed their goals, they told me about their wish to send their children to private grade school and high school. They wanted to pay for 100 percent of college costs for their children, too, because their parents had helped both of them through school. They also wanted to retire in their early 60s and buy a vacation home in Florida one day. None of the goals they expressed to me were surprising. After all, who doesn't want to provide a great education for their kids, retire relatively early, and buy a second home? I explained to this couple that we would need to have a second meeting after I had the chance to review their financial information in greater depth.

Immediately after the meeting, I already knew I would have to be the bearer of bad news with this young couple. They just finished sharing their life's dreams with me, and I had to explain to them that they couldn't afford all of these goals. An analysis is exactly what they needed to see it for themselves, though. It's hard to argue with math.

We met once again to review their financial analysis to determine if and how they may be able to achieve the dreams they had joyfully expressed just a few weeks earlier. I began the meeting by asking them, "Do you want me to tell you what you *want* to hear, or do you want me to tell you what's in your best interests?" They answered as most couples do, "Please tell us what's in our best interests." Once they opened the door for me to be brutally transparent with them about their goals, I explained to them they can't afford to do everything they desire, at least not on their current incomes. I could see it in their faces I had just dropped a pile of bricks on their dreams. They were surprised. After all, they were making good money and so many of their friends were already doing the things they sought out to do. Then I went through my analysis, justified by facts and figures.

Their household income was about $195,000 pretax. They were earning salaries well above the national average at the time, especially for their ages. They were only saving 5 percent of their incomes to their retirement plans through work, so this wasn't enough to come close to their goal of retiring in their early 60s. They didn't have enough life insurance to cover the needs of their children should one or both of them die early. They also didn't have enough disability insurance. Tom had a basic disability insurance plan through work, but Sally didn't have any coverage whatsoever. They hadn't begun saving for their upcoming education costs yet — grade school, high school, or college. At almost $10,000 per year per child for grade school, more than $15,000 per year per child for high school, and anywhere from $15,000 to $30,000 per year per child for college, they were faced with very large education expenses. I didn't even bring up the vacation home. It wasn't necessary.

After I brought up some of these concerns, Sally mentioned they were spending so much money each month already. How could they afford to increase retirement savings, acquire the insurance they need, and begin saving to education plans? "Unfortunately, I don't see how you can either," I responded. "If you want to accomplish these goals, something has to be modified." I explained that they could adjust their goals a bit to take financial pressure off their incomes. For example, retirement in their late 60s versus early 60s. They could pay for private grade school and high school, but not 100 percent of college, too. Their children could help with college by using loans, and we would come up with a plan later for how the kids could pay off those loans quickly after graduation. Tom and Sally could also cut some personal expenses to make room for the needed insurance and retirement savings.

Then, I brought up a topic I knew they didn't want to discuss, but it had to be broached. "I know you bought your home last year, but if you truly want to accomplish the dreams you told me about, you should consider selling it for something less expensive," I said. The room fell silent. Sally then turned to Tom, who was blankly staring at my desk, and said, "I knew we shouldn't have bought that house." They already knew I may bring up this topic and had prior concerns of their own. They didn't express these concerns with me initially. They only expressed hope and excitement for how I may be able to "solve" their list of goals on their fixed incomes.

They were spending more than $4,700 per month on a 30-year mortgage payment. This includes real estate taxes and homeowners' insurance. That's more than $56,000 per year. Although they made about $195,000 per year as a household, that income after taxes was about $138,000. They were spending about 40 percent of their after-tax income on a mortgage payment. When that much of your income is gone thanks to a mortgage payment, you have to live on what's left. They still had to pay for two children, day care, auto insurance, food, cars, utilities, travel, health care, and more.

They explained to me that they were easily approved for the loan on their home thanks to their incomes and excellent credit. I wasn't surprised at all they were approved. The bank doesn't care if you're saving well for retirement. The bank doesn't care if you want to pay for your child's education. The bank doesn't care if you have enough disability insurance. The bank is there to lend you money and determine if you can pay back the loan over time. Could they afford the mortgage they were given? Yes, of course. However, they couldn't afford that big mortgage, *plus* all their other goals and savings needs. You can only stretch your money so far.

By the end of our meeting, we discussed a plan to downsize their monthly mortgage payment to about $2,800 per month. That meant they would need to sell their home for something less expensive — a tough decision that many would struggle to entertain. However, that would give them about $1,200 per month that could go toward starting college savings plans. They may not be able to pay for 100 percent of college, but they would be able to help. This would allow them to increase their retirement plan savings at work and target retirement in their mid-60s instead of their early 60s. They would also be able to buy a car in a few years without feeling completely stretched. The vacation home turned into, "I guess we could just rent a place on the beach twice a year." They also discussed other changes in their spending to make room for the insurance they needed to protect their family.

The mood greatly improved from the start of the meeting. The load of bricks I had dropped on their goals were being used to create the foundation of a new financial plan. They knew they weren't heading in the direction they thought they were, but now they had a plan for how to work toward their cherished goals. I explained that if they followed this plan we created together, they would technically be buying their dream home. A dream home is a home that fits the budget and allows you to work toward the dreams you have in life. While some people may want a large or expensive home more than they want education goals or an early retirement, I've found most people place greater importance on life goals that bring themselves or their loved ones financial freedom. Homes with large mortgage payments often choke monthly budgets of the discretionary cashflow needed to fund these goals. Doing this over 20 to 30 years as someone services their mortgage means decades of time may be lost before being able to fund their goals with more cash. As you learn to think like a multimillionaire, your new definition of a dream home must be redefined. It's a reasonable home based on your income that allows you to accomplish your financial dreams.

This example couple I shared with you isn't unique. I have countless stories such as this where families find themselves driving the same cars as their coworkers, buying the same homes as their friends, and promising their children they will pay for 100 percent of college before a college is even picked. The difference between the example couple and those who make large financial decisions without a long-term plan is that, one day, the tables may turn. The couple who makes the difficult decision to sell their home, increase retirement savings, and make room for buying their next car will likely one day be the couple their friends and coworkers admire. The friends and coworkers who buy nice cars today, possibly on five- to seven-year loans, and live in nice homes may not have as much to show for it later in life. Without a true plan in place, they may have traded their long-term life goals for those materials items in life that people tend to associate with success.

It's normal to feel the need to drive a nice car and live in a nice home. Our modern society tends to value visual symbols of wealth. Someone who drives a 10-year-old car, lives in an "average" home, and spends moderately isn't someone we assume is wealthy. We assume they aren't successful because we can't see their success. Even as a financial planner, I struggled with this early in my career. In my early 20s, I already appeared young and inexperienced. By also being seen driving a car fit for a high schooler, potential clients may immediately assume I'm not only inexperienced but also unsuccessful. I felt the pressures of materialism in the choice of my next car. Eventually, this became a non-issue and clients learned that I practice what I preach when it comes to spending money on depreciating assets.

Whether you currently rent, you're considering buying your next home, or you fear you may have purchased a home that's keeping you from your long-term goals, let's focus on finding that dream home. Let's also put something into perspective. In 1975, the average single-family home being built in the U.S. was 1,645 square feet. Forty years later, that average jumped to 2,687 square feet[7]. That's an increase of 63.3 percent in 40 years. It's normal for the *price* of homes to increase over time. That's part of inflation, just as it's normal for average incomes to increase, the price of a coffee to increase, or the price of a car to increase. What's not normal is for the *size* to increase over time. Imagine if the *size* of the average car increased 63 percent over 40 years. Our entire system of roads in the U.S. would need to be rebuilt. See the difference? As the average size of the American home increased, along with the price, do you think people started paying for them with cash? No. Instead, most families take out larger and larger loans to buy these larger and larger homes.

I find the greatest contributor to this trend is society. We justify buying these homes because our friends are doing it, too. Plus, the bank approves us for it. We only have to use as little as 3.5 percent of our cash as a down payment and borrow the other 96.5 percent. Bucking the societal norm is the most difficult part of buying your dream home. You must combat these societal "norms" and live like a future multimillionaire. Just as people survived just fine in 1975 buying averages homes at 1,645 square feet, you will, too. Your friends and coworkers may enjoy larger homes today, but who do you think will be in a stronger financial position later in life?

If you're in a situation where you've received an inheritance, bonus, or small lottery, you may be asking yourself if you can use these funds to buy a larger home with a smaller mortgage versus buying a larger home with a larger mortgage. In essence, you may be considering putting a larger down payment, such as 30 percent, 50 percent or more, on this home that would require a smaller mortgage. A smaller mortgage requires a smaller payment, thus allowing more of your income to be saved and invested each month. Although there's nothing wrong with this strategy, I'll share with you what I would do in this situation.

Back in 2016, my wife and I discussed buying a different house. Our family was growing, and I wanted to have a shorter commute to my office. The home we had been living in since we were married was well within our budget. We were spending less than 10 percent of our income on the monthly mortgage payment. This allowed us to save and invest 20–30 percent of our income each year for retirement, college, and other goals. When we started searching for our next home, we knew the budget we should stay within to be able to continue saving well for our future. Once we found that special home, we had a decision to make. How much money should we use as a down payment? We had the ability to buy the new home with cash after selling the old home and some other assets. That may sound appealing to buy a home with cash and never have a mortgage payment. We, however, only put down 20 percent on this home — the minimum required to avoid private mortgage insurance and have a reasonable interest rate on our mortgage. The other 80 percent of the house was purchased using the bank's money. We used a 30-year mortgage. So why would someone who can afford to buy a house with cash use a loan?

Imagine if we did sell some assets and use our cash to buy our home free and clear. Although not guaranteed, our investments had been steadily growing at the time. Our hope was that we would continue seeing that growth long-term. It wasn't worth selling something with potential growth, plus it would have triggered taxes. But what about the cash from selling our prior home? The reason we didn't use all of our cash on making a large down payment is because we used that cash to add to investments and college savings plans instead. If we would have used the cash for a larger down payment (and a smaller mortgage), yes, we would have saved money by borrowing less from the bank. However, the interest rate of the mortgage was less than the amount of growth we anticipated long-term on our investments. In other words, the growth we anticipated from our investments was greater than the interest cost of the mortgage over time.

Let's drive this example one step further by using simple math. Let's say you want to buy a home worth $100,000. You happen to have $100,000 of cash in the bank from a recent inheritance. You can simply buy the home with cash, thus avoiding any interest charges from a mortgage. That sounds appealing. However, the other option would be to put only $20,000 of your cash into your home purchase and borrow the remaining $80,000. That would leave you with $80,000 of cash in the bank still since you bought the home using the bank's money.

If the interest rate on this mortgage was 6 percent and you used a 30-year mortgage, you would end up paying about $93,000 of interest over the full 30-year period. Now you know the potential cost of this mortgage over 30 years. In other words, if you pay for this home with cash, you will *save* about $93,000 of interest cost over 30 years. As for the $80,000 of cash left in the bank by using the mortgage, let's assume you invest it in something that earns an average return of 3 percent over 30 years. After 30 years, your 3 percent investment would be worth about $194,000. If we assume this hypothetical investment actually earned an average of 6 percent over 30 years, which is the same interest rate charged by the mortgage, you would have nearly $460,000 at the end of 30 years. Even after accounting for your starting investment amount of $80,000, you would be ahead, even if your average return was only 3 percent over 30 years. So how in the world can a 3 percent return "beat" a 6 percent mortgage over 30 years? After all, the mortgage rate is twice as much as the investment rate. The answer is — compounding.

Mortgages use different math than investments. A mortgage uses something called amortization, while investment returns offer the potential for compound growth. If compounding is like a snowball rolling down a hill, amortization is like a marble rolling down a hill. It's not going to grow. If you really want to focus on the technical aspects, amortization is linear while compounding is exponential. The easiest concept to remember is that a low-rate mortgage isn't a bad thing to pay off *slowly* if you can compound your money elsewhere. In short, low-rate amortized debt isn't a bad thing. Businesses use these types of loans all the time to finance growth.

Although I was able to justify my decision on our house with math and experience, I was also willing to take at least a small amount of risk. Borrowing money from the bank while leaving other assets to potentially grow over time was a risk. If my business failed and my investments lost value, I would still owe the bank its money. However, after completing the math on my options, I believed it was an appropriate risk to take. Any investment involves some type of risk and taking risk is one of the only ways to grow wealth.

This decision my wife and I made to buy a home with only 20 percent cash and mortgage the rest occurred when we were in our early 30s. As you'll learn in the following chapters, we knew time was on our side and our opportunity to grow wealth was greatest at our young ages. We needed a home that would still allow our investments to continue growing and allow us to continue saving 20–30 percent of our incomes each year for our goals.

This book is focused on "younger people" because of the potential opportunities. While someone at the age of 60 could certainly change their housing expenses to improve their cashflow, that cashflow simply doesn't have as much time to be invested and potentially grow for future goals. Someone at 60 may live another 25 years or more, but the fertile ground for growing wealth is greatest early in life. The ideal age to implement the "dream home" concept is immediately after graduation from high school or college. Building a lifestyle that always focuses on a reasonable home and making room for monthly investing may afford you significant financial freedoms later in life.

For those of you who currently rent and would like to purchase your first home, you may be wondering what amount of money is most appropriate for an initial down payment. I generally recommend an initial down payment of 20 percent. For a home valued at $300,000, that means a down payment of $60,000. This may seem like a daunting task to save up tens of thousands of dollars depending on your income, so let's walk through a few strategies.

The reason I recommend a 20 percent down payment is because most mortgages require this level of down payment to avoid something called private mortgage insurance (PMI) in the U.S. Canada, Australia, the U.K., and other countries have similar mortgage insurance programs by other names, but many share the 20 percent threshold. Mortgage insurance is an additional cost added to a mortgage payment because the mortgage provider is taking additional risk by creating or guaranteeing the mortgage. If you only place a 5 percent down payment on a home and borrow 95 percent on a mortgage, if your home's value declines by 7 percent, your home may then be worth less than the mortgage balance. It would be "under water." This means if you stop paying your mortgage and default on your loan, the mortgage provider may take possession of your home so it can sell it and recoup the loan. If the provider can't sell your home for the same amount you still owe, it may be forced to take a loss. This is the greatest risk to the mortgage lender. However, when someone puts down 20 percent as a down payment, it means the mortgage lender is taking less risk.

Mortgage insurance protects lenders if you default on your loan. In the U.S., it works differently between conventional mortgages and other types, such as Veterans Affairs loans for veterans, Federal Housing Administration (FHA) loans, and U.S. Department of Agriculture loans. I won't cover all the differences here but know that your individual situation will determine which loan type is best for you. For conventional loans and FHA loans, which are the most common in the U.S., smaller down payments generally mean higher mortgage insurance costs. If the idea of paying additional costs with your mortgage doesn't sound appealing, below are a few ways you can focus on a larger down payment.

- Conventional lenders may offer special loans that require no mortgage insurance, even when making down payments less than 20 percent. The flip side is that the interest rate is generally higher.

- You may be able to secure two loans — one for your down payment and another for your traditional mortgage. Many banks have programs that fit this strategy. This approach may affect your rate on the larger mortgage but would avoid mortgage insurance costs.

- You may also consider borrowing from family to reach a 20 percent down payment. If you're fortunate enough to have this option and you already saved up a 10 percent down payment on your own, borrowing another 10 percent from family at little to no interest may save you mortgage insurance costs and interest.

- If the strategies above don't sound appealing, you can also aggressively save up your own money for a 20 percent down payment to reduce your mortgage costs. You might also search for a less expensive home.

Although I recommend a 20 percent down payment when buying a home, if you decide to use a lower down payment, remember the concept of the dream home. Forget about what types of homes your friends are buying because they may be buried in debt. Forget about how much the bank says you can afford because it may stretch your budget too far. Forget about the nicer homes a real estate agent may want to show you because they earn more if you spend more. Focus on buying the home that allows you to accomplish your financial dreams.

Forget the Budget

When I bring up the topic of creating a budget, some people cringe. In fact, a survey by OnePoll found that one in five Americans would rather spend time in jail than create a budget[8]. Some people don't know how to start one, some don't want to know how much they spend, and some simply don't care enough. Creating a budget probably isn't what most people think of when they have spare time on a Saturday morning. It's no surprise that two in five Americans have never had a budget before[9]. Many recognized financial professionals will tell you that creating a budget is very important. I hear recommendations like this regularly on social media, TV, and radio.

Dave Ramsey, a financial personality with a popular radio show, often recommends creating a budget. He has said, "A budget is telling your money where to go instead of wondering where it went." The creation of a budget is also something most nonprofits, government agencies, and corporations do each year. After all, they need a plan for where their limited assets will be spent. So, does every household need to create and maintain a budget? Absolutely not.

Think about what a budget is meant do to. It's a way for us to review how much money we make and where that money will be spent. The main purpose is to watch your spending and ensure you don't add debt by spending more than you make. A budget can also help someone save more for goals, such as retirement or college. So far, the budget sounds like a reasonable tool to have. However, a budget has a significant weakness. At the end of the day, it's a promise. Promises can easily be broken. Worse yet, that promise is one we make to ourselves. If you promise your mother you'll come over for dinner because you haven't seen her in a while, you'll likely keep that promise because you don't want to disappoint her. If you don't have mom to keep you honest, though, it's easy to break the promise.

Another way to look at budgeting is like dieting and counting calories. You can have every good intention of eating a salad instead of fried chicken tenders for dinner, but when given those two choices, it's tempting to pick the chicken tenders. Once we fall to temptation, we break our promise to ourselves and break our diet at the same time. It happens easily. But what if we decided to remove the delicious chicken tenders from the list of meal options? If we're hungry and salad is the *only* option, I don't know about you, but I'll choose salad over hunger any day. With budgeting, it's easy to overspend and run up a credit card balance for something we really, really want, even though we know we shouldn't do it. In the same way that you can remove the bad food option from the equation and force yourself to eat healthier, we can force ourselves to make wise financial decisions, too. The key is to remove the choice.

Let's assume you work at a company that has a retirement plan. This plan allows you to save money for retirement each pay period. Let's also assume you're not saving enough for retirement yet. If you complete a budget and *promise* yourself that you'll save more for retirement each month, assuming you have the money available, there may be months where it doesn't happen because you broke your own promise. However, if you automatically put part of your income into a retirement plan each month, you don't have the *option* of missing a month. Because the retirement plan is automatic and happens without you taking action each month, it's stronger than a budget. It's stronger because you may have to pay taxes and penalties for touching that money after it went into the retirement plan. It's not like swiping a credit card.

Even if you don't have a retirement plan option available at work, you can set up your own investment account where you automatically have money taken out of your bank account each month. In the U.S., that might be a Roth IRA, a traditional IRA, or a brokerage account. If you live outside the U.S., you may have similar types of accounts available, but brokerage investment accounts are fairly universal. The point is to remove the option of saving for retirement or not saving for retirement. Force yourself to save each month, even if it's only a small amount. As long as you don't build credit card debt, you've accomplished the same outcome as a budget, but without wasting an hour on a Saturday morning. As a financial professional, I don't have a budget. Instead, I force myself to save 20 percent or more of my income regularly and live on what's left. That strategy is stronger than a budget, which is why I don't have one.

Although I may suggest "forget the budget," there are times when having one makes sense for someone. For example, let's say you're skilled in a few areas of life, but money isn't one of them. If you struggle with money, you may have outstanding credit card debt that continues to grow. If you've had credit card debt for longer than one year, especially if the balance isn't decreasing, then you need a good old-fashioned budget. Dedicating some time to this exercise will help you take control of your spending and where your money is going. You can make it easy by using free budgeting apps or websites. The key here is to create a plan for applying extra cash toward your high-interest debt each month. This may require you to make sacrifices, such as limiting fancy coffees, dinners, or clothing.

I once received a call from someone who wanted help "getting back on track" with her finances. She explained to me that she had a good paying job and didn't live lavishly but had racked up more than

$10,000 of credit card debt. I asked her how long she had carried a balance on credit cards, and she said more than five years. This told me something else was going on and it wasn't an expensive life event, such as a divorce or illness. When I asked her about her spending, she said she had cut out numerous expenses to save money. She then told me she had just returned from a trip to Europe with friends and it "set her back quite a bit." This told me what I needed to know — she had a hard time committing to living within her means.

Sometimes our spending habits are so toxic to our financial lives that they require drastic action. In the same way that alcohol or drugs can be abused, so can credit cards. Many people drink responsibly, but some simply can't control themselves. For what it's worth, I don't place any judgment on them. It's part of being human. When it comes to credit cards, being in debt is not acceptable, just as driving a car after drinking two bottles of wine is not acceptable. Somehow, our society has normalized the idea of carrying credit card debt and paying double-digit interest rates. It's nearly the worst thing you could do with your finances. In the wake of the Great Recession of 2008–2009, the average American had $5,856 of outstanding credit card debt. A decade later, when the economy was on significantly stronger footing, the average had increased to $6,194[10].

Earlier in this chapter, we discussed how compound interest is like a snowball rolling down a hill. It continues to grow and grow. Paying interest on credit card debt is just the opposite, but it's still the snowball effect. Instead of *you* benefiting from the growing snowball, a bank or credit card company benefits instead. Create a mindset that owing money on credit cards is not acceptable. If you can't pay it off the next month, don't spend the money. Find another option. I don't care if you have friends and family who don't think it's a big deal to carry a credit card balance. It's not acceptable because high-interest credit card debt can destroy someone's financial goals. Just because the average household has credit card debt doesn't make it okay.

If you happen to be in credit card debt today, and you've carried a balance for more than a year, give the budget a try. If creating a budget doesn't seem to work, then it's time to take a more drastic approach. In the same way that we can force ourselves to eat healthier by staying away from fried chicken, if you can't seem to manage your credit cards properly, it's time to quit them. This may seem like an extreme position, but if you don't do it, you may waste years of your life where you could have been growing wealth. In other words, what is more extreme — quitting on credit cards or being burdened with debt for years? As you'll see throughout this book, time is one of the best assets you can have. If that time is wasted by paying off credit card debt and paying high interest rates, it will become harder and harder to make up for that lost time.

If you do decide to quit your credit cards, you may find living without them isn't so bad. There are many ways of paying for goods and services without a credit card these days, especially with smartphone apps connected to bank accounts. If you're worried your credit score might not improve as much if you don't have any credit cards, that may be true. Making timely payments month after month on credit cards can help show the credit bureaus that you're "responsible" about making payments. What's more important, though — possibly having a somewhat higher credit score or never paying another dime of interest on credit cards again?

If you're wondering what someone would do if they ran into financial difficulty without having access to a credit card, this is why it's important to have an emergency fund. An emergency fund is bound to be used at some point because emergencies simply happen. You should expect the unexpected to happen. If you have a single income in your household, you should have at least six months of fixed and variable expenses saved in an emergency fund. If you have a dual-income household, you should have at least three months of fixed and variable expenses in an emergency fund. These are minimum thresholds, so you're welcome to keep more cash for emergencies.

While credit cards can be ruinous for some people, they can be rewarding for others. I use credit cards to pay for just about everything. I pay off the full balance every month, though. In turn, I enjoy the rewards that come with some of my cards. My wife and I have earned thousands of dollars in rewards over time by using our credit cards responsibly. Everyone knows credit card companies make money through charging interest, but they also make money through transaction fees. These fees are charged to businesses that allow customers to pay using credit cards. You might notice some small businesses will charge you extra if you pay by card. That's because it may cost the business between 1–3 percent to accept your card payment. These fees are split among the banks, credit card networks, and processing companies that make up the credit card industry. This is also how your credit card provider can afford to offer you rewards, even if you pay your card off each month.

Because most businesses allow customers to pay by credit card these days, most have adjusted their pricing to account for credit card processing fees. That means, unless a business offers a discount for paying with cash, I'll be paying the same price for the same product with or without my credit card. This is why I would rather use my card and earn the rewards. If you have trouble with credit cards, forget about the rewards. They're not worth it if you can't pay off the debt.

If you decide to give budgeting a try, it may help to track your spending and determine where cuts could be made to increase your emergency fund, pay off high-interest debt, or save more for goals. If you don't see much wiggle room in the budget for cuts and still need more cash in your emergency fund, consider selling something in your home that you don't truly need. For example, if you have a food dehydrator that you haven't used in years, but you keep it around because you would love to make beef jerky one day, sell it for cash. Maybe you have clothing that's worth some money to a second-hand store. Just about everyone has something they don't need any longer that could be sold for instant cash.

If you're someone who's fairly disciplined about spending and you rarely carry a balance on credit cards, if ever, focus on saving a portion of each paycheck for your financial goals and make it automatic. In the same way that someone who eats healthy every week doesn't need a "diet," someone who's saving well and staying away from credit cards doesn't need a budget. For those who have a hard time with spending and credit card debt, a budget may be a worthy exercise. Keep in mind, you may not need to keep a budget forever. You may find yourself creating new habits and living a lifestyle that no longer requires a budget. If that happens to you, go out and celebrate. Order some chicken fingers and put them on your credit card.

Target 10 Percent

Mark Twain once said, "The secret to getting ahead is getting started." Twain has countless quotes associated with his name and is lauded as one of the greatest authors in modern history. He authored *Tom Sawyer and Huckleberry Finn*, among his famous writings. While his name is associated with wisdom and publishing prowess, a lesser-known fact about Twain is he once went bankrupt. If Twain had saved well for his future while also pursuing his business and book ventures, he may not have endured such financial instability.

People often ask me how much they need to save toward their financial goals. I really wish it was as simple as a straight answer. Determining how much to save for your own financial goals requires a deeper conversation about those goals, your income, your taxes, your existing assets, etc. With that said, I do often quote a baseline savings amount to people that are looking for just that — a starting point.

I recommend saving at least 10 percent of your household pretax income toward your long-term goals. I've found that saving 10 percent of your income or more on a consistent, annual basis greatly increases your chances of reaching your goals. That statement is general, but it's appropriate because your goals are likely correlated to your annual income. Someone who makes $50,000 per year isn't likely to have the same long-term goals as someone who makes $500,000 per year. The person making $500,000 per year is allocating $50,000 per year (10 percent) toward savings and investments because they're more likely to have a lifestyle that requires a larger amount of wealth. One key to the 10 percent saving rule is having enough time for the savings to accumulate and grow.

If you have an employer with a retirement plan available, you may have the option of saving a percentage of your income into the plan directly through your payroll department. It's easy and simple. Depending on your industry, you may also be forced to save into a pension plan with a percentage of your income. Either way, if you're only saving 3 percent of your income, that's fine. Saving 3 percent is better than saving 0 percent. Try to target a saving rate of at least 10 percent. It may take time to reach this level depending on your situation, but it can be done. If you're already saving 10 percent of your income, try increasing it to 15 percent. I have yet to meet anyone in my career who said, "I wish I wouldn't have saved so much when I was younger."

One of the reasons I'm such a big fan of employer group retirement plans is because you can pick a percentage of your pay to save and it can automatically adjust as you receive raises. If you receive a 5 percent raise in pay, you'll be saving the same percentage, but at your higher pay rate. More money will be saved. Unlike other types of investment accounts outside of work, you don't have to remember to make a contribution each month, and you don't have to adjust the amount as your income changes.

For those of you living in the U.S., let's cover two other options available to grow wealth through investments — individual retirement accounts (IRAs) and brokerage accounts. Brokerage accounts are simply investment accounts without special retirement rules associated with them. With IRAs, you'll have the option of using a traditional IRA or a Roth IRA. Both of these IRA types have annual contributions limits. You can only put in so much each year. Depending on your age and your level of income, you may also be limited on the amount you can contribute. There are quite a few tax rules involved with IRAs, so instead of going down a technical rabbit hole, let's cover one important difference between them — taxation.

Pretend you're retired and you need money for a new car. You call your financial planner and tell her you need $50,000. She explains that you can take money from your traditional IRA, but you'll owe income tax. You may need to withdraw $65,000 to have $50,000 because the difference is the tax you may owe. On the other hand, you can take money from your Roth IRA and you'll owe no income tax. If you need $50,000, she only needs to withdraw $50,000.

You may be thinking the Roth IRA is a good deal with that example. Personally, I'm a big fan of the Roth IRA because growth that occurs in the Roth can be distributed tax free as long as you follow the rules of the Roth and your retirement age when you take it out. There aren't many opportunities for people to grow wealth free of taxation. That doesn't mean a Roth is for everyone though. The downside of a Roth is you don't receive a tax benefit when you put money into it. The potential tax benefit happens on the "back end" when you take it out.

With a traditional IRA, the taxes are the opposite. You can receive a tax benefit on the "front end" when you put your money into it. As long as you properly follow the rules of the traditional IRA, you would be deferring income taxation on the money you put in. You could then invest that money and defer taxation, even on the growth, until you take it out at retirement age.

So, which one is better for you? I don't know, we've only just met. It greatly depends on your situation, but if you think your income tax rate will be lower when you're retired, the traditional IRA may make more sense. If you think you'll be in about the same tax bracket or higher, the Roth IRA may make more sense. Some people also use what I call "tax diversification" by having both. This way, you would have the flexibility of choosing between the two depending on how taxes change or life changes. Also, if your employer offers both a pretax option and a Roth option in your retirement plan at work, although the rules are different than IRAs, the same basic concept on taxes applies. You can pick the option that defers taxation into the future or the option that pays taxes right away but allows the growth to occur tax-free.

The example I gave earlier of the retiree needing money is something you should consider. If you only have pretax money when you retire, you may owe income tax on every dollar you take out. Personally, I'm using creative strategies to put money into Roth IRAs for my wife and me because I want the flexibility and tax-free growth. A good financial planner can review your personal situation and help you determine which option makes sense and at what amount.

Regardless of the type of account you use to save and invest your money, the most important part is to save and do so automatically. I meet people all the time who say they wish they would have saved more when they were young. I even met a young woman who started saving 15 percent of her income when she was 23 and she was disappointed in herself for not starting earlier. Because of the magic of compounding, that's the right mentality to have. Too often, I see people delay saving and investing because they don't prioritize it, losing precious time they can't get back.

Let's say you went to college and took out student loans. Then you graduated and landed a job with a fair wage. You found an apartment, so you didn't have to live with your parents. Because of your rent and student loan payments, you could only afford to save 3 percent of your income. You received a raise and bought a new car since your college-mobile was on its last leg. Your raises for the next few years went to increasing your lifestyle — more dinners with friends, travel, new clothes. Then came the wedding and children. With kids, you find it hard to save more than 5 percent of your income.

I do understand that budgets can be tight, and life isn't easy. However, what if this young person had stayed in her parents' house for a while and forced herself to save 8 percent right away? Then she received a raise and decided to drive her car for just one more year, allowing her to save 10 percent by the age of 24. Once you force yourself to live without the money, you figure out *how* to live without it. Aside from going into debt, there's literally no way you can spend more than 90 percent of your income because 10 percent is going into an investment account for your future. You figure out how to live on the 90 percent. One day you'll need to live on 100 percent of your life's savings, so if you want it to be a meaningful amount, target at least 10 percent aggressively and do it early.

Good debt vs. bad debt

The Great Depression was the longest and deepest economic depression ever experienced in the U.S. The effects were also felt by many other nations around world. It began in 1929 and lasted more than a decade, ending during World War II. It spread throughout the industrialized world, partially thanks to the gold standard that was shared by the U.S. and many other nations at the time. After the end of World War I in 1918, the United States began to experience significant economic expansion, also known as the Roaring '20s. It was a time of optimism, social change, and financial growth. The Dow Jones Industrial Average, an index that measures the value of some of the largest publicly traded stocks in the U.S., was up more than 26 percent in 1924, followed by another year of growth at 25 percent the following year. Then came a modest gain in 1926, followed by 27 percent in 1927, and a whopping 49 percent gain in 1928[11]. The rapid growth of the stock market was met with enthusiasm and celebration for most investors. Then, the party came to an end.

During the worst of the Great Depression, unemployment in the U.S. was nearly 25 percent. Roughly one in every four people were unemployed. That statistic is significant. When that many people are out of a job with little to no income, they can't spend on consumer goods. Factories stopped producing those goods because demand had decreased. This meant more people were laid off from factories and no longer had income to spend. A healthy employment rate is crucially important for a developed nation. Unfortunately, 25 percent unemployment was disastrous.

You may have heard about a program called the New Deal in the U.S. The New Deal was a comprehensive package of government spending, stimulus, laws, and programs enacted throughout the 1930s to bring the U.S. out of the Great Depression. The Social Security

Administration is an example of a program created under the New Deal. The combination of government spending for World War II and the New Deal are widely thought to be the reasons the U.S. was able to recover from the Great Depression. While this history is commonly taught in school, you may not be as familiar with the economic struggles that began before the official start of the Great Depression in 1929.

In 1920, 30.2 percent of Americans still lived on farms[12]. Farming still accounts for a significant portion of U.S. employment. As mentioned, economic expansion occurred in the U.S. after the end of World War I. However, during World War I, which started in 1914, many farms were destroyed across Europe. The demand for farm products increased dramatically. The U.S. government was one the largest customers for American farmers thanks to the need to feed military service members. By the end of World War I, approximately 4 million people had served in the war[13]. Everyday Americans were even encouraged to start their own gardens for food due to shortages. In an effort to meet growing demand, farmers expanded their operations and purchased additional acreage. Those without sufficient cash borrowed money for their expansions. It was a prosperous time for farmers and farming communities.

As World War I ended, so, too, did the demand to feed and clothe overseas armies. Many farmers had already expanded their herds and crops and continued to bring their products to market. Products such as wheat, cotton, tobacco, and corn were in abundant supply. With oversupply comes a decrease in prices. Farmers found it more difficult to pay their loans due to decreasing revenues. The loan defaults began. Banks were forced to foreclose on farmland. Then came the Great Depression in 1929 that made the situation even worse. Added to this financial stress for American farmers was the Dust Bowl of the 1930s, which was a period of severe drought and dust storms for large parts of the Midwest. If the loan issues of the 1920s were like a punch to the gut to farmers, the Great Depression was a kick while they were down, followed by a sack of potatoes being dropped on them with the Dust Bowl. Many farmers lost their farms, homes, and livelihoods.

Imagine being a 12-year-old child during this period while living on a farm. Your family experienced exciting growth and prosperity. Then, everything changed and banks started foreclosing on multiple farms in the area, including your family's farm. It would be a traumatic experience for most children to have their lives turned upside down this way. In fact, you would probably grow up thinking it's never a good idea to borrow money, especially to finance the family farm. After all, the bank may have been the enemy in your childhood when the family farm was lost. You would probably teach your children why debt is bad and to never put yourself in that situation with a bank.

While the 1920s seem like distant history, the lessons passed down from that generation still have a profound effect on the perception of debt today, at least in America. Some debts are toxic for your finances, such as credit cards with high interest rates. However, not all debt is bad. If all debt were bad, why would so many successful companies in the S&P 500 index have debt? As a reminder, the S&P 500 measures the performance of 500 of the largest publicly traded companies in the U.S. As of 2023, AT&T, the telecommunications giant with more than $121 billion in revenue, had approximately $136 billion in debt[14]. Toyota had around $217 billion in debt with $271 billion in revenue. Ford, General Motors, Comcast, Disney, Microsoft, Apple, and Caterpillar each had debt as of 2023. Why would these successful companies with highly intelligent people running them decide to have long-term debt? It's because some debts are bad and some can be used to your advantage.

We discussed earlier why I decided to purchase my home primarily with debt. Thanks to a low rate and a tax deduction, the interest costs aren't hurting my family because I'm free to use my cash for investment opportunities. I'm leveraging my time by focusing on long-term growth rather than paying off a low-interest rate debt. This is generally the same reason a corporation would use debt, despite making billions of dollars in revenue.

Let's assume you own a manufacturing company that produces medical equipment. You want to start a new line of business from a new product you've created. In order to bring this product to market, you'll need to expand your existing factory, purchase new equipment, hire new employees, and acquire raw materials. Based on your research, you estimate that you'll need $1 million to launch this new product and expect to earn 15 percent on your investment. You then reach out to your bank to ask about commercial loans and they offer you $1 million at 8 percent interest for 10 years. The loan can also be paid back early with no penalty if you wish. You decide to borrow the money, despite the cost you'll incur due to interest, because you feel you can still generate a profit. You expect your rate of return to be higher than your rate of interest. This is a simple yet prime example of how and why businesses of all sizes use debt. Without it, new products may never make it to market or would take substantially longer to launch as cash is saved over time.

It's easy to see this example and understand why a business would want to take on debt, but when someone considers the same strategy for their own personal assets, emotions come into play. Would you borrow money at 5 percent and invest it if you felt you could earn twice that rate in return? It's a difficult decision when it's your own hard-earned money and you're not used to thinking like a business. While personally borrowing money from the bank to invest in the stock market is a risky move, deciding to *not* pay off low-rate debts early such as a mortgage and investing the money instead can make great financial sense over time.

Some financial experts will tell you that all debts are bad. They write books on how to pay off debt as quickly as possible and never use debt again. My approach is different. Consider using debt to your advantage, but only "good" debt. Good debts are low-rate mortgages, business loans, or student loans. The list of bad debts is larger and includes payday loans, credit cards, auto loans, boat loans, and personal loans used for buying depreciators.

With student loans, borrowing $300,000 for a career that pays an average of $70,000 per year obviously doesn't make financial sense. In general, I believe it's acceptable to borrow money for a college education if you or your family don't have the cash. If you borrow $30,000 to be able to make $70,000 per year instead of $50,000 per year, it's easy to justify the debt to have more earning power over your lifetime. However, is it truly worth it financially if you borrow more than $100,000 to earn a PhD in a field that may only pay $70,000 per year? You may be able to earn a different degree for far less and still make $70,000 per year. I completely understand career choices involve more than just money, but tweaks can still be made on the college cost side for careers that have low to moderate average pay.

I've met attorneys who went to prestigious universities to earn their degrees. Many of them had more than $100,000 of debt. Some had spouses who were also attorneys and had about the same amount of debt. While an attorney typically makes more than the average person, not every field of law is created equally. Family law attorneys may have a much different income than corporate litigation attorneys, for example. It's possible an expensive, prestigious university may create friends and contacts that help in someone's career. However, outside that possibility, some career paths are very hard to justify with significant student loan debt. Remember, if you can't pay off student loan debt quickly and must make payments for 20 years, that cashflow can't be invested for your future. That means you lost precious time that can't be recovered. Student loan debt is fine, but only to a point.

In the budgeting section of this chapter, I cover credit cards, using them responsibly, and possibly quitting them when they're a problem. Now let's talk about what to do if you find yourself with credit card debt you've already accumulated. If this doesn't apply to you, the following strategies may allow you to offer advice to a friend one day who's in trouble. Everyone knows it's unwise to accumulate this kind of bad debt. Despite this, I've met countless people who've found themselves in trouble with credit cards. It can happen to anyone of any age with virtually any income level. The trouble usually starts with a large purchase that can't be paid off the following month, such as a home remodeling project or an unexpected car repair. Then, they continue charging expenses to the card while carrying a balance month to month. Then, another large expense is added from an unforeseen event, such as a health issue or broken appliance. Sometimes, it's a vacation they knew they shouldn't have added to the credit card, but they felt they had earned it. The debt has grown so much that it's difficult to fix.

No matter the specifics, if you currently have credit card debt that can't be paid off within three months and your interest rate is relatively high, it's time to take action. By the way, a relatively high interest rate is one that's equal to or higher than the rate you think you can earn on your investments. If you can't control your debt, consider using a service called credit counseling. In some countries this is called debt counseling or financial counseling. Credit counseling may sound like laying down on a couch and talking about your first childhood memory of money, but it's really more like cash flow and debt management.

Credit counseling services will generally help you understand your income and expenses so you can clearly see your cash flow. Then, they help you consolidate your debts and lower your interest costs. For example, they may help you consolidate three credit cards and one auto loan into one single loan payment, while also negotiating with your credit card companies to lower your interest rate. Negotiating the terms of your loan with a credit card company isn't something even I know how to do as a CFP®. It's likely these credit counseling services have special contacts with credit card providers and know the right words to say. Many credit counseling services are nonprofit organizations. They may charge a fee for their services to cover their costs, but their fee may still be worth it if they're able to greatly simplify your debt payments and reduce your interest costs. If you find a similar service that recommends ceasing all payments on your debts to scare your creditors into thinking you're unable to pay, be aware that your credit score may suffer considerably. Most nonprofit credit counseling services won't recommend strategies that aggressive.

If you have bad debt that needs to be addressed but don't want to use a credit counseling service, here's how you can do it yourself.

First, write down the amount you owe. This may be a mix of mortgage, auto loans, credit cards, etc. Next to each debt, write down the interest rate. If you have a debt with an introductory interest rate, such as zero percent for 12 months, write down the rate you'll pay after the introductory period. Next, write down whether each debt is fixed or variable. A fixed interest rate will remain constant through the loan, while a variable interest rate can float or change over time as interest rates in the economy change.

Now, rank each of these debts by their interest rate, putting the highest interest rate at the top. For those with introductory rates, if you don't think you'll pay off that debt by the time the rate increases, use the rate it will eventually become as you rank each debt. Once you've ranked the highest-rate debt to the lowest rate, you now have your list of debts ranked by importance. The highest rates are the most important debts to pay off, while the lowest rates are less important.

As you find yourself with extra money in the bank, whether from a bonus, a raise, a gift, or selling something you don't need, use it to pay down the No. 1 debt on your list. You may be tempted to pay down the largest debt, the smallest debt, or pay down each debt with a little extra. Ignore the balances and focus on your priority list based on the highest interest rate, not the balance. If you tend to live without any extra cash each month and you have bad debts, it's time to have a hard look at your expenses. Find something you can live without to pay off this debt or you may miss out on precious time to build wealth. I can't stress this enough. You're making someone else rich by paying high interest rates.

Whether you currently have bad debts or not, remember that debt can be a tool. It's not all bad, especially when it comes to running and growing a business. If you prefer to live a lifestyle where no debt is ever used, more power to you. It's not a bad strategy, but also not necessary. Plenty of successful people leverage debt, but they do it wisely. Relying on personal loans, auto loans, and credit cards to buy depreciating assets at high interest rates is something you should avoid if you want to succeed financially. Pay off bad debts aggressively — as if your life depends on it — because your time is too valuable.

Credit

Early in my life, I had a credit card with a very low maximum limit. It was roughly $3,000. I only used it for international travel because it didn't charge extra fees for currency conversions. After having this card for many years, I decided to increase the limit in case I needed to make larger purchases. After applying with the company for an increase in the limit to something significantly higher, I was approved for a whopping $250 increase. This obviously wasn't what I had in mind. I called the company to speak with someone about the issue and a representative said there was nothing she could do. Her company used a computer algorithm to automatically make credit decisions about limit increases. In frustration, I explained that my credit score was excellent, I had no outstanding credit card debt, I had never been late for a payment of any type of debt in my life. I honestly didn't need a credit card because I had plenty of money. To no avail, she reminded me there was nothing she could do and sent me on my way. I then applied for a new credit card and was approved for more credit than I would ever need.

This example illustrates how the credit system in the United States doesn't always make sense. More and more decisions are being made by computer systems than a person relying on common sense. As a businessman, I completely understand why this trend is occurring. We must be mindful of how the system works and what we can do to leverage it to our advantage.

As a reminder, "building credit" is the process of showing others you're financially responsible over time. It's a report card of sorts for your ability to manage money. Credit bureaus are large institutions that act as the collectors of our financial data. In the U.S., it can include:

- The types of debt you may have open (credit cards, mortgage, auto loan, etc.)
- The limits on each debt

- The amount owed on each debt
- How many times you've made a late payment
- If you have any debts in collection
- The age of your debts (how long you've had them)

These credit bureaus then use this information to give you a credit score. Your financial activities shape this score over time, either positively or negatively. For example, if you have 10 credit cards and most of them are near their limit, but you make your payments on time, that's not going to help your score. It's crucially important to maintain good financial habits with your debts and bills so you can increase your score over time.

The irony in the credit scoring system is it shouldn't matter for some Americans. For example, a man once drove past an exotic car dealership and decided to stop in to admire the cars. He was a successful businessman and always thought about buying such a toy. A salesman approached him and before the man knew, he was going for a test drive in an orange sportscar that could go from zero to 60 in three seconds. Exhilarated by the experience, he decided to buy it. Because he didn't plan for this large purchase, he hadn't had time to transfer the appropriate amount of cash into his checking account. The salesman recommended financing because it was zero percent interest. The man agreed and applied for financing. However, because this successful businessman never used credit to buy anything, he didn't have any credit history whatsoever. He always paid cash and was a multi-millionaire. Therefore, his credit score was too low to be approved for the loan, despite being extremely well qualified. He decided not to buy the car and thanked the salesman for the experience.

This is an example of how the credit scoring system doesn't always make sense. The businessman in this story could have written a check for 10 exotic cars but wasn't approved to buy even one because of his credit score. He had lived a life without credit, which is impressive, and was penalized for doing so. This is why most people must work on building good credit if they ever want to use it. Although credit scores are used largely for credit decisions, they can also be used by the following:

- Phone companies
- Utility providers
- Employers
- Insurance companies
- Agencies reviewing your financial status for government benefits
- Landlords

Because your credit scores can affect your life so greatly, from the ability to buy insurance to landing a great job, it's important to take intentional steps to maintain and improve it. Aside from making payments on time to creditors, which is the most important factor to having a good credit score, here are other factors you should consider.

First, monitor how much of your maximum credit you're using. For example, if you have a credit card with a $10,000 maximum limit, try not to use more than 30 percent of it. It might seem strange, but a $10,000 limit means you shouldn't have more than a $3,000 balance. If you use more than 30 percent of your available credit, this tells creditors that you may depend more on credit and less on cash. This may or may not be true, but it's something to consider when using credit. If you find yourself adding larger purchases to a credit card that would exceed the 30 percent limit, consider increasing your maximum credit limit or immediately paying down the debt if you have the cash.

Second, the age of your credit accounts can help your score. Let's say you have a credit card account that's been open for seven years, but you're thinking about switching to a different credit card company. If you close the credit card of seven years, you may negatively affect your score. This doesn't mean you should maintain five different credit cards, but it does mean you should consider keeping the longest-standing card to show creditors that you can maintain good credit habits over the long term.

Third, having a mix of credit accounts can help your score. For example, having an auto loan, credit card, student loan, personal loan, and mortgage may show that you can manage a diversified pool of credit. Each type of debt is different, such as having fixed payments versus variable payments. This may seem counterintuitive because taking on debt isn't usually a good idea. This concept of diversified credit is more informational than something I recommend acting on.

Fourth, try to avoid applying for multiple new credit accounts in a short period of time. This may indicate you're in financial trouble if you're applying for two new credit cards and an auto loan all within a few weeks. Creditors may see this as a risk. This may also occur when shopping for a mortgage. If you apply for a mortgage with numerous banks or mortgage brokers, each may be checking your credit, which is reportable to the credit bureaus.

Maintaining and monitoring your credit has become easier over the years as new laws and new technologies have emerged. For example, many large banks now provide free apps or online tools that estimate your credit score and help you monitor it. These tools have been a significant help to consumers to provide transparency to a credit scoring system that used to be more of a mystery.

In the U.S., you can also review your credit report for free once per year by federal law. Please keep in mind that your credit *report* is different than your credit *score*. Your credit report shows historical information that's used to build your score. For example, your credit report may show how many credit accounts you currently have open and if you've ever missed a payment. It's important to check this report once per year for errors. If you notice something that doesn't look correct, you may be able to appeal to the credit bureaus to have it fixed, which may help your score. The only website that provides free credit reports by U.S. federal law is www.annualcreditreport.com. Other websites exist that charge a fee for credit reporting services, so be sure to use the correct site. If you were already familiar with this site, have you used it in the last year? Knowing is one thing, but doing is another.

Overall, we live in a society that depends on the credit scoring system. It may seem strange that debt must be used to establish and enhance this, but it's simply a factor of how the system works. Be mindful of what "ingredients" are used in building your score and use discipline in your approach.

Chapter 3

Insurance

In this chapter:
- Building and protecting wealth
- Life, health, disability, home, & auto
- Common misconceptions

While this book focuses on creating and growing wealth, leaving your assets unprotected is like heading into battle with only a sword and no shield or armor. Even the most skilled swordsman will face human error and bad luck at some point. Managing wealth includes both creating it *and* protecting it. Without proper coverage, you may be putting your wealth at risk. Insurance is one of those topics that can solicit strong opinions and even emotions. What I've always found interesting on the topic is how some people consider one type of insurance different than others. Some people say they hate life insurance, while they would never think twice about buying homeowners insurance. In its purest form, insurance is aleatory, which means it's a gambling contract. When a risk is present in your life or your business, you can choose to pay a fee, or premium, to another party to accept part or all of the risk instead of you. You *transfer* the risk to them, and they ask for payment in return. All insurance works this way at its core.

The first forms of insurance started as far back as ancient Babylonia during the time of King Hammurabi. Merchants who shipped their goods via rivers and seas would sometimes borrow money to finance their operations. Within the Code of Hammurabi Law, a merchant could pay an additional fee to a lender to guarantee that the loan would be forgiven if the shipment was lost at sea or stolen. The additional fee can be thought of as a premium payment to receive a guarantee against loss or theft. If a merchant borrowed money to ship wheat to another city and the shipment was lost at sea due to a storm, the merchant wouldn't be obligated to pay back the loan thanks to the extra gold coin he paid for the guarantee. This type of contract was supported by the laws of the Old Babylonian Empire. There are many other examples from ancient civilizations that typically focused on transferring risk from the perils of maritime trade.

Modern insurance can be highly complex, with long contracts, riders, exclusions, and counterparties. An industry with roots in nautical trade has bloomed into health insurance, disability insurance, long-term care insurance, pet insurance, and more. You can even find body part insurance, wedding insurance, and multiple birth insurance these days. If insurance is the ability to transfer risk from one party to another, if you don't believe it's necessary, you can try other risk management options. I can think of a few alternatives to wedding insurance, for sure.

There are four strategies for managing risk. You've already learned one of them, which is transferring risk. This is the concept of insurance. Another risk management strategy is reducing risk. Think of this like choosing to drive 40 miles per hour in a car instead of 80. You still have risk from driving but cutting your speed down to 40 represents a reduction in risk. A third risk management option is risk avoidance. If you fear driving over bridges, you might decide to drive the long way around instead and completely avoid this risk. Someone who fears rollercoasters may decide to avoid them and spend time at bumper cars instead. The fourth risk management option is risk acceptance. If you decided to forgo wedding insurance on your big day, you practiced a form of risk management by accepting the risk your significant other may not show up for the ceremony.

While some forms of risk seem fine to accept, others require a more complex answer. That answer may be some form of insurance at some level of risk transfer. The good news about having a robust global insurance industry today is that many options exist to customize an insurance policy and how much risk you want to transfer or accept. Let's discuss six common types of insurance and how you may decide to use them or avoid them.

1. Life insurance
2. Health insurance
3. Disability insurance
4. Long-term care insurance
5. Home and auto insurance
6. Pet insurance

Life Insurance

Many people see life insurance as a way to pay for burial or cremation expenses, but it's more commonly for the replacement of someone's income. If you have three young children and only one of two parents in your household works, you may have a significant risk of losing the working parent's income. What if you don't have kids, though? What if you're not married or if your spouse would be fine financially on his or her own if you died? Is life insurance needed in that example? There would be emotional harm if someone died, but if there wouldn't be any *financial* harm, it's possible life insurance may not be needed.

During a meeting with two of my clients years ago, who are husband and wife, we discussed their whole life insurance policies. We'll discuss this type of life insurance soon. My clients were each about 58 years old at the time. They both had purchased whole life insurance policies on themselves when their children were young. At the time, they were concerned with losing the other spouse's income in the event of a tragedy. Now that their two children were grown and financially independent, I asked them why they continued to pay for these whole life policies. They were both healthy and expected to live well into their 80s or 90s. They explained that these policies had been with them for decades and enjoyed the comfort of knowing they were insured to cover burial expenses. I then pulled up information on their total net worth. When including cash in the bank, retirement accounts, real estate value, and vehicle values, their net worth was more than $3 million. At the time, average burial costs were around $10,000. I then showed them a retirement projection that assumed the other spouse had died. They were expected to be fine financially on their own. They quickly realized they had reached a point in their lives where those old policies weren't needed any longer. There was no longer a risk.

We're often taught at a young age that life insurance is something everyone should have. Everyone should have life insurance because everyone has a risk of dying. It's true that we're all at risk of dying prematurely, but life insurance is meant to protect against the *financial* risk of losing someone. That includes final expenses such as a burial or cremation, plus losing someone's income that's needed to pay down debts, save for college, cover bills, etc. If someone is single with no kids and no one is dependent on them, do they need life insurance? If they have a car, a small investment account, and some cash in the bank, that may be more than enough to cover final expenses. Therefore, what value would life insurance offer? If there's no financial risk to anyone if that person's income is lost, life insurance probably isn't necessary. In other words, if you sold your car and rode the bus to work every day, would you still pay for auto insurance? Absolutely not. That's because the risk of owning and driving a car went away. Therefore, insurance to protect against that risk isn't needed. If you determine there's no financial risk to anyone if your income stops coming in, you may not need life insurance.

Now, let's talk about those who do need life insurance. If your income went away and someone would be harmed financially, it's time to calculate how much life insurance you need. Asking a licensed insurance professional how much life insurance you need is a bit like asking a real estate agent how much house you can afford. The more you buy, the more they make. There's obvious bias. It doesn't mean they're bad people. It simply means someone can't be completely unbiased when their compensation changes based on their recommendation. Therefore, I recommend the "trust but verify" method. Ask for a recommendation from an insurance professional but verify their recommendation on your own or with an online calculator. Independent fee-only financial planners who don't sell life insurance can generally help with this calculation, too. If you want to calculate this on your own, visit GrowthInfo.com/life for an easy-to-use life insurance calculator. Remember to consider more than just burial or cremation expenses. Should college expenses be covered by life insurance? How long would you want to replace someone's lost income? Should the mortgage be paid off or would the surviving spouse need to move to a different house? These factors all contribute to determining how much life insurance you may need.

If you currently need life insurance, remember to reassess your situation at least every five years. If you acquired $1 million of life insurance when your kids were under the age of 10, but they're now in their 30s and on their own, it's possible you no longer need life insurance. It's also possible you still need insurance, but at a lesser amount. Some life insurance carriers allow you to reduce your policy value, thereby reducing your premium cost. They understand it's better to allow you to reduce the cost or you may cancel the policy completely. Overall, remember that life insurance is meant to protect against risk. Once the risk is gone, you may no longer need it. Instead of keeping it to pay for your final expenses, remember you may have plenty of assets that can be sold to pay for these expenses, plus one heck of a party. Life insurance doesn't always need to be around for life.

One possible exception to only having life insurance when there's a risk is if you want to secure a policy while you have good health. Before I was married or had kids, I decided to buy a relatively small 30-year term life insurance policy. That's because I was in great health and knew I could lock in a preferred rate for 30 years. That meant if my health changed a year later, I would still be able to keep my low-rate 30-year term policy. While the chance of someone's health changing significantly from age 20 to age 30 is low, it's something to consider if you're in good health.

You'll notice I purchased a term policy when I was younger, not a policy that has cash value. By nature, insurance policies don't typically include the "growth" of cash or the accumulation of value over time. Think about your homeowners or renters insurance. It doesn't accumulate cash. Think about your auto insurance or your health insurance. Those policies don't give you cash when you surrender them. The idea of having an "investment" component combined with insurance is distinct to the life insurance industry. What's unique about life insurance is it's the only type of insurance you're guaranteed to use at some point in your life. It isn't a question of "if" but a question of "when."

Term life insurance is the simplest and purest form of life insurance. You may acquire a 20-year term policy for a $500,000 death benefit. If you die in Year 18 of the 20-year term, as long as you didn't violate the contract (which is rare), your family or estate will receive $500,000. However, if you live beyond 20 years and the policy expires, you don't receive anything. No cash value component exists with term life insurance. Remember, that's not necessarily a bad thing to live more than 20 years and not receive anything from a life insurance policy!

I personally prefer term life insurance over other types of life insurance for two reasons — it's easy to understand and the cost is generally lower than cash value-type life insurance. Term insurance is purely a contract to pay a lump-sum amount of money if you die during the term. The insurance company calculates the risk of you dying during the term period and charges you a premium for taking on the risk. That's it. By using the lowest-cost option for life insurance, your money can be used to pay down debt or grow your nest egg.

While term insurance was the original style of life insurance offered commercially, eventually three more types of life insurance were created:
- Whole life
- Universal life
- Variable universal life

With these types of policies, the insurance carriers essentially "marry" a term-life policy with a cash-accumulation vehicle. The cash-accumulation vehicle differs between each of these three types, but one benefit of this "marriage" is the Internal Revenue Service (IRS) typically allows the cash to grow tax-deferred. This means the typically isn't taxed until you withdraw gains from the policy. Here's a high-level description of each one so you can have a basic understanding of each.

Whole life — With whole life, you can receive dividend and interest that often accumulate inside the policy. The growth of this cash inside the policy depends on the success of the insurance company but can also change based on interest rates. From my experience, whole life tends to be the most common type of cash-value life insurance sold by agents. There are many different riders and options to customize whole-life policies, which can be both convenient and confusing.

Universal life — With universal life, the cash value accumulates based on interest rates. Unlike whole life, universal life generally doesn't depend on dividend payments from the life insurance company that issues the policy. Because cash can grow from interest, if rates are low, don't expect much growth. Also, because these policies rely on interest rates, you may be able to acquire a guaranteed policy. This means you can receive a guarantee that the policy will never lapse as long as you make your guaranteed premium payments over time. This is one reason people use universal life.

Variable universal life — With variable universal life, which I'll call variable life, the cash value can accumulate in what looks more like a mutual fund. Variable life policies use the "chassis" of a universal life policy but offer a menu of investment options to invest your cash value. This type of cash-value life insurance is the closest category to resemble a traditional investment and because it's "married" with term life, so you may enjoy tax-deferred growth. The greatest risk to this category is the fact that your investment choices may lose money. You can lose your principle, just like any other investment.

With all cash-value life insurance, keep in mind that they often require more premium than a simple term-life policy. That's how the policy begins building cash value — the extra dollars over and above the cost of the insurance are put into the cash value "bucket" to potentially grow over time. Think of it like the insurance company forcing you to save part of your premium into the cash-value bucket. Many people choose to buy term-life insurance and invest on their own. There are times, however, when cash-value policies make sense. They're more common in businesses for liquidity if an owner dies or for families with very large estates. In other words, the average person is probably fine with term life. More complex cases or families with significant wealth may need cash-value life.

Keep in mind, these cash-value-type policies pay an upfront commission to the agents and advisors who sell them. This doesn't mean they're poor choices to consider. It simply means the alure of a big payday can sometimes direct these professionals to recommend whole life, universal life, or variable life over other options like term life. Typically, the higher the premium, the higher the commission. If someone recommends a cash-value life insurance policy to you, you'll need to ask tough questions on why term insurance isn't being recommended. I've seen so many people with policies they don't truly need because they were convinced to buy them. Folks who sell life insurance have to make a living, so it's on you to make sure you're not buying something you don't need.

Health insurance

In 2018, a new company was formed by Amazon, Berkshire Hathaway, and JPMorgan Chase. The company was called Haven and was formed to reinvent the health care industry in the U.S. The titans behind the new venture, Jeff Bezos, Warren Buffett, and Jamie Dimon, each had a unified vision of making health care more accessible, less complex, and less costly to the American people. I can remember the excitement in the marketplace about this new company. The thought of these three business leaders coming together to improve an overly complex system was thrilling. Less than three years later, the company failed. The COVID pandemic didn't help, but the complicated health care system in the U.S. is so entrenched that not even Bezos, Buffett, and Dimon could change it.

Health insurance in the U.S. involves federal regulations, state regulations, employers, in-network physicians, out-of-network physicians, third-party billing groups, insurance carriers, copays, deductibles, tax rules, and more. It's probably the most complex personal insurance in the U.S. This chapter covers some of the most important info to know without writing an entire book on the details.

The most important point about health insurance is making sure you never have a lapse in coverage. I've known people who have gone months without health insurance with no issue, but the risk of having an accident or illness that costs tens or hundreds of thousands of dollars is too great to go uninsured. Young, healthy people are often the most likely demographic to risk going without coverage, but it's simply not worth the risk.

In 2019, Scott Parness learned firsthand about the risk of being uninsured. The 39-year-old woke one day with a pain in his abdomen. He went to the emergency room where doctors discovered he had appendicitis. He soon went into surgery to remove his appendix. A few days later, Shannon felt pain in the area where his appendix was removed. The pain continued to grow until it was unbearable. He returned to the same hospital where a CT scan revealed a brick-sized blood clot in his lower abdomen. After yet another surgery and four days in the hospital, he was released. Then the medical bills began to arrive. He was charged $35,906 for the first surgery, plus $44,326 for the second surgery. He was also charged for services by the surgeon, anesthesiologist, and radiologist. Unfortunately, due to being uninsured, Shannon was faced with paying these bills himself. While it's possible someone may live without health insurance and face zero health care costs, the financial risks can be significant.

A common question I receive is what type of health insurance plan to choose. If you work for an employer that offers health insurance, you're familiar with open enrollment — the period of time where you can pick various benefits, including different health insurance plans. Two common categories of health plans are high-deductible plans or PPO/HMO plans. A higher deductible means you'll have more out-of-pocket expenses before your health plan generally begins to pay a benefit. Therefore, these plans usually have a lower premium expense each month. A high-deductible plan can be designed as a PPO or as an HMO. I won't go into the differences between a PPO and an HMO in this book, but the primary difference is how you access different types of physicians.

If you have poor health and rack up health care expenses every year, a high-deductible plan may not be for you. Having a higher deductible means you're taking on more of the risk if you need care. Generally, if you believe you'll pay the full deductible for a calendar year, you may want to opt for the lower deductible plan. That may not always be the case, especially if your employer puts money into a Health Savings Account (HSA), but it gives you a general idea.

One of my favorite features of a high-deductible plan is the ability to use a HSA. The HSA is a type of account that provides potential tax benefits and a way to save for health care expenses. The basic idea of an HSA is to save money into the account so you can then use it to cover your high deductible during an expensive health care event. If your health insurance plan deductible is $4,000 and you have $4,000 in your HSA, you can use these dollars to cover the full deductible without draining the cash in your bank. Once the deductible is met, your health insurance plan should generally begin paying for your costs. If you save into the HSA and don't spend the money, you can carry the balance forward into the next year. It's not a "use it or lose it" account. The balance is owned and controlled by you, not an employer. If your employer contributes to your HSA on your behalf, too, those dollars are generally yours to control also.

The HSA can provide a triple tax benefit, depending on where you live in the U.S. First, you may receive a state income tax deduction on the dollars you contribute to the HSA. The IRS dictates the maximum

amount you can contribute to the HSA, so visit GrowthInfo.com/
taxes to check on the most current maximum. Some states don't assess
an income tax, and a few states that do have state income taxes don't
allow the HSA deduction. Second, you can receive a federal income
tax deduction on the dollars you contribute to the HSA. The higher
your federal income tax bracket, the higher your potential tax savings.
Third, you can receive a FICA tax deduction. FICA is Social Security
and Medicare tax in the U.S. Employer retirement plans offer state and
federal income tax deductions, but not a FICA deduction. Thanks to
this potential triple tax benefit, the HSA can be a great tool to use if a
high-deductible health plan is right for you. I'll also share one of my
favorite tax planning strategies using the HSA in Chapter 5.

There's plenty more on health insurance, but the most important
concept to remember is not to have a lapse in coverage, especially
if you're in between jobs. If you secure temporary health insurance
or something called COBRA, acquire proof of insurance before you
assume you're covered.

Disability insurance

Brad Laing is a writer from California. At 20, he was your typical college student. He enjoyed parties, visiting friends, and traveling during
breaks from school. During spring break, he and his friends drove two
hours from their university for a party. Like many college-age parties,
drinks were plentiful. Brad was smart, though, and had a designated
driving for the evening, a friend of his who had to work early in the
morning. As the party drew to a close, he and his friends hopped in
their car to drive back home. Brad fell asleep as they drove down the
freeway under the moonlight.

Suddenly, the car jolted. Brad woke up to find the car had run
into the center divider on the freeway. His friend had fallen asleep at
the wheel. Now the car was disabled in the middle of the dark California interstate. Brad and his friends panicked. They exited the car and
tried pushing it to the shoulder so it wouldn't cause an accident. As
they did, a car came up behind them and slammed into theirs. With

little time to react, the force slammed the disabled vehicle into Brad, launching him into the air. He landed roughly 20 feet from where he was just standing. One of his uninjured friends ran to his aid, finding Brad covered in blood. His body was disfigured.

Help soon arrived; Brad was rushed to the hospital. Doctors put him into a medically induced coma, which lasted two weeks. He had broken his nose, jaw, and collarbone, and had a traumatic brain injury. As he recovered, he found his short-term memory was shot, struggling to recall what he did the prior day. He thought to himself, "How am I supposed to graduate from college? Who would hire me for a job?"

After one month in the hospital and another month in an intensive rehabilitation center, he was released. He was told it may be a year until his brain returned to normal, but he may never be 100 percent again. He went on to graduate from his university and shares his story so others can appreciate the health and good things they may have in life.

Anyone can relate to Brad's story. Have you fallen asleep in a car at night while trusting someone to drive you home safely? I certainly have. Brad was unfortunate in his luck that evening and will live forever with the consequences. We can control many variables in our lives, but not all of them. Accidents simply happen. If we're lucky enough to survive such accidents, we must survive the consequences, too.

In the year prior to the initial COVID epidemic, there were nearly 1.9 million car accidents in the U.S. that involved an injury[15]. This excludes the car accidents that lead to a fatality. Millions of people are injured in car, bus, and motorcycle accidents each year. If those injuries are bad enough, they may cause either a short-term or long-term disability. In addition to car accidents, cancer is another leading cause of disability that can affect someone of any age. Because of these risks, it's important for young people to consider disability insurance.

Disability insurance at its core is meant to protect someone's income in the event they can no longer work. I've found disability to be one of those risks that people highly underestimate. Becoming partially or totally disabled isn't something people generally want to think about in the first place. Add the fun topic of disability *insurance* to the mix and you can see why it's often avoided.

Imagine you own a home worth $500,000. Would you protect it against fires, tornadoes, and flood damage? I rarely find someone who goes without insurance on their home. After all, the financial loss from these perils could be hundreds of thousands of dollars. Homes are also quite visible. You can see the drywall, brick, and electrical work that would need to be replaced from damage. The risk of disability is much less visible.

Imagine that you earn $75,000 per year in salary at the age of 30. If you became totally disabled and could no longer work, what would the potential damage be in terms of lost income? Assuming you couldn't work at all, your lost income from age 30 to 65, without assuming any adjustments for inflation, would be $2.625 million. Compared to our earlier example, that's five homes. The number is much higher when you include inflation. So, why do so many people place greater importance on homeowner's insurance than they do on disability insurance if the risk could be exponentially higher?

Aside from the earlier examples of homes being more visible and disability being an event few people want to think about, some people assume they're covered with their employer's disability insurance plan. Some people treat this type of insurance as a "check the box" task. As long as they have something they can call "disability insurance," they move on. Unfortunately, unlike term life insurance, which is very straightforward, disability insurance is more complex.

For those employers who offer disability insurance, some only pay benefits for five years. That means if you become disabled, the benefits may only pay out for five years. For a 30-year-old who becomes totally disabled, what about the gap between age 35 and age 65? That's almost a lifetime of working potential left. This is why you can't just check a box when it comes to disability insurance. Some employer disability plans pay for benefits to age 65, but I find many only pay for five years or less.

Another consideration for employer plans is taxation. If your employer is paying for your disability insurance and deducting it as an expense, you'll likely owe tax on the benefits of the policy. Assuming our 30-year-old makes $75,000 per year and needs to collect on her policy due to a disability, she would owe income tax on her insurance benefits. Depending on where you live and other taxable income sources in your household, that could take a significant bite out of your benefits while you're adjusting to life without work.

Another point to know about employer disability plans is they typically only cover a fixed percentage of your income, such as 60 percent. Many also have maximum limits. For example, if you make $200,000 per year, the employer plan may not actually cover 60 percent of your income due to maximum limits. For someone making $75,000 per year, a 60 percent benefit would be $45,000 per year. Then take out income taxes if they apply and the amount of net income would be even lower. If you're someone who finds it difficult to live on your current level of income, imagine a 40 percent pay cut or worse. This is why disability insurance is so important to understand.

There are generally two types of disability insurance — short and long term. Short-term disabilities are usually those that last six months or fewer, while long-term disabilities are those that exceed six months. I usually think of long-term disabilities as lasting many years or decades. While being out of work for three months would be difficult for many families, I don't worry much about a short-term loss of income. This is why someone should have an emergency fund — to make it through an emergency without racking up debt. In my opinion, a healthy emergency fund is an acceptable alternative for short-term disability insurance.

Because long-term disability insurance through an employer is often limited by a certain percentage, such as 60 percent of salary, plus the plan may only pay out for five years, consider supplementing an employer's plan with your own private disability insurance. This means acquiring your own policy that has nothing to do with your employer. It also means you must pay for the premium on your own.

Aside from having your own policy to offer more protection, it also means your benefits may be tax free if you collect on the policy one day. Paying your premiums with after-tax dollars means you're not deducting the cost of the policy. In turn, you're likely to receive tax-free benefits.

In the U.S., if you're wondering about Social Security and how it plays into disability coverage, it does have a system to pay benefits in the event of a disability. However, it doesn't function like traditional disability insurance. If you work and pay taxes into Social Security, you may be eligible for Social Security disability insurance. Think of it like regular Social Security income you may receive at retirement age, but it's available earlier if you have a qualifying disability. Social Security also offers something called Supplemental Security Income, or SSI. SSI doesn't have a work requirement like Social Security disability insurance, but it's generally provided for individuals with a minimal amount of income and assets. SSI has a lower average benefit to recipients also. For either program through Social Security, you're not guaranteed to receive disability benefits. You must qualify under their definition of disability. If you do qualify, you may find it difficult to live on the benefit. As of 2022, the average Social Security disability benefit per recipient was $1,358 per month[16]. This benefit increases with inflation over time, but that only keeps up with increasing costs. In other words, I wouldn't depend much on Social Security to help you.

If you buy your own private disability policy to supplement what you have at work, there are a few points you need to know. First, you need to know how your employer plan works. You can acquire this info from your employer. Second, don't feel like you need enough insurance to cover 100 percent of your pay. In fact, most insurance companies will only insure up to 80 percent or 90 percent of your pay because they want you to share some of the risk. Depending on your situation, insuring between 60 percent and 80 percent of your pay is normally the sweet spot. Third, buy a policy with a strong definition of disability.

Some policies will pay out a benefit if you become totally disabled, while others will pay out if you can't perform the duties of your own occupation. For example, if you're a dentist and lose your vision, you can't perform the duties of your occupation any longer. However, you may still be able to work as a receptionist in a dentist's office. Two common definitions of disability are "own occupation" and "any occupation."

Imagine being in a car accident that leaves you with permanent damage. Doctors tell you there's nothing further they can do to remedy the severe tremor you've developed in your hands. Prior to the accident, you worked as a nurse for a large hospital. Now you can't return to your job because you can't safely treat patients without a steady hand. Drawing blood, working medical equipment, and dressing wounds is no longer safe for you or the patients. You make the difficult decision of filing for disability benefits through your company's disability plan because you can't return to the job you love. After the insurance company reviews your medical records, it determines you don't qualify for disability benefits, citing that you can still work in the medical field in a different function, such as medical transcription or billing. These alternative careers pay less than half of your prior salary. With two children at home depending on you, you decide to sue the insurance company for denying your claim. Unfortunately, after 18 months of litigation, the insurance company wins because your disability insurance policy required you to be unable to perform the duties of *any* occupation for which you were trained and educated.

There are countless stories of people suing their insurance carrier over disability insurance claims. Part of the reason is because of how complex these policies can be and people not understanding the terms of the policy. For both employer disability plans and individual policies, pay special attention to the definition of disability. For my own disability insurance, because I don't have a policy through an employer, I have a policy that covers roughly 70 percent of my income. I made sure the definition of disability is "own occupation" and not "any occupation." This stronger definition of disability is more expensive than "any occupation," but in my case, I see no reason to go cheap when protecting my family. I needed a policy that would protect my income and my family in the event I could no longer perform the duties of my career. My policy also covers a partial disability, such as being limited in my ability to work in my own occupation. It doesn't require me to be totally disabled in my own occupation to pay a benefit. You may be able to find a policy with this type of coverage, too.

If you're wondering if the cost of disability insurance is worth it, consider the cost as a percentage of your income. Insurance should cost a small amount relative to the risk. If a policy costs 3 percent of your income to protect 80 percent of your income, that's acceptable in my opinion. It may not feel that way if you look at it in dollar terms but use percentages to put the cost into perspective. As you grow older and have fewer years left to work, the risk generally becomes lower and lower. If you're 62 years old and plan on retiring at 65, a loss of income is less detrimental than it would be 30 years earlier. This is one reason why disability insurance can be costly for younger people. Depending on your situation, disability insurance might be more important than life insurance or homeowners' insurance.

Home and auto insurance

When I was 17, I was involved in a terrible car accident. It was the first day of summer and I was hanging out with my friends on a sunny afternoon. One of them needed to run to his house, so two of us tagged along for the ride. I was sitting in the back of my friend's car. As we headed down the road toward his home, he picked up speed. We were going well over the speed limit, as teenagers do sometimes. That's the last moment I remember.

I awoke in the hospital, drunk on pain medication though an IV. I tried moving my head, but I was in a neck brace. My family members and a few friends were there in the hospital room. I looked down and saw bandages covering my left arm. Then, I went back to sleep. By the time I woke again, I was in a different hospital. Not only do I not remember the ambulance ride to the first hospital, I don't remember the helicopter ride to the second. There were staples in my head, stiches on my face, bandages on my arms and legs, and a neck brace to help my fractured vertebrae heal. To this day, the faint marks on my arms, head, and knees tell the story of what transpired that summer. Luckily, everyone survived the accident.

Not only did I learn the importance of driving the speed limit that day, I learned how auto insurance works at a young age. One ambulance, a helicopter, two hospitals, and multiple doctors' visits meant my parents had plenty of bills coming. I was also in a neck brace for the rest of the summer and couldn't work my normal summer job. You could say it was the most expensive summer of my life. Fortunately, my friend's auto insurance policy included coverage to pay for these medical bills and lost wages. Every cost was covered.

Imagine if you were driving a car and accidentally caused an accident. If you were at fault, you may be liable for injuries that occurred during the accident. What if you injured a family of four on their way to dinner? Do you know if your auto insurance policy would fully protect you? Without proper coverage, you may be personally liable for these costs, which may include property damage, lost wages, and medical expenses.

If you already have auto insurance, pull up your policy details and look for your coverage limits. For example, you may have a certain amount of coverage for floods or vandalism to your vehicle. You may also have coverage for uninsured or underinsured drivers. The most important coverage, in my opinion, is bodily injury liability. Yes, having coverage for denting someone's Corvette is important, but an entire Corvette is unlikely to cost more than a low six-figure sum. Injuring multiple people to the point where they spend days or weeks in the hospital, they can't work, and require months of physical therapy can cost significantly more.

If you look for the bodily injury liability limit on your vehicle, you may find you have one limit if you injure a single person and another limit for the entire accident if multiple people are injured. For example, if you have $100,000 of protection per person and $300,000 per accident, if three people are injured with $100,000 of damages, you maxed out the policy. Damages above your maximum cover may be your responsibility, not the insurance company's. If you cause an accident and injure people severely, the costs could be in the millions.

A friend of mine called me years ago after she received a letter from an attorney asking for $250,000 due to a car accident she caused. She hit a man on a motorcycle and was clearly at fault. The man walked away from the accident, seemingly unharmed. To her surprise months later, she received this letter. She was crying and shaken from the thought of losing everything she had at the time to this man who was threatening a lawsuit. We immediately called her auto insurance agent and asked about her bodily injury liability limits on her car. Unfortunately, she had only $50,000 of per-person coverage at the time of the accident. This means the difference of $200,000 was on her shoulders to potentially pay. Luckily, the man and his attorney didn't pursue the lawsuit and took what they could from her insurance carrier. It was enough to make her realize the importance of having higher bodily injury liability coverage.

On my personal vehicles, I have the highest amount of bodily injury liability coverage I can acquire. You may be happy to learn it's relatively inexpensive to increase bodily injury in most cases. I didn't stop there. I also added what's called an umbrella liability policy. An umbrella policy is an additional layer of protection that can go above and beyond your underlying policy limits. As the name suggests, an umbrella policy "covers" your underlying assets, such as multiple vehicles. It can even cover your home, boat, hunting ground, and other property. This means I have a certain level of coverage on my vehicles, with an additional seven figures of coverage with my umbrella. While it's unlikely I'll ever cause a car accident that produces that level of damage, it's still possible. If you have multiple drivers in your household, especially teenagers, you might strongly consider an umbrella policy.

While vehicles pose the greatest risk, in my opinion, it's also possible someone may fall on your property, such as your home or apartment, and sue you for damages. This is where your bodily injury limits on your homeowners policy would apply, plus your umbrella policy limits if you have one. Also, if you rent instead of own, don't go without renters insurance. It's normally inexpensive and can cover you from theft, property damage, and someone suing you after an injury at your place.

Consider where you may be at risk. Do you have a swimming pool that isn't property fenced off? Do you have a trampoline someone could jump on while you're not at home? Have you inherited hunting property that someone could enter and become injured? Assess where you may need a shield or armor and take steps to protect yourself and your family as you grow your wealth over time.

Chapter 4

Estate Planning

In this chapter:
- Creating a legacy
- Wills, trusts, and probate court
- Powers of attorney

When I mention the words "estate planning," they may trigger thoughts of someone on their deathbed or family members sitting in a room while an attorney reads their late father's will. While these movie scenes may include *aspects* of estate planning, the topic involves much more than death, dying, and inheritance. Most of this book focuses on growing and maintaining wealth, but if certain aspects of financial planning aren't implemented, the hard work that goes into creating wealth may be lost to inaction.

I often call estate planning "legacy planning" because it's more about creating a legacy. No, I don't just mean putting your name on a stone building in the middle of a college campus. I'm talking about ensuring your wishes are carried out if tragedy strikes. Tragedy may come from a death, but also from a disability. Legacy planning is also about more than money. If you have children, they're an important part of your estate plan, especially if they're underage or have special needs. If you have aging parents or other family members who depend on you, legacy planning considers the implications for their lives should something happen to you.

The first important concept to understand with estate planning is probate court. If you're familiar with probate court, you may have dealt with it firsthand due to losing a family member such as a parent. I hope most of you haven't had to experience it. In the U.S., probate court is the court system set up in each state to handle someone's financial affairs if they die. Probate courts may also be involved in family matters such as guardianship for children. Most people try to avoid probate court for three reasons — time, cost, and privacy.

When someone dies and their assets must go through probate court, it may take months or more than a year for assets to be processed through the court system, especially with real estate. Probate courts may have high caseloads to work through, which leads to delays in handling someone's estate. More complicated estates with numerous different assets can also take longer to process. Imagine dealing with probate proceedings for months while also mourning after the loss of a loved one.

Aside from the time issues, probate court can also be costly. Among court fees, appraisal fees, accounting fees, and attorney fees, your hard-earned money can be lost due to probate court costs. Depending on the state, some probate courts assess flat fees, percentage fees, or a combination. Larger estates tend to pay more than smaller estates, but I often see amounts of 3–7 percent being lost to probate costs. Imagine this amount of your money being spent on court costs instead of being given to your loved ones. If you own assets in multiple states, such as a home in Miami or rental property in Las Vegas, you may also have to deal with multiple probate courts. This is called ancillary probate and adds another layer of complexity and cost to the issue of probate court.

Aside from time and cost issues, probate court can also be public. As with many court records, probate court proceedings can leave your estate open to public record. Try looking up Marilyn Monroe's will online. You may find a copy of it in a few places. That's because Monroe's estate, including her will, went through probate court. She left specific amounts of money to her half-sister, her acting coach, her mother, and her therapist. Each received different amounts and it was all made public thanks to probate court. If you don't want your family's affairs shared online, plus the time and cost issues, proper estate planning can help avoid probate altogether.

You may be familiar with a trust. People often assume trusts are for billionaires. While that may be true, trusts are used by everyday people all the time. One of the reasons they're used is to avoid probate court. Trusts are private documents that typically don't require the intervention of probate court. Because trusts are private and can be used to handle estate matters privately when someone dies, the time, cost, and privacy issues of probate may not apply.

The most common type of trust is called a revocable living trust. Think of it like a separate entity that you control. Your trust can own your home, your investments, and your business. Even though your revocable trust may own your assets, if you own and control your trust, your assets held in your trust are still yours. You can still live in your home if it's owned by your trust. You can still drive your car if it's owned by your trust. You can still withdraw money from your bank account if it's owned by your trust. There are other types of complex trusts we won't cover in this book, but a revocable living trust is fairly easy to use and allows you to maintain control over your assets while you're living.

If you were to die, your trust document details what should happen next. If you're married, your trust may say your spouse should assume control over your trust. If you're not married, your trust may list who should receive your assets when you die. Your trust may also list who oversees making these decisions after you're no longer around. You might designate a sibling or a parent, for example. It's because of this person, called a trustee, that your assets can be distributed to various people without the need for probate court.

Another reason revocable living trusts are used is to protect young children from their own financial improvidence. Imagine if you inherited $1 million at the age of 18. You would be considered an adult in most states, so you would be able to accept this inheritance and put it into your own bank account without another adult's approval. You could also spend the money on whatever you want without another adult's approval. At 18, I probably would have blown part of it in Vegas, another part of it on a sports car or two, and the rest on parties with my closest 200 friends. I would have done foolish things with that kind of money. Therefore, this is why I personally have a revocable living trust in place.

If my wife and I die while the kids are young, the trust stipulates when and how they can access the money in it. Our trustee has the power to tell our kids "no" if they ask for money from the trust and it's not for education, health care, or something they truly need. We're able to control the money from beyond the grave. We can sleep at night knowing the kids will be protected and we can avoid probate court. This is one reason why so many people rely on revocable living trusts.

You may also be familiar a will. Unlike a trust, a will is a document that lists what should happen to your assets at death but is used by probate court. Because it's a tool *meant* for probate court, it means you generally must go through probate court, including the time, cost, and privacy issues, for it to be used. Wills do *not* avoid probate court. So why would someone create a will if it doesn't avoid probate court? First, a will is generally less expensive to create that a trust. Wills are usually simpler than trusts, requiring less time for a legal professional to draft. Second, a will doesn't normally require any administrative work like a trust, such as ensuring your newest vehicle is titled in the name of your trust. Lastly, and most important, wills include guardianship provisions for minor children. Wills are generally the legal document of choice to name a guardian for minor children should the parents die. Unlike trusts, which are more for the treatment of *assets*, wills can name who will care for your minor child until they're of legal age. This is one reason why people often have wills, even if they have a revocable living trust.

While we've discussed a few scenarios of someone dying, estate planning should also consider disability. With a trust, I gave the example of a trustee who steps in place to oversee assets after a person dies.

A trustee can also step in for someone who becomes incapacitated, such as after a serious illness or car accident. Assets owned and controlled by a trust may then be controlled by the trustee of your trust whom you pick to oversee your affairs. In other words, if you're in the hospital and can't make financial decisions, an alternate trustee of your trust may be able to step into your shoes to keep your affairs in order as long as they're owned by your trust.

There's also another type of document that can allow someone to act on your behalf if you become incapacitated. It's called a durable power of attorney, or POA. Depending on the state, POAs can be for financial and legal decisions, medical decisions, or both. This is an important document to have in place if you care about your legacy.

Terry Schiavo once lived in St. Petersburg, Fla. At the age of 26, she went into cardiac arrest while at home. It was Feb. 25, 1990. She was rushed to the hospital where doctors were able to stabilize her. Sadly, she experienced severe brain damage due to a lack of oxygen to her brain and was left in a state of comatose. Doctors tried many different therapies to bring Terry back, but she was in a vegetative state for years. After waiting and hoping Terry would come back, her husband made the difficult decision to have her feeding tube removed. It had been roughly eight years since she experienced the incident and showed no signs of returning to the person she once was. He believed his wife wouldn't have wanted to live this way. Then, Terry's parents learned of the plans to remove her feeding tube and asked the courts to step in to stop her husband.

The legal battle that ensued over what to do with Terry involved multiple legal motions, petitions, appeals, and challenges. It escalated to include members of Florida's state congress. Then, Florida Gov. Jeb Bush became involved. Next came members of the U.S. Congress. Even president George W. Bush and the Supreme Court were involved. It made national headlines and caused vigorous debate as to who had the right to decide Terry's fate. Some believed it was terrible to give up on Terry. Others thought it was a compassionate decision to allow her to die peacefully. No one knew what Terry wanted because she couldn't voice the opinion herself.

Ultimately, the courts sided with Terry's husband and agreed that Terry would not have wanted to live in a prolonged vegetative state. On March 18, 2005, roughly seven years after Terry's husband asked to have her taken off life support, her feeding tube was removed. Terry died a few weeks later. It had been more than 15 years since her cardiac arrest put her in the hospital.

This tragic story played out on televisions across the globe. I remember this story personally and will never forget Terry's name. I try to imagine what it must have been like for her friends and family to watch this real life drama unfold for years in the public eye. For this very reason, my wife and I both have durable POAs for medical decisions. We've given each other the legal capacity to make difficult medical decisions. The last thing I want to do is merely give my wife the legal ability to make such a decision without knowing what I want, though. This is why we each have health care directives. Some also call them living wills or advanced directives. My health care directive says what I would like to have happen if I'm in a difficult medical situation. This way, my wife doesn't have to guess and live with the decision. It's my decision. I've given her the legal ability to carry it out based on my written wishes.

Aside from the medical POA, we also have financial and legal POAs. One document appoints someone for medical decisions and the other appoints someone for both financial and legal decisions. This way, if I'm unable to take care of our household finances, my wife can use her POAs to act as my "attorney in fact" and make decisions on my behalf. This might include renewing our auto insurance if it requires both my signature and hers. If she needs to cancel a subscription service that's in my name, the POA should give her the ability to do it. Although we're married, it doesn't mean she automatically has the legal right to sell a car that may be in my sole name. With the POA, though, as long as the document is written correctly, she does have that legal right.

Having POAs and health care directives are wise for anyone who's legally an adult. This includes college students going to college for the first time. Imagine sending your 18-year-old daughter to college in a town five hours away. She meets a new boyfriend who seems troublesome. Then, you don't hear from your daughter very often. Then, you can't reach her at all. Fearing the worst after weeks of no communication, you call the college to inquire about her, but the college tells you they can't release any information it may have on her because she's legally an adult. You may be her parent, but that doesn't override her legal rights. If she's seeking mental health services or drug addiction treatment, the college is unlikely to tell you. That is, unless you have a POA for your daughter. While some parents may prefer to keep this information private, many others may prefer to know if their child is in trouble at the age of 18. This is one reason I often speak about medical POAs when parents send their children to college.

Wills, trusts, and durable POAs are examples of specialized documents created by estate attorneys. However, there are a few simple estate documents you may be able to use without the cost of an attorney. These documents aren't available in every state because they're based on state law, but they're available in many states. All three of these documents are meant to protect your assets from probate court.

The first is something called payable on death, commonly referred to as POD. PODs are typically used for bank accounts. If you own a bank account and it's only in your sole name, what happens to that bank account if you die? Without a POD, it will likely be subject to probate court, even if you're married. If I have a bank account in my sole name and I die, my bank isn't going to care if my wife walks into the branch with our marriage certificate and says the money should go to her. Maybe I wanted the money to go to charity or directly to our children. The bank will then ask for court instructions that the account should be given to my wife, which requires probate. However, if I have a payable on death designation added to the bank account, it tells the bank that my wife should receive my cash at my death. If done correctly, it can avoid probate court. Even for bank accounts you may own jointly with someone, what if you and the other owner both pass in a joint disaster? For this reason, many spouses still use PODs for joint bank accounts. You can even appoint a trust as the beneficiary through a POD.

What's great about PODs is they're free. If your bank tries to charge you for a POD designation, find a new bank. My wife used to work at a bank and never received training on PODs. She said they weren't used very often by customers at her bank because most people weren't aware they existed. It's possible some banks don't educate their customers on this document because it adds a recordkeeping burden, so be sure to ask about it.

Another simple estate planning tool that's normally free to use is a transfer on death agreement, or TOD. Similar to the POD for bank accounts, TODs can be used with vehicle titles and brokerage investment accounts. When you buy your next vehicle, you may have the option of adding a TOD designation to the title. Before I was married, my car titles would be registered in my sole name, but with a TOD to my brother in case something happened to me. Even married couples can include a TOD along with their joint ownership of a vehicle. For states that allow TODs for vehicles, some require that the vehicle be paid off with no loan attached to it. Other states don't have this rule and allow the TOD regardless of whether you buy your vehicle with a loan.

TODs for brokerage accounts are more like PODs for bank accounts. You simply contact your financial institution where you hold your brokerage investment account and ask them to add a TOD designation to your account. It's generally a separate form and not part of the account setup. Once it's completed, you'll likely see the letters TOD behind the account's registration, such as "John Smith individual TOD." This indicates a TOD has been added to your account. If you don't ask for the TOD, it might never be set up.

Lastly, if you own a piece of real estate, you may be able to protect it from probate using something called a beneficiary deed. A beneficiary deed is similar to a TOD, but for real estate. It's a little more complicated than a TOD, but much less complicated than a trust. A beneficiary deed is normally a few pages long and adds instructions for passing your real estate to another party if you were to die. The beneficiary deed is normally created by an attorney, but you may be able to find templates online if you're a do-it-yourself type. The beneficiary deed must also be recorded with your title in your county or city records department. I've relied on attorneys to help draft and file beneficiary deeds on my properties in the past rather than doing it on my own. Well worth the nominal cost in my opinion.

Keep in mind, if you appoint a minor child or someone who's mentally disabled as the beneficiary of a POD, TOD, or beneficiary deed, it may force probate court intervention. After all, a 7-year-old can't sign off to accept ownership of a car title. You should consider assigning a mentally competent adult or a trust as a beneficiary when using these types of documents. If used properly, they can be effective estate-planning tools with minimal to no cost.

Estate planning is one of those areas where people often procrastinate because it requires contemplating difficult circumstances. Without planning, it can be the difference between creating a legacy and protecting your family or leaving a mess for someone else to deal with. Working with attorneys will be discussed later in this book, but use this motivation to take action and begin putting a legacy plan in place.

Chapter 5

Tax Planning

In this chapter:
- Lifetime tax planning
- Easy tax strategies
- Sophisticated tax strategies

A bright college student was sitting in a lecture hall while her professor discussed tax strategies. The professor had just finished discussing the differences between tax avoidance and tax evasion. He then asked the students if they could describe the difference back to him. No one raised their hand. The professor asked again if someone could clearly explain the difference between tax avoidance and tax evasion. The bright college student raised her hand. The professor called on her, and with a grin, she replied, "jail."

The U.S. tax code, commonly referred to as the Internal Revenue Code, is a highly complex set of rules governing anything from income taxes to the depreciation schedule for a dishwasher. It's more than 6,800 pages long[17]. Hundreds of thousands of CPAs exist in the U.S. to help organizations and individuals comply with accounting principles and tax rules each year. While I could write a very long book about the tax code, I'm going to give you some of my favorite tax-planning techniques I and many of my affluent clients use.

Tax planning involves using legal methods of reducing taxes. Some tax-planning strategies help reduce taxes in the short term, while others help reduce taxes over the long term. People tend to focus their attention on tax reduction today, but I encourage you to think about tax reduction over your lifetime. I regularly meet people who aren't fully utilizing tax-reducing strategies, either because they aren't aware of them or they don't have enough time to implement them. Tax planning may seem dry at times, but it's important to learn some of the basic strategies if you want to reduce your tax burden over time. First, there are a few categories of taxes you need to know about in the U.S.:

- State income taxes
- Federal income taxes
- FICA taxes
- Self-employment taxes
- Capital gains taxes

Income taxes tend to be the most significant tax expense for most people. If you live in a state that assesses its own income tax, it's an additional expense on top of federal income taxes. Since the federal income tax was first established in the U.S. in 1913 to help finance World War I, Americans have paid these taxes on a graduated scale. This means different tax rates apply to different levels of income. If federal taxes were based on a flat rate, similar to how many states assess income taxes, someone making $100,000 of income and another making $50,000 of income would each pay the same rate. The person with the higher income would still pay more in total taxes, but the tax rates would be the same for both. With a graduated tax system, not only do higher income earners pay more in total taxes, they pay more in taxes at higher and higher tax *rates* as their incomes increase. Because of this graduated scale, tax planning can play a significant role in reducing taxes as your income grows into higher and higher tax brackets.

One of the simplest ways to reduce your income taxes in the short term is to use a pretax employer retirement plan such as a 401(k) or 403(b). These plans allow you to defer portions of your income on a pretax basis, which means you don't owe federal income taxes on those dollars in the year you put them in the plan. If I defer $10,000 of my income into a pretax 401(k) plan this year, I still have to pay FICA taxes on those dollars this year, but not federal or state income taxes. That's because I've used a legal method of deferring my income into the future. One day, when I retire, I can draw that money out of my 401(k) plan at which time I'll pay taxes on it. I estimate I'll be in a lower tax bracket when I retire, so it makes sense for me to postpone paying taxes on those dollars today in favor of paying taxes on them later in life. I may also be able to control my taxable income when I retire depending on what sources I have to fund my lifestyle.

One downside to this technique is I can't touch my money until I'm retirement age. Otherwise, I'll be charged an early withdrawal penalty. There are some exceptions to this rule, but plan on keeping retirement plan dollars out of reach until you're retirement age. Still, a retirement plan allows you to save for your future while also enjoying a reduction in taxes. If this concept makes you excited, remember that the IRS sets a maximum amount you can defer into an employer retirement plan. The amount typically changes each year, so visit GrowthInfo.com/taxes to see the current limits. If you want to maximize your savings for retirement and minimize your taxes, consider deferring the maximum amount to your retirement plan.

In Chapter 2, I covered the differences between pretax retirement accounts and Roth-type retirement accounts. While pretax retirement accounts help reduce taxes today, Roth retirement accounts help reduce taxes tomorrow when you're retirement age. If someone is in a relatively high tax bracket and believes they'll be in a lower tax bracket in retirement, it may make sense to rely heavily on pretax retirement savings. If someone is in a lower tax bracket, Roth dollars may make more sense. The decision of which type of account to use is very unique to each person, so I recommend speaking with a professional first. What I've provided in this chapter may help you understand your options at the very least.

So, what are FICA taxes? FICA stands for Federal Insurance Contributions Act. These taxes are in addition to income taxes. FICA taxes include Social Security taxes and Medicare taxes. Most Americans pay these additional taxes to help fund the Social Security system and the Medicare system. As of the date this book was published, the Social Security tax rate is 6.2 percent and the Medicare tax rate is 1.45 percent. In total, the FICA tax rate is 7.65 percent. If you're employed, your employer must also pay another 7.65 percent in FICA taxes. It's an expense to the employer. For those of you who are self-employed or thinking about being self-employed, you have to pay both the employee part of FICA and the employer part of FICA. This extra employer FICA is called the self-employment tax. This means a self-employed person may need to pay a total of 15.3 percent in FICA taxes in *addition* to their other taxes.

There aren't many ways to reduce FICA taxes, but one possible way is by using either flexible spending accounts or health savings accounts. With both FSAs and HSAs, dollars you contribute to these accounts can reduce your income for FICA, federal tax, and possibly state tax, as well. For states that allow income tax deductions for these types of accounts, that equates to a triple-tax deduction. If those dollars are then spent on qualified expenses, such as dependent daycare expenses for FSAs and healthcare expenses for HSAs, no taxes are due when you draw back out the money. That essentially means you were able to turn taxable income into tax-free income to pay for your expenses.

With FSAs, you can't invest the dollars after contributing them. With HSAs, you can. One of my favorite tax-planning strategies is using HSAs like a retirement account. Here's what I do personally. I have a high-deductible health insurance plan for my family, which means I qualify for using an HSA. I contribute the maximum amount the IRS will allow for a family each year, which then reduces my taxable income. After contributing to the HSA, I then invest the money like I would any other investment account. The company I use for my HSA allows me to pick from hundreds of mutual funds, exchange traded funds, and more. Assuming my HSA grows in value over time, I'm growing an account that can be used tax free to pay for qualified health care expenses in the future. If I retire at 65 and live until

95, that's 30 years of health care expenses. Without the HSA, I would have to pay for those expenses from my investments, likely triggering taxable income. With enough saved in the HSA, I can use those dollars tax free and avoid drawing those expenses from my other investments. The HSA allows me to enjoy a tax benefit today *and* a tax benefit tomorrow.

While this HSA strategy sounds appealing, it also assumes you don't spend from it until later in life. In reality, if you put $3,000 into an HSA and then your child twists their ankle playing soccer, you may need to take that money back out to cover the cost. What I do is keep plenty of cash around for emergencies so I can afford to spend from my cash instead of spending down my HSA too early. If you don't have much cash saved up yet, this strategy may be a bit difficult if you run into health care expenses. It's an important strategy to consider, though, given how significant the tax savings can be over your lifetime.

If you save $5,000 each year into an HSA and leave the money to invest, assuming a growth rate of 5 percent for 30 years, you would have more than $330,000 available in your HSA. That means you would have plenty of money to spend on your health care expenses in retirement, tax free. In other words, if you don't use this strategy, you may be missing out on a significant tax benefit.

It's important to note that reducing your FICA taxes means you may be reducing your taxable Social Security wages. Your eventual Social Security benefit is normally based on your earnings history over your lifetime. If you decrease your Social Security earnings on paper in an effort to reduce taxes, it may also lower your Social Security benefits a bit. In my opinion, I would much rather have the reduced taxes. I don't plan on Social Security providing a significant benefit to me in the future for multiple reasons, so I place more importance on reducing my lifetime tax bill over increasing my Social Security benefits.

Another tax strategy is something called a backdoor Roth conversion. It's fairly technical and advanced, so be sure to speak with a professional first unless you're confident you know the rules. I'll cover the high points here with more details listed on GrowthInfo.com/

Roth. Outside of employer retirement plans, people can generally save to traditional IRAs, which are pretax, or Roth IRAs, which are after-tax. If you reach the IRS maximum saving to a retirement plan at work, you can still save to an IRA up until the maximum. In other words, employer retirement plans and IRAs don't count against one another. Within the complex tax code is a rule about contributing to a Roth IRA. Some people aren't allowed because they make "too much" income. This is called the Roth IRA phaseout rule. If someone reaches this phaseout due to their income, they're not allowed to contribute to a Roth IRA.

This is where the backdoor Roth conversion comes into play. If someone's income is phased out, they can't contribute to a Roth IRA, but they can generally still contribute to a pretax traditional IRA. If they contribute to a traditional IRA and then do what's called a conversion, they may be able to turn that traditional IRA contribution into a Roth. Conducting a traditional IRA to a Roth IRA conversion involves a special rule called the IRA aggregation rule. The rule is beyond the scope of this book, so be sure you understand it before you attempt a conversion. Overall, the backdoor Roth IRA strategy is something you should be aware of that may allow you to save to a Roth IRA and grow tax-free wealth over time, even if your income has caused you to be "phased out" of contributing directly to a Roth.

Peter Thiel is one of the cofounders of PayPal, the global online payments company. He was also an early investor in Facebook. His investments have helped make him a billionaire. In 1999, he purchased 1.7 million shares of PayPal in his Roth IRA. That's a significant number of shares. However, because he purchased them for one tenth of a penny per share, it only cost him $1,700. PayPal obviously became a success, rocketing the value of his Roth into the hundreds of millions. As he made more investments within his Roth, it grew to be worth billions of dollars[18]. Yes, that means he owns a Roth IRA with billions of dollars of tax-free wealth in it. If you think that's outrageous, remember he followed the laws. He used them to his advantage. His investment in PayPal could have gone up in smoke. Instead, he took the risk, it paid off, and he did it in a tax-advantaged way. That's what I'm trying to teach you here. If you aren't using a Roth whatsoever, you may be missing out on tax-free opportunities for your future.

If you begin aggressively saving toward accounts such as 401(k) s, IRAs, and HSAs, you may find yourself completely maxed out for each of them. If you want to continue saving your money, what else could you use? The simplest option is to begin saving to a brokerage account. Yes, you can invest in a private business, but that's for another chapter. With a brokerage account, you can save unlimited amounts of money into it each year. You can also draw the money back out at any age without a penalty. You can't, however, enjoy a tax deduction like you can for the other accounts we've covered. Instead, you'll need to pay a special tax, called a capital gains tax, on any gains you realize year to year on your brokerage account. Other taxes might apply, too, but capital gains are the most common. If you buy XYZ stock and it happens to double in value, should you sell it, you'll generally need to pay capital gains taxes on the gain you realized.

Capital gains taxes fall into two categories — short term and long term. Short-term capital gains are taxed as ordinary income. In other words, short-term capital gains taxes normally trigger federal and possibly state income taxes, but not FICA taxes. Long-term capital gains taxes are normally taxed more favorably and have their own tax brackets altogether. Long-term capital gains taxes change over time depending on changes in tax law, but remember that long-term capital gains are normally lower than short-term capital gains. Typically, the key to enjoying long-term capital gains taxes is holding an investment for at least 12 months before selling it. If you have to sell an investment and you're a few weeks away from holding it for a year, it may make financial sense to wait before selling. Enjoying the lower tax rates on capital gains can amount to significant tax savings over your lifetime if you establish a sizable portfolio in brokerage-type accounts.

If you end up with a portfolio over time that includes money in pretax, tax-free, and taxable accounts, you may be able to use a strategy called asset placement. Asset placement involves owning certain investments in certain specific investment accounts based on the tax treatment. For example, if you own a mutual fund that focuses on international investments, you may be able to receive something called the foreign tax credit. It's a credit on your taxable income if you also paid taxes to a foreign government on the same income. However, if you own this international mutual fund in your IRA, you generally can't use the foreign tax credit. Instead, the fund would need to have been owned in your taxable brokerage account to be able to use the credit. For this reason, if you're going to own international investments, you might consider owning them in a brokerage account.

Another asset placement example is buying growth-oriented investments. If you own $1,000 worth of a high-growth investment and $1,000 worth of a low-risk bond, you probably want the high-growth investment to be held in your Roth IRA because it can grow tax-free. Remember what Thiel did with his Roth. Bonds tend to be lower risk and have lower returns, so there may not be a reason to take up space in your Roth IRA with bonds if you have pretax accounts. Another way to look at this is putting investments that can take off like a rocket in your Roth if you have one since that rapid growth may be tax-free. If you put an investment in your pretax retirement account and it takes off like a rocket, you must pay income taxes on all that money when you take it out. Put the rockets in the Roth.

It's common for people to underestimate the impact of taxes on their investments. That is, until they retire and begin drawing from those investments. If you have $1 million in a pretax 401(k) or traditional IRA, you may think you have $1 million in the account, but you really don't. Uncle Sam still has a tax lien on those dollars. You haven't paid him yet. Therefore, depending on your tax bracket when you take the money out in retirement, you may only have the equivalent of $600,000. Think about this while you're young because you can't go back and make changes once you've reached retirement age. The time to plan for these issues is now, while you're young, not in your 50s or 60s. Tax planning doesn't happen in April when you file your tax return. It happens year-round and over the course of your lifetime.

Another tax strategy involves charitable giving. You may already know that giving money to a qualified charity means you may be able to deduct your gift from your taxable income. What you may not know is that you can also give away something like stock to a charity. If you currently don't give to charity, I don't judge you whatsoever. This strategy is for those who currently give to charity or a church, or wish to give to charitable causes in the future.

When my wife and I give money to charity, we rarely give cash. Instead, we give away appreciated securities, such as stocks or mutual funds. If done correctly, we can receive a tax deduction on the value of the stocks we give away, plus we can avoid the capital gains taxes. Let's say you own XYZ stock and you originally paid $1,000 for it. Now XYZ has grown to $2,000 over the course of two years. If you want to give $2,000 to charity, you can either give cash from your bank account or you can give away your XYZ stock.

You probably don't want to sell your XYZ stock and then give the proceeds away to charity because you would owe taxes from selling it. By donating the actual stock, you can give $2,000 to charity and receive a potential tax deduction for it, *plus* you donated the capital gains taxes you would have paid if you had sold it instead. In a nutshell, you gave $2,000 to charity and avoided paying capital gains taxes because you donated stock instead of cash. If you don't want to lose your XYZ stock because you think it will keep going up, just use your cash to buy it again. After all, if you didn't give away the stock, you would have given away $2,000 worth of cash. Use the cash to buy XYZ shares again after you've donated them to charity. The easiest concept to remember here is that giving away appreciated investments instead of cash may offer you greater tax benefits.

Selling stock and donating the cash		VS	Donating stock directly	
$50k Current value	**$30k** Cost basis		**$50k** Current value	**$30k** Cost basis

Long-term capital gains tax paid	-$4,760	$0	Long-term capital gains tax paid
Resulting charitable donation	$45,240	$50,000	Resulting charitable donation

This illustration is hypothetical and assumes a 23.8 percent tax on capital gains and net investment income. Charitable deductions may be limited depending on your income.

This tax-planning section of the book covered some basics as well as some more advanced strategies, but these techniques can equate to significant tax savings over time if they apply to your situation and they're done correctly. There are multiple rules and nuances to these strategies that I didn't cover here in the spirit of brevity, so be sure to speak with a qualified financial planner or tax expert before making any changes to your situation. Overall, start thinking about tax planning as a lifelong process and not an annual event. If you use some of these strategies, you may be able to significantly reduce your lifetime tax bill.

Chapter 6

Retirement Planning

In this chapter:
- Retirement then and now
- Mental retirement
- Rethinking the definition of retirement

How far in advance do you plan your social calendar? I'm talking about events like birthday parties, anniversaries, and vacations. How far out is your longest-planned event in your calendar right now? Weeks away? Months away? Maybe a year away for something like an international vacation? It's rare to see someone plan something further than a year away. Most people aren't wired to plan that far in advance. Our ancient ancestors were wired to think about their next meal. Our genetics give us instinctive skills such as our fight or flight mechanism, our automatic reflexes, and our language skills. Planning for the long term isn't exactly an essential skill needed for survival. This may be one reason why many people struggle with planning for long-term goals such as retirement.

If you're 35 years old and would like to retire at 65, you still have 30 years left to work. That's a significant amount of time. Can you realistically picture what your life will be like in 30 years? I find most people struggle with this question because it's simply too distant. This is one reason why retirement planning can be challenging. We think we can worry about it later because we have plenty of time. It's much different than an impending deadline. People are usually motivated by deadlines that approach in days or weeks, but not decades. Have you ever procrastinated on a school project that was due in two weeks? We all have. Now imagine having 30 years to work on that project.

This concept of planning for retirement is distinct to the modern age. Saving for 30 to 40 years for a retirement that may last decades more wasn't a concern for most Americans in the 19th century. In fact, life expectancy in the mid-19th century was only 39[19]. Most people worked until they died. Those who stopped working but kept living were either very wealthy or disabled. By the year 1900, life expectancy rose to 48. By 1935, it rose to 60. Rising life expectancies were helpful to the American economy. Workers could continue to work and fuel economic growth as various industries grew and needed labor. Extending life expectancies was only helpful to a point, though, especially for factories.

Factory owners found older employees were slowing down operations. Compared to their younger coworkers, older employees were unable to work as quickly in a labor-intensive assembly line. Maintaining muscle mass and range of motion simply becomes harder over time. A factory in the early 1900s was more likely to require someone to have greater upper-body strength and quick hands than modern factories. Older employees also required more sick days and kept factories from employing younger people in their place. For these reasons, companies began encouraging their older workers to retire. Many older workers didn't want to stop working either because work gave them purpose, or they couldn't afford to retire. That's when employers began providing an answer to the affordability issue — a pension plan.

Pensions, which generally provide a guaranteed monthly income for as long as someone lives, had existed prior to the industrial revolution. They were primarily given to veterans and were paid for by the governments that sent them to war. In the U.S., this began to change with the creation of pensions for police officers. The first example of a modern public pension was for the New York City Police in 1857[20].

Then, pensions for firefighters began to grow in popularity. In 1875, American Express created the first private pension for its employees.

The industrial revolution shifted significant amounts of labor from farming to factories. As life expectancy increased during this period, so did the number of pensions. If life expectancy in 1935 was 60 years old, a worker who was fortunate enough to live to the age of 60 may have retired and collected their pension for a few short years. These companies felt the cost of paying for a pension was less than the cost of keeping older workers on the factory floor.

During this period, Social Security was born. Created in 1935 by Franklin D. Roosevelt, Social Security was touted as a program that would help the elderly, the unemployed, and the widowed. While that may be true, it was also created for the same reasons as factory worker pensions. Social Security was created during the Great Depression when the unemployment rate grew to more than 20 percent. With one in every five working-age Americans unemployed, Social Security was there to help older workers retire, or remain retired, while younger workers with growing families could increase their chances of finding employment.

As the decades rolled on and life expectancy continued to increase, employers found their pension plans were costing them significantly more. Where a retiring worker once lived for a few years on a company pension, many of these retirees were now living a few decades on the same pension. The concept of paying for a person to retire was no longer profitable. The Social Security system also found it was paying significantly more in benefits than originally intended, thanks to longer and longer life expectancy rates. It's no surprise that the 401(k) plan, which is now the most popular retirement savings vehicle in the U.S., was created in 1979[21]. Employer pensions began to freeze and no longer be offered to employees due to the costs and risks to employers. The answer to the retirement savings question became the 401(k) plan, where employees were largely on their own to save for their futures.

I'm not here to judge the factories of the past or the governments of the present. Some may believe employers have a duty to provide retirement benefits to their workers, while others may think capitalism requires the free market to determine when and how such benefits are provided. Instead of attaching labels to the actions of the past, I'm equipping you with the tools for navigating the future. It's possible Social Security will look wildly different in the future. It's possible 401(k) plans will be replaced by a different benefit decades from now. What I encourage you to focus on is creating your own wealth and your own retirement income. When you have financial independence, you don't need to depend on a pension. When you have financial independence, you don't need to depend on Social Security. When you have financial independence, you have financial freedom. Cash is king, and I want you to have plenty of it.

As I've mentioned throughout this book, time is essential to building wealth. If someone has 30 years left to build a nest egg for retirement, it may take them the entire 30 years to do it. Yes, you can still build a nice nest egg over 20 years, but adding an extra decade of time may *double* someone's wealth. Another way to look at this is considering the cost of procrastination instead of the value of saving early. If someone's wealth may double over 10 years, depending on their rate of return, then procrastinating by 10 years may *cost* them half of their potential wealth in the future. You may be costing yourself significant wealth if you don't take action. This concept really hits you when you think about the cost of procrastination instead of the value of starting early. No one wants to miss out or experience loss. That's precisely what happens when you wait years before growing your nest egg. You experience the loss of time. You lose out on potential growth and compounding.

If you want to test how this works for yourself, use the rule of 72. The rule of 72 allows you to divide the number 72 into a hypothetical rate of return to estimate approximately how long it would take to double a portfolio's value. A rate of return of 7 percent would allow a portfolio to double in roughly 10.3 years. A rate of return of 8 percent would allow a portfolio to double in roughly nine years. While invest-ment returns aren't static each year and also have a risk of losing value, the rule of 72 is a great way to illustrate the importance of saving early for retirement.

Rule of 72	
Rate of Return	Years to Double
1%	72 Years
2%	36 Years
3%	24 Years
4%	18 Years
5%	14 Years
6%	12 Years
7%	10 Years
8%	9 Years
9%	8 Years
10%	7 Years

To help motivate you to save for your retirement, I recommend setting milestones. It's much easier to work toward a goal that's a few years away than to work on one that's decades away. Ideally, these mile-stones can be set by working with an independent financial planner. A CFP® can help create a customized plan for what your future may look like based on your goals. Then, working backward from your retirement age, milestones can be set. For example, if you may need $3 million at the age of 65 to retire and live a certain lifestyle, you can reasonably set milestones at ages 60, 55, 50, etc. As you continue working backward to your current age, you can see your trajectory and what may need to be done in the next few years to reach your next milestone.

If you prefer to do this on your own instead of working with a pro, Fidelity has published a guideline chart based on your age. It focuses on having a multiple of your income at various ages. Keep in mind, this is a general guideline that assumes everyone can use the same methodology. In reality, two people with the same level of income and the same age may have vastly different goals for retirement. One may prefer the quiet life in the country with low expenses. Another may prefer two homes and exotic travel. These two individuals will have vastly different retirement savings goals. With that said, if you prefer to use the rule of thumb for now, here are the Fidelity milestones based on a multiple of your annual income. According to their guidelines, you need three times your annual salary saved by the age of 40 and 10 times your annual salary by the age of 67.

Age	Multiple of Salary
30	1x
35	2x
40	3x
45	4x
50	6x
55	7x
60	8x
67	10x

Within this book, I discuss ways to create wealth by both saving and investing and also by creating your own business. Remember, a business can be a large company with 200 employees, a small business with just you and your spouse, or a side hustle that supplements your income. Individuals who own businesses have an opportunity when it comes to planning for retirement. Retirement planning can look different for business owners. Here's an example:

Monica owns a digital advertising business. She started it 10 years ago and now makes $1 million of gross revenue. She draws a salary of $100,000 to pay herself from the business. Then, she pays for other expenses such as employees, insurance, rent, etc. After her expenses, which include the salary she pays herself, she makes another $100,000 in profit from the business. Between her salary and profits, she makes a total of $200,000 from the business. Ignoring inflation and any changes in Monica's revenues, if she decides to retire from the business, she may still be able to earn $100,000 in profits from her business. She would no longer have a salary if she's no longer working in the business, but she would still have her profits as the owner. She would likely need to hire a new leader if she stepped down, so let's assume she would pay that person the same salary of $100,000. Even if she needed to pay this new leader $100,000 and share 25 percent of her profits, she would still have $75,000 of profit with little to no ongoing effort.

Monica would be able to retire while still enjoying profits from her business; something an employee with no ownership can't do. Also, Monica would still own the business. If she wanted to begin selling her business, she could arrange for a series of payments over time, such as 10 years. If Monica believes the business may continue growing, she might create an agreement to sell the business over time based on annual revenue. This would allow her to receive cash for her retirement needs over a decade that may also increase with inflation as her business grows. During that time, Monica might decide to consult other businesses based on her own experience with growing and running her company. She could turn that experience into an hourly consulting fee to help cover her retirement expenses.

These are just a few simple examples of how business ownership may unlock additional opportunities as you approach retirement. I have many clients who are similar to Monica. They own profitable businesses and have the flexibility to leverage various strategies to create the retirement future they want. With some of my clients, retirement isn't even a goal. They love what they do to a point that retirement isn't in their vocabulary. In fact, to them, retirement means something bad happened — an illness or injury. To them, they love what they do and can't imagine a life without working in the business.

If you think that sounds strange, you're not alone. Some people can't wait to reach retirement age and either slow down or stop working forever. Others enjoy the challenge of work and the social engagement that comes with it. Whether they own a business or not, some people simply enjoy working. Imagine if you could have the best of both worlds. What if you could have the fulfillment that comes with work, not to mention the income, but also the leisure of a retiree? If you could find that middle ground that satisfies your needs, would retirement still be a goal?

When I speak with people about retirement goals, I hear about travel, spending more time with family, and seeing old friends. I hear about sports cars, gifts to charity, and paying for their grandchildren's college. I hear about hunting property, big anniversary parties, and leaving an inheritance. These are some of the most common things people tell me about as they express their most cherished dreams. I'm happy to report these dreams don't all need to wait until age 65. It's possible to save for your future and enjoy these dreams along the way. The concept of saving and saving every year until you retire and *then* spending time on your dreams is one way to do it. Plenty of people plan for a traditional retirement in this way. My own retirement goals are much different.

Imagine if I save aggressively for most of my life, limiting travel and experiences with my family along the way, all to reach that point in my 60s where I can flip the switch and begin enjoying my wealth. What if I die a year after retirement and never have a chance to enjoy it? I've seen this happen to people. What if my health declines right before my retirement date? Cancer can happen to anyone. It's just not worth it to me. Instead, I'm focused on having balance in my life that allows me to have some of those cherished life goals while I'm healthy and relatively young, while enjoying the income and engagement that comes from a career I love.

I often recommend saving aggressively while someone is young and living well within their means. That doesn't mean someone can't begin to enjoy more of the fruits of their labor in their 30s, 40s, and 50s. It still requires living within your means. However, at 40, someone may choose to either increase their retirement savings rate from 12 percent of their income to 15 percent, or choose to keep their savings rate at 12 percent and have fun with their excess income instead of saving it. This means they may have a smaller pile of cash when they reach a traditional retirement age, but this may give them a more

enjoyable path to work longer. Then, less money may be needed when they quit work. Remember, you can shape your own retirement.

If you were completely retired today, what would you do with your time? If you would like to travel more, how often would you realistically travel? You may be the adventurous type who wants to backpack from Europe to Asia over the course of months, but I find most people enjoy travel for one to three weeks at a time. Then, they're back home for a while. They might travel again a few months later. This equates to traveling roughly four times per year. If you own a business and have employees, you can likely take enough time off to travel four times a year. If you work for an employer, with 15 days of paid time off per year, that's three weeks of travel per year. If you travel during paid holidays and weekends, you may be able to stretch that to four trips per year. If so, you may be traveling just as much as the average retiree.

What else would you do with your time if you were retired today? Buy a sports car? Spend more time with friends? Buy a hunting property? All of these goals can be accomplished well before you're 65. They simply take financial planning and creativity. You can save for a sports car over time. You can spend more time with friends by making it a priority. You can buy hunting property with a few others and share it with them, cutting down on the price tag and the property taxes. Most of the retirement goals people express to me are really lifetime goals. They simply focus on *enjoying* them once they're retired. If you can begin living a lifestyle where you can accomplish these goals well before retirement age, would you work longer?

There's a classic story you may have heard about a fisherman. He was taking out his boat one day when a newly retired CEO stopped to speak with him. The CEO had just purchased a boat and had questions about fishing. The younger fisherman explained his daily routine for catching fish and taking care of his boat. As the CEO listened, he asked the fisherman if he ever considered expanding his operation. The CEO suggested the fisherman could use his knowledge to hire and train employees to catch fish and sell them to local restaurants. He explained that he could have a fleet of 20 fishing boats in as little as 10 years. He could focus on reducing costs and increasing revenue in preparation to sell the business. Then, the fisherman would have millions of dollars. The CEO explained having that amount of money would mean the fisherman wouldn't have to work another day in his life. He could relax all day and fish as much as he wanted. Just as the CEO was finishing his explanation, he stopped midsentence. He realized the fisherman already had exactly what he wanted.

While you may be able to go through life without saving a penny and pay for everything with your income, there may come a day when you can no longer work. Our bodies slowly decline over time and working becomes more difficult, especially in our 70s and 80s. Also, you may change your opinion about work and grow tired of it. What you enjoy now may be much different 30 years from now. This is why I still advocate for building a nest egg over time, especially if you want to reach financial independence. The overall theme is to think differently about when and how you will reach your goals, as well as what it means to retire. For me, I may officially retire and completely stop working one day. What's more likely is that the type of work I engage in will change, allowing me to enjoy the activities of a retiree with the challenge and income of work. This creates a balance between work and play that encourages someone to continue working, well into their later years.

If you have an interest in starting a business and having a side hustle, I've given you blueprints in the coming chapter for doing both. Pursuing either may help you with your retirement goals. If you don't have an interest in business ownership of any kind, I have a suggestion for you, especially if you can't wait to retire. I suggest finding an industry that provides a competitive wage with satisfying work so you don't feel like you need to retire yesterday. For now, let's assume you have a job that pays well enough that switching careers doesn't make sense.

I recommend something I call mental retirement. I met a couple years ago that had never worked with a financial planner. They were in their mid-50s and were heavily focused on retiring. They had saved aggressively when they were young and lived well within their means when buying vehicles, making updates to their home, and deciding how to spend their cash flow. As they told me about their goals, they wanted to retire as soon as possible because of the stress they both had at work. They both worked for the same large corporation, dealing with similar issues such as tight deadlines, unproductive meetings, and difficult bosses. As I analyzed their expenses, their goals, and their assets, I found they were well on their way to retiring as early as 60. In fact, if they were willing to reduce some of their expenses, they could retire next year. This already accounted for how expensive their health insurance costs may be if they retired before being eligible for Medicare. They were thrilled.

We met again weeks later to answer any questions they had about the analysis I had performed. To my surprise, they said they were feeling much better about their working conditions after our last meeting. They went on to explain that knowing they could reduce a few expenses and retire soon was so comforting to them that they felt much less stress at work. They even said they may be willing to work longer than anticipated if they can maintain this new mentality. This new mentality was the confidence in knowing they can walk away from work at any time and still be able to reach their goals. They entered meetings at work knowing it could be their last if they wanted to quit. They interacted with their bosses knowing they can put in their two weeks' notice at any time. They came to work every day with a new level of confidence they lacked before. They were no longer working by obligation. They were working by choice.

This mentality is powerful. Once you've determined that you can retire without working ever again, you look at your situation much differently. You may respectfully voice your opinion more. You may ask for more flexibility in your schedule. You may simply say "no" to requests that would otherwise cause your stress level to skyrocket. Once this new retirement mentality sets in, you may find yourself having more satisfaction in the same work environment. If so, you may decide to work longer in that role, either full time or part time. This means you may enjoy the additional security of income while enjoying a lower-stress life that includes spending time on your lifetime goals.

As you've learned in this chapter, retirement planning isn't a cookie-cutter approach. It's clay that you're able to mold, especially if you have the benefit of time to mold it over decades. While you're young, save aggressively. You'll be thankful you did when you're older. Along the way, though, you don't need to continue saving every raise or bonus you receive. Live a little. You don't need to work on your bucket list when you're older. You can work on it during your lifetime, especially if you create a lifestyle that allows you to balance work and play. Balancing work and play in your 40s and 50s may mean you have less wealth in your 60s, but if you enjoy how you're spending your time, you may continue this balance well into your 70s or 80s.

Chapter 7

Investing

In this chapter:
- Intelligent risk
- Investment options
- Asset allocation

In this chapter, I'll cover many aspects of investing. For some of you, this may be exactly the information you need to make smart investment decisions. For others, it may seem a little technical. If any part of this chapter seems a bit technical for you, keep going. I've sprinkled in strategies for making investing easy. Also, it's important info to learn, even if you only pick up the basics.

Wayne Gretzky, one of the greatest ice hockey players of all time, once said, "You'll miss 100 percent of the shots you don't take." His quote is quite fitting for this chapter. When you imagine some of the most successful people in the world, past or present, whom do you imagine? Bill Gates? Elon Musk? Warren Buffett, Jeff Bezos, Steve Jobs, or Mark Zuckerberg? It's likely the successful person you imagined became successful by taking certain risks. I can't think of anyone who built significant wealth using a government bond. Living like a multimillionaire means accepting some level of risk with your money — one of the key ingredients to building wealth.

Intelligent Risk

First, let's break down risk into two categories — intelligent and impulsive. An impulsive risk is one that lacks thoughtfulness or planning. An example of impulsive risk is trying to become wealthy by gambling. Although it's possible to profit from an evening at the casino or buying a lottery ticket, gambling is a risk I would avoid. The chances of winning consistently through gambling are extremely low. It's alright to spend some time at the roulette tables but do so as part of your entertainment budget and recognize that your money is likely to disappear.

As for intelligent risk, an example is creating a business plan and investing in that plan. Another example is investing in the stock market or buying real estate as part of a diversified portfolio. Intelligent risk is intentional and part of a well-thought-out strategy. You won't be flush with cash in a day like you would with a winning lottery ticket, but you can still have the opportunity to accumulate significant wealth.

With intelligent risks, it's possible to have a high or low degree. You may contemplate investing in a private company that specializes in biotechnology with only a two-year track record. This type of early-phase company can be considered high risk, especially because it's in the biotech sector. At only two years old, this company may not yet be making a profit. It may be working on a new cancer or arthritis drug with promising potential. However, once clinical trials start, if this company isn't able to show results that meet government standards, this new drug may never be approved. The company may then need to ask investors for more money. If the company doesn't acquire enough funding, it may have to close its doors. On the other hand, if the company creates a breakthrough drug, you may enjoy profits on your investment equivalent to a lottery win.

Another example of intelligent risk is investing in a 10-unit rental complex along with three other investors who have more than 20 years of experience with rental property. Unlike the startup biotech company, if a tenant in one of the 10 units decides to trash the place, you and the other investors may have to pay for the damage. You may still have nine other units rented by profitable tenants, though. Plus, the building itself is unlikely to drop significantly in price, barring an economic recession. Having three other investors or business partners in this rental complex with decades of experience also helps lower your risk as an individual investor.

There are certainly risks with both the biotech company and the rental property, but the risks are quite different. It's also fairly obvious that your return on investment could be much higher with the startup than with the rental building. The startup may receive a 300 percent return on investment, while the rental may receive a 20 percent return on investment. With that said, the startup may go bust and all of your investment may be lost, but the apartment complex is unlikely to lose all its value.

This brings up the topic of risk-adjusted investing. The goal of risk-adjusted investing is to pick an investment opportunity that may provide the greatest potential for growth, but with the lowest possible level of risk. Finding an investment with *low* risk and the potential for *high* returns is like finding a unicorn. If someone recommends an investment to you that has low risk and high-return potential, be skeptical. High-growth potential means high risk. Low risk means low-growth potential. It's a classic tradeoff between the two, as shown in the diagram below.

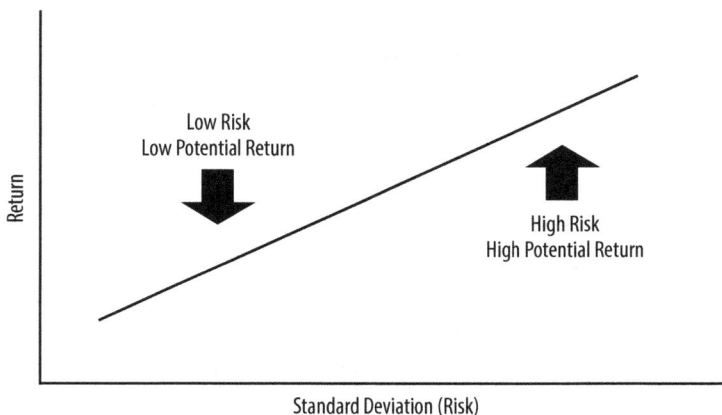

Because growth requires you to accept some level of risk, you may be able to pick between two investments that offer different levels of risk and potential return. Imagine this in simple terms. If you found two investment opportunities, both may have a different level of risk and expected return. Let's assume Investment A has an expected return of 12 percent, but you must accept eight units of risk to possibly reach that return. Let's assume Investment B has an expected return of 10 percent, but you must accept five units of risk to possibly reach that return. On the surface, a 12 percent rate of return looks more attractive than a 10 percent rate of return. However, on a risk-adjusted basis, Investment B is more attractive than Investment A. In this simple example, you expect a 1.5 percent return for every unit of risk with Investment A. However, you expect a 2 percent return for every unit of risk with Investment B. The challenge with this process is that this information can be difficult to quantify.

	A	B
Return	12	10
Risk	8	5

Risk-adjusted investing is important for you to know in concept. Rather than teaching you the equivalent of a finance class on risk analytics, I want to teach you this concept as you consider making business decisions. Measuring risk is easier with investments that trade on the market, such as stocks or mutual funds. It's more difficult with private investments, though, if you're not a tenured investor. Instead, consider what may reasonably go wrong with a private investment or business venture versus the potential return on investment.

Let's assume you want to start investing in rental real estate and have no experience in it. You can calculate fairly accurate projections on what return you may expect from rental income under normal tenant, repair, and market conditions. To project your risks, think of everything that may go wrong. You could have a tenant who may destroy your property and flee the area. You could face a lawsuit from an injury that occurs on your property. You could even experience a downturn in the real estate market.

Once you've considered reasonable potential risks versus the return you may expect from this rental property, you should be able to pick between this venture or another. If you expect an 8 percent return on this rental property after paying taxes, insurance, repairs, etc., and you expect to earn 7 percent on a different investment with different risks, use your best judgment to determine which one offers you the highest return given the risks you may face.

When I invest my own money, I consider the risk-adjusted return I expect on the investment. I also look for investment opportunities that have asymmetric risk and reward. This means I want an investment that has significantly more upside than downside. If I invest $100,000 in something that may gain $20,000 on the upside or lose $15,000 on the downside, that's a reasonable tradeoff. A potential 20 percent return is a solid return. However, I'm looking for more reward. I would rather invest in something that may gain $400,000 or lose all $100,000. If the investment doesn't do well, the most I can lose is $100,000, or 100 percent of my investment. However, if it does well, I may quadruple my money. The upside is much higher than the downside. This is what I mean by asymmetric risk and return.

Taking on this kind of risk is not for the faint of heart. As a financial planner, I typically don't recommend investing this way to my clients. Many of my clients have reached their peak earnings years and are closing in on retirement, if not retired already. For many of them, this type of risk isn't acceptable. While I'm young, though, and have time on my side, not only am I willing to accept very high levels of risk, I seek it out. My wife and I also live well below our means, which allows us to have more cash to invest.

As I seek investment opportunities with asymmetric risk and return, I keep in mind that I need to invest in more than one. I also keep in mind that some of them won't work out. For example, if I have $200,000 of cash to invest, I may invest $50,000 in four different opportunities that have high-growth potential. I do this with the knowledge that some of them are likely to do so poorly that I never see those dollars again. It's simply part of investing with high risk. However, if one of my investments breaks even and one of them makes a 400 percent return, I will have $300,000. If you're curious about the math, that's $50,000 from the one that broke even and returned my money back, plus $250,000 from the one that did well. The one that did well made a $200,000 profit on top of my $50,000 original investment, giving me a total of $300,000 between the two investments. Even if the other two investments crashed and burned, I still made a profit of 50 percent overall.

This may sound simple, but it takes a certain tolerance for risk — a certain mindset. It's possible all four of those hypothetical investments would have done poorly. In my mind, I plan on continuing to invest in more and more ventures with high potential reward with the hope that one or more will provide a significant return. I once invested $350,000 of my own hard-earned money into a technology venture that didn't pan out. It made a little money but overall it was a bust. At the time, that investment was quite a bit of money for my family. It had the potential for significant growth, though, and fit my risk-reward target.

If the idea of losing $350,000 brings tears to your eyes, let me tell you about a man named Bill Bartmann. After dropping out of school and spending time in a gang, Bartmann was a 17-year-old alcoholic. He once fell down a flight of stairs while drunk, becoming paralyzed. He was bound to a wheelchair after physicians told him he wouldn't walk again. Against their wishes, he pushed himself physically and slowly regained his ability to walk. He went on to gain his GED certificate and eventually earned a college degree. Then he earned a Juris Doctorate and became an attorney.

After investing in real estate, Bartmann shifted his focus from law to business. That led him to start a debt collection company, Commercial Financial Services. His company was successful and became the largest consumer debt collection company in the U.S. at the time. In 1997, he was listed in *Forbes* magazine as one of the riches people in America. A year later, his company was being investigated for questionable business practices. Bartmann was found not guilty, with one of his shareholders confessing to the crimes and acknowledging Bartmann wasn't aware. Still, Bartmann's business was destroyed and went into bankruptcy. He lost billions.

Just as he didn't let his paralysis keep him down, Bartmann started a new company with the same niche. He also wrote multiple books about business and entrepreneurship. His goal wasn't to regain his title of billionaire, but to bring the company he loved back to life and enjoy any success that may follow. He did just that and regained significant wealth before he died in 2016[22]. He had lost significantly, but used his skillset, determination, and tolerance for risk to create a successful business once again. Over his lifetime, he used asymmetric risk and return to his advantage. While there was no guarantee either of Bartmann's businesses would pan out, he saw an opportunity and took the risk because he saw the upside potential.

If the thought of investing in something that may turn into dust isn't appealing to you, you're not alone. It's certainly not for everyone. There are plenty of wealth-building options available for those who prefer to work steady jobs and build a nest egg over time. In Chapter 2, we discussed the concept of targeting 10 percent as an annual rate of savings. Regardless of how much you decide to save and invest each year, consider taking an appropriate level of intelligent risks with your savings to grow your wealth. When taking on risk to target growth, there are many options available to investors. Below are some examples:

- Individual stocks
- Individual bonds
- Mutual funds
- Exchange-traded funds (ETFs)
- Real estate investment trusts (REITs)
- Annuities
- Cash-value life insurance
- Derivatives

Individual Stocks & Bonds

With individual stocks, you have the option of purchasing shares of companies on a stock exchange, generally with the click of a button. Later in this book, we'll discuss starting a business. Many of the large companies you may follow, such as your favorite tech companies, began as small startups. Then, they grew and likely had investors to support additional growth. Eventually, they listed their shares on a stock exchange, officially becoming publicly traded companies. Owning a share of a publicly traded company versus owning a share of a *private* company isn't much different. Because publicly traded companies trade on an exchange and have liquidity, they generally have less risk than private businesses that aren't liquid. Liquidity generally offers you the ability to sell your shares within seconds on an exchange, as long as another party is willing to buy them from you. With private company shares, the number of parties willing to buy your shares may be limited or even nonexistent.

If you decide to invest in individual stocks, keep in mind that these companies can lose money just as easily as private companies. After all, they're businesses and subject to lawsuits, bad press, poor leadership, and new competitors. As a financial professional, I sometimes hear from people that they enjoy owning XYZ stock because it's low risk. In my opinion, there are no low-risk stocks. If it's stock in a company, which represents equity in that company, it's not low risk. Low-risk investments are money market funds and CDs at the bank, not stocks. It's fair to assume that stock in an established grocery store is lower risk than stock in a biotech company. Still, I would never label any stock as low risk. Aside from the risk of something negative occurring with individual companies, if the general stock market declines during a recession, so too may your share in XYZ stock. If you've heard the phrase, "A rising tide lifts all boats," think of each publicly traded company as boats in the same ocean. If the entire tide is going down, it's likely to influence your favorite stock, even if that one stock is doing exceptionally well. This is why I don't consider any stock to be low risk.

Stock investing is also one of the most popular ways to build wealth over time. There are plenty of multimillionaires who have stock investing to thank for their wealth. By purchasing individual shares of company stock, you have rights as an owner of the company. You typically have the right to receive dividends the company decides to pay its shareholders and to participate in the growth (or decline) of the share price. You may also have voting rights, such as whom to elect to the board of that company.

One reason stock investing is so popular is because you can let your money go to work while you go to work. While you're busy at a nine-to-five job, your shares may be growing over time. It's as easy as buying shares online from your couch or having a professional handle it for you. Buying stocks can be exciting but remember that diversification is important when investing. Buying just one or two stocks and hoping for the best means taking on a higher level of risk than buying multiple stocks. Below are examples of large publicly traded companies that went from big to broke. Collectively, they represented hundreds of billions of dollars before their decline.

- Blockbuster – 2013
- CIT Group – 2009
- Conseco – 2002
- Enron – 2001
- General Motors – 2009
- Lehman Brothers – 2008
- MF Global – 2011
- Washington Mutual – 2008
- WorldCom – 2002

Because individual companies have inherent risk that you generally can't control as a shareholder, I avoid more than 10 percent of my portfolio invested in one stock unless. If you prefer to speculate and only buy a few stocks, remember that this increases your risk.

With individual bonds, the experience is vastly different than with stocks. As a bold holder, you're essentially acting as a bank. If

XYZ company needs money for a new research and design project, it may elect to borrow it. Borrowing from a bank is one option for a company, but borrowing from the public is another. This is when bonds are issued. If you decide to buy a bond from XYZ company, you agree to give your money to XYZ in return for its promise to pay back the bond in the future, plus interest. It's like a CD at the bank, but in reverse. Unlike CDs, though, bonds aren't protected by the Federal Deposit Insurance Corporation (FDIC). If XYZ company declares bankruptcy, you may not receive your money back on your bond.

Buying individual bonds is more complex than buying individual stocks. In fact, most individual bonds are bought and sold through professionals, unlike individual stocks that are simple to buy and sell through a smartphone app. It can be done but involves a different market and skillset. Also, with bonds in general, don't expect to reap high returns. Bonds involve less risk than stocks because bondholders are more likely to receive their principal back than stockholders when a company fails. Bonds are meant to keep up with inflation and *protect* wealth versus *grow* wealth. You probably won't use bonds if you're trying to aggressively grow your wealth, but it's important to know about them in the scope of investment options. You'll likely use them one day.

Mutual Funds

With mutual funds, you can purchase a group or "basket" of underlying investments. Think of it like buying 50 to 100 stocks at once instead of buying them each individually. This can instantly help with diversification and may be why mutual funds are so popular among investors. In fact, there are more than 9,000 different mutual fund options available in the U.S.[23]. Mutual funds come in vastly different shapes and sizes, so understanding what's "under the hood" will help you determine if a mutual fund is worth buying. It's likely you already have exposure to mutual funds if you work for a company that offers a group retirement plan.

Mutual funds generally fall into five categories:
- Stock funds
- Bond funds
- Money market funds
- Allocation funds
- Specialty funds

As you may have guessed, stock and bond funds invest in stocks and bonds. However, 10 stock funds may own vastly different baskets of stocks. Some may own U.S. large-cap stocks, which are some of the largest publicly traded companies in the country, while others may own small-cap international stocks, which are small companies in other countries you likely wouldn't recognize. Each category of investment involves different risks and growth potential, but, in general, stock-based mutual funds will have higher risks and potential rewards than other categories.

Investing in a stock-based mutual fund versus individual stocks can make investing much easier because you may instantly own upward of 500 stocks or more. This diversification is important if a company or two performs poorly. Think of investing like a glass window. Buying a single stock is like having one large window. Buying a mutual fund is like having many different glass panes that form one large window. If a baseball were to come crashing through your window, it's much less expensive to fix one small pane than an entire large window.

This concept of diversifying and having smaller windowpanes instead of one large window is the basic lesson of asset allocation. Asset allocation means putting your assets into different types of investments in an effort to do two things — increase your expected return and decrease your expected risk. It's the closest thing to having your cake and eating it too when it comes to investing. It's not guaranteed, but it's such an important strategy that you'll find it taught in every university that offers a financial planning degree. I use asset allocation in my own portfolio. Instead of putting all my eggs in the stock market basket, I also own real estate, cryptocurrency, private equity, infrastructure, and more. Within stocks, I don't just invest in the S&P 500, which is all U.S. large cap. I also own mid cap, small cap, international, and emerging markets. And within each of these categories, I may own hundreds of individual investments at any time. It's alright if you don't recognize some of these terms. The point is to recognize that diversification is really important.

Below is an example of how someone may decide to diversify their investments using asset allocation. Think of it like a recipe with multiple ingredients. If you follow a recipe that's focused on growth, you might have four parts U.S. large cap, two parts U.S. mid cap, etc. As you change the recipe, you change the potential outcome. Sometimes, people assume they have to have the best possible ingredients in their recipe — for example, the best stocks in the market. Instead, I believe the *recipe* is more important than the ingredients. If you enjoy homemade salsa, you know a good recipe requires salt, tomatoes, onions, pepper, cilantro, etc. The right mix of ingredients can make for the perfect salsa. What if we change the recipe and make it 30 percent salt, 40 percent onions, and 30 percent everything else? I don't care how good the ingredients are at that point; no margarita in the world is going to make up for this terrible salsa. Even if we have the freshest ingredients on the planet, the recipe is off. This is why I focus more on the recipe, which is my asset allocation, than the ingredients, which are the individual investments. I certainly spend time picking good investments that meet my high standards, but my first emphasis is on the recipe.

ASSET ALLOCATION

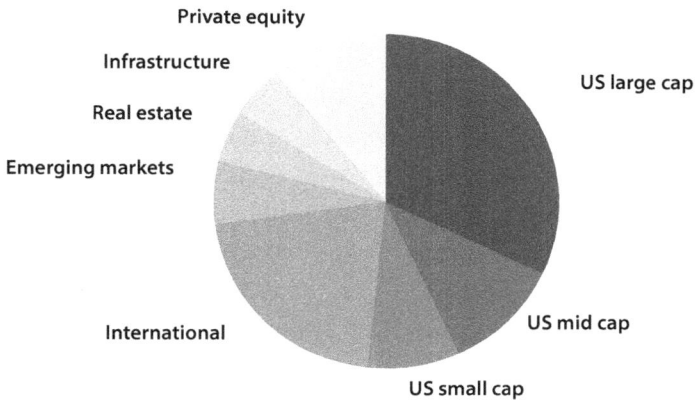

Private equity

Infrastructure

Real estate

Emerging markets

US large cap

International

US mid cap

US small cap

Hypothetical mix of investments using asset allocation. Asset allocation does not guarantee a profit or protect against loss.

So why does asset allocation have the potential to increase returns and decrease risk over time? Below is a simple example. This shows three different assets or investments. This also shows hypothetical performance for each asset over two years. Asset 1 is fairly volatile, but also has the highest average return. Asset 2 also has some volatility, with an average return less than Asset 1. Asset 3 is steady with an average rate of return of 10 percent, but it has the lowest average return among the three. Something is missing from this chart, though. Don't be fooled by past performance. Past performance is something many people focus on to make future decisions because they think good performance will continue in the future. This can be a misleading way to make investment decisions. What's missing from this chart is what happened to the dollars. It's like looking at a two-dimensional object versus a three-dimensional object. The chart below is missing a third dimension — the money.

	Asset 1	**Asset 2**	**Asset 3**
Year 1	45%	(12%)	10%
Year 2	(20%)	35%	10%
Average Return	**12.5%**	**11.5%**	**10%**

Hypothetical returns for illustrative purposes only.

The following chart shows what happens to the money in our hypothetical. Asset 1, which had the highest average rate of return, actually had the smallest return in dollars. After all, that's what really matters. Asset 3, which had the lowest average return, wound up with the most dollars. In the first chart, you may have assumed Asset 1 was the best. It's a common choice because people think performance is all about high percentages and past performance. In this chart, you may assume Asset 3 is the best because it gave the highest return in dollars. Remember what I said about diversification? What happens if we spread our eggs into each of these three baskets? In that case, the dollars grow even higher than any of the three assets by themselves. By investing in all three — by putting all three ingredients in our recipe — our dollars grew even higher.

	Asset 1	Asset 2	Asset 3
Average Return	12.5%	11.5%	10%
Starting Cash	$100	$100	$100
Ending Cash	$116	$119	$121

Hypothetical returns for illustrative purposes only.

	Assets 1, 2, and 3 combined
Starting Cash	$100
Ending Cash	$124

If you're wondering if this is smoke and mirrors, try the math yourself. It's not guaranteed and sometimes all three assets may perform poorly. Yet, if each performs differently through different market cycles over time, you may end up having lower overall risk and greater overall return using asset allocation. In my portfolio, I'll have investments that do poorly sometimes. Maybe it's because the investment didn't meet expectations or maybe it's because the entire market for that type of investment did poorly. Even high-quality real estate did poorly in the 2008 crash. Knowing that I'll have parts of my portfolio that perform poorly at times means diversification is working. If all my investments go up and down together, diversification isn't working. Diversification is important to me because I know how asset allocation works. Now you do, too.

When someone uses diversification, they may choose mutual funds to help pick the ingredients for the recipe. Mutual fund investing with stocks, bonds, and other categories involves a built-in mutual fund management team. This team oversees the day-to-day monitoring and management of the underlying basket of investments. This is another attractive feature for mutual funds if you don't have the time, patience, or expertise to manage a portfolio of stocks on your own. The management team also makes decisions regarding which investments to buy and sell over time on your behalf as a shareholder in the fund.

A common misconception about mutual funds is that the management team will help investors steer clear of market downturns and recessions. Most mutual funds have mandates they have to follow. For example, if a mutual fund advertises itself as a "U.S. large-cap growth fund," it will focus on buying and managing a basket of stocks that fit that description. If the management team thinks a recession is coming, it's not its job to speculate and sell all the stocks in the fund. Some mutual funds advertise themselves as "tactical" and do have the ability to make drastic changes, but most don't. Therefore, keep this in mind when investing in mutual funds. Know the fund's mandate so your expectations can be set properly.

Having a mutual fund management team also means there are skilled professionals being paid to do their job. This is why mutual funds have expense ratios. The expense ratio is generally a percentage fee that's paid to the mutual fund company to do its work. This expense comes directly out of the balance of the fund on a monthly or quarterly basis. Also, you normally don't see the dollar amount of the fee listed on a statement. In other words, you're unlikely to see "management fee: $531" on your statement. You can find out the expense ratio costs, but when the actual expense is *deducted* from your shares in the fund, it generally doesn't show up as a transaction. It happens behind the scenes. In my opinion, it's worth paying this expense ratio fee if it's reasonable compared to similar funds and it brings value to a portfolio. I'm happy to pay a fee for something of value.

Mutual fund expense ratios that seem much less expensive than their peers may be because they're a different breed. Some mutual funds focus on active management, while some are passive. An active mutual fund conducts research and tries to outperform a benchmark by buying or selling investments throughout the year. This active management requires more analysts, more trading, and more work. Passive funds, on the other hand, tend to buy more of a static basket of investments and hold them long term. The passive approach requires less trading, less research, and less work. Therefore, active funds tend to be more expensive than passive funds.

If you're wondering which option is better between active and passive mutual funds, it depends on a number of factors. In my opinion, some categories of investments warrant active management while others are fine being passive. Below is an example of various asset classes and my thoughts on using active or passive funds.

- U.S. large cap – passive
- U.S. mid cap – passive or active
- U.S. small cap – active
- U.S. real estate – passive or active
- Emerging markets – active
- Developed international large cap – passive or active
- Developed international small/mid cap – active
- International real estate – active
- U.S. corporate bonds – passive or active
- U.S. municipal bonds – active
- U.S. high-yield bonds – active
- International bonds – active

I've had people debate active versus passive management with me. As you can see, I don't favor one over the other. It simply depends. For example, if you want to invest in U.S. municipal bonds, you probably don't want a passive approach that owns municipal bonds throughout the entire country. Can you think of a few states in the U.S. that have struggled financially? I can think of a few states I wouldn't trust to borrow my money. I can also think of a few that are growing rapidly and manage their fiscal policy well. If you believe in passive investing across the board, you might end up investing in the entire municipal bond market throughout the U.S., perhaps including those states that may be risky borrowers. Personally, I would rather have active management in this case because I feel it is worth the expense to be selective and do the research.

Overall, before you pick a stock or bond mutual fund, consider what the fund will own, how that may change over time, the expense ratio, and whether it's actively or passively managed. There are plenty of other factors, too, but these are important ones.

With money-market mutual funds, you're buying into a basket of lower-risk investments like CDs and government bonds. Most people use money-market funds to protect their principle and earn interest. These funds generally have lower risk than bond mutual funds because of the underlying investments. You might use a money market mutual fund for emergency dollars you want to keep liquid. Also keep in mind that money-market mutual funds are different than money-market *accounts* at banks. You may prefer to use an FDIC guaranteed money market account at your local bank. Money market mutual funds generally aren't FDIC guaranteed.

Next up is allocation funds. With allocation funds, your money may be diversified into different investments, all in a single fund. For example, an allocation fund might own 55 percent stock, 40 percent bonds, and 5 percent real estate. This can be attractive if someone doesn't want to pick multiple different funds. Some allocation funds are aggressive, some are conservative, and some are in between.

Another type of allocation fund is something called a target-date fund. Target-date funds have seen significant growth in popularity since their introduction in the group retirement plan industry. Unlike most allocation funds, a target-date fund actively changes its mix of investment over time. For example, if you're 30 today and plan to retire in the year 2060, you may choose a 2060 target-date fund. Because 2060 is decades away, the fund will focus on higher-risk and higher-growth investments. Over time, though, it will become more and more conservative, selling stocks in favor of bonds and safer investments. This is also what I call an "auto-pilot fund." If you genuinely don't enjoy investing on your own, this may be a great option. People who don't work with a financial planner might choose the auto-pilot option and focus their time on working hard and saving aggressively.

Not all target-date funds are created equally. If you were to compare two 2060 funds from two different investment firms, you may notice they choose to invest in a different mix of investments, although they're targeting the same timeframe. Therefore, it's important to do a little reading to find out how much stock you'll own within the fund if you choose to invest in it. Also, target-date funds generally don't use tactical strategies to ramp up risk during good markets and taper back during bad markets. If you choose a long-term target-date fund, plan on experiencing volatility and keep a long-term mindset. Also, I wouldn't choose multiple target-date funds. I see some people pick two or three target-date funds and think they're diversifying their money. Generally, the point of these funds is to use only one.

The last category of mutual funds is specialty funds. These can vary wildly from fund to fund. Specialty funds can be focused just on one country, such a China, Brazil, or Israel. Some may focus on sectors such as technology or health care. Some focus on alternative asset classes like real estate, midstream energy, or commodities. Some even have complex options and derivatives strategies. If you're interested in specialty funds, you might use them with the consultation of a professional. A pro may have the experience and expertise of understanding these types of funds and how they might be used as part of an overall portfolio.

Exchange Traded Funds (ETFs)

With ETFs, you can trade a basket of stocks, bonds, real estate, and more, but do so more like a stock. Mutual funds can't be purchased during the normal trading hours of the stock exchanges. Instead, mutual fund orders, both buys and sells, are completed at the *end* of the trading day. What if the market has wild swings throughout the day? If you want to buy while the market may be down at 10:00 a.m., ETFs may be a better choice. They trade throughout the day like stocks. This is one reason some may prefer ETFs over mutual funds. ETFs also allow you to acquire hundreds of underlying investments within a single ETF, helping with diversification.

Unlike mutual funds that may have a management team that actively manages the underlying investments of the fund, most ETFs do not. Instead, most ETFs are created to be fairly static baskets of investments. For example, an S&P 500 ETF may own all 500 stocks that are tracked in the S&P 500. If one stock were to drop out of the S&P 500 index and be replaced by another, the ETF would likely follow suit. Although some ETFs advertise themselves as actively traded, because most are passive, the expenses for ETFs are usually lower than mutual funds that own similar investments.

If you're wondering which type of investment vehicle is better between ETFs or mutual funds, it depends. What may help you choose is the list of asset classes covered earlier and whether active or passive management is preferred. For example, you may choose to use a passive, cost-efficient ETF for U.S. large-cap exposure, whereas an active mutual fund might be used for emerging markets exposure. Personally, I own both mutual funds and ETFs in my portfolio.

Real Estate Investment Trusts (REITs)

If I had a dollar for every time someone told me they wanted to start investing in real estate, I would have suitcases full of them. Real estate is one of those popular areas of investing because it's visible. Unlike investing in a mutual fund, with real estate, you can walk up and touch the property you bought. It's a familiar asset, so it's less intimidating.

Real estate still has risks, though. I think about it every time I see an article in the news about a landlord who had their property trashed after their tenants had a huge party. Clogged pipes, broken doors, holes in the walls, and destroyed carpet are just a few examples of how someone can destroy your property's value if it's not respected. If you're interested in real estate, but don't want the risk of having just one or two properties, consider using a REIT instead.

REITs are popular vehicles and invest in various types of real estate. This may include residential, commercial, or industrial real estate. Some REITs invest in many types of real estate, while others are focused on specialty properties such as hotels, retails stores, and even ski resorts. REITs may look and feel like regular stocks. They often have specific ticker symbols like stocks and can trade throughout the day like stocks.

Many investors purchase mutual funds or ETFs that focus on REITs. In other words, the mutual fund may be purchasing the REITs for you and all you have to do is purchase the fund. This tends to be a more popular choice than purchasing REITs directly. If you're wondering why REITs even exist if you can own real estate within a mutual fund or ETF, there are special rules that govern REITs. The rules are beyond the scope of this book but know that REITs must follow these rules to be considered a REIT. If those rules are followed, REITs can enjoy preferential tax treatment.

One fact to know about REITs is some financial professionals may recommend them and receive a commission. If a financial professional asks you to complete special forms to invest in a REIT, ask him or her if a commission is being generated from it. Sometimes a commission applies and sometimes it doesn't, depending on the REIT. Earning a commission doesn't mean the financial professional is a bad person. It's simply an important question to ask to determine if other factors may be involved in the recommendation.

Investing in REITs that trade on a stock exchange can give you exposure to real estate investing that's much easier than buying and renting out properties on your own. For example, I've helped many clients analyze their current rental real estate — mostly single-family homes and condos. This analysis includes reviewing the values of each property, the incomes they generate, the taxes owed on each, historical repair information, etc. Sometimes, I find these rentals have healthy returns, such as 6 percent after tax from rental income, plus appreciation of 2–3 percent. I also have found that some have paltry returns of 2 percent from rental income plus appreciation. Going through the motions of analyzing each property someone may own seems like a simple task, but it requires the owner of the properties to be completely unbiased and question themselves. It can be a difficult task for even the most business-minded investors. If you own a rental that's paying you income each month, that may feel good, but if it's not generating the kind of returns you might find elsewhere, don't settle for less. Being comfortable with your money isn't the same as being smart with your money.

Investing in REITs may provide a solution for real estate investing without the complications, risks, and time commitment of buying individual properties. You don't have to fix a hole in the wall or a broken pipe with a REIT, nor do REITs typically complicate someone's tax return like direct rentals do. REITs can also provide the diversification of hundreds of properties versus buying individual properties. Investing in individual properties can certainly be lucrative. You've probably met or heard of people who have become wealthy investing in real estate. The point here is to understand there are other ways to invest in real estate that are simpler and provide diversification to a portfolio.

Annuities

Annuities are issued by insurance companies and, frankly, they're complex. They're also typically sold by insurance agents because they're insurance products. Some financial advisors hold insurance licenses and can act as insurance agents, so financial advisors may offer them as well. Before investing in annuities, ask the agent or advisor if they'll be paid a commission on the annuity. Compensation to a professional from these products can be complicated, as some may pay a commission while others are fee-based with no commission. Commission compensation is most common, though. If someone tells you they'll be paid directly by the annuity company, that means they'll be paid a commission. It may not sound like a big deal if they'll be paid from the annuity company, but remember, the insurance agent and the annuity company aren't working for free. They're making money on your money, so you need to ask questions. A handsome commission can be a big motivator for recommending an annuity to you.

One benefit of investing in annuities is their tax-deferred nature. If you invest in a mutual fund or REIT, you may owe taxes on capital gains or dividends each year. This "tax drag" on gains and dividends adds a layer of cost in the form of taxes. However, annuities can provide tax-deferral and postpone the taxes into the future. Think of annuities as empty boxes. They're technically not investments; they're shells. Then, you can put various investments *inside* the box — mutual funds, ETFs, REITs, etc. As you earn dividends or capital gains on the various investments inside the box, as long as you keep your money in the box, you generally don't have to pay any taxes.

Because of this tax-deferral benefit, in the U.S., the IRS requires investors to keep their assets inside of the annuity "box" until the age of 59 and a half. Otherwise, if you remove the assets at an earlier age, you may owe a 10 percent early withdrawal penalty, plus income taxes. There are some exceptions to the age 59-and-a-half rule that are beyond the scope of this book, but I've found them to be rare in real life.

There are generally three types of annuities:
• Variable annuities
• Fixed annuities
• Indexed annuities

Variable annuities are the traditional "box" analogy mentioned earlier. Insurance companies that offer variable annuities typically offer a menu of investment options from which to pick. These investments may also be called subaccounts but resemble mutual funds. Variable annuities may be beneficial if you want tax-deferral and waiting until age 59 and a half to take the money out isn't an issue. Before investing in variable annuities, aside from asking a professional how they're compensated, ask about the expenses of the annuity. Tax-deferral comes with a cost, which includes the cost of the annuity "box" itself, plus the cost of the underlying investment options.

Fixed annuities resemble a bond with a tax-deferral shell around it. Fixed annuities pay a stated interest rate for a period of time that comes directly from the insurance company. You might find a five-year fixed annuity that pays a rate of 4 percent. If you leave your dollars in the fixed annuity year to year, you don't have to pay taxes on the interest. Unlike CDs or U.S. government bonds that may have FDIC insurance or guarantees from the U.S. government, fixed annuities are backed by the claims-paying ability of the insurance carrier. In other words, you don't want to buy a fixed annuity with an insurance company that may go bankrupt next year. Given their more conservative nature and the fact that you can't remove the money until age 59 and a half, fixed annuities are more common for retirees than younger people trying to grow their wealth.

Indexed annuities are the most complicated type. They resemble variable annuities in that they offer the ability to grow your assets when the stock market appreciates. You can't actually invest your money in the stock market with these types of annuities, though. Instead, insurance companies allow you to "track" various stock market indices. For example, an indexed annuity may track the S&P 500 stock index and allow you to participate in growth if the index appreciates over a certain period of time. If this occurs, you may see the value of your indexed annuity increase. However, there may also be a cap on your growth potential, such as 8 percent per year. Insurance companies are using complex derivatives strategies to create this arrangement. If it sounds complicated, it is.

Because indexed annuities don't actually include stock-based investments, they can be sold by insurance agents without a financial advisor's license. Also, they typically pay a commission to the agent. Because of the commission, which may be 5–8 percent or higher, plus the allure of being able to participate in the growth of the stock market, these products should be scrutinized. I've met countless people who were sold indexed annuities and truly didn't understand how they work. They typically have a surrender schedule for a period of six to 10 years, too. This means if you want out of it within that period of time, you may pay a penalty to the annuity company of 1–10 percent. I once met a woman who was 81 years old who was sold an indexed annuity. She had no idea she was locked in it for five years! Imagine if she needed the money back to pay for health care costs at her age. If someone recommends this type of product to you, proceed with caution.

Derivatives

The last category of investment is derivatives. This is the most complex investment category, and most people stay away from them because of this. Some also have high risk for high-potential reward. These include options and futures. I'll share a high-level overview of these so you can know what someone's talking about if you're not familiar with them.

As the name implies, options offer the ability to buy or sell an investment, such as a stock, at a certain price for a certain period of time. Depending on the type of option contract, it may have unlimited risk exposure. Yes, *unlimited* risk exposure. Not all options have that level of risk, but some do. If you decide to try options trading, consider speaking with a professional first and doing plenty of reading. Even for professionals, this can be a complex way to invest.

Futures allow someone to buy or sell an asset at a specific time in the future for an agreed-upon price. These are common in the farming industry. A farmer may not know what the price of corn or wheat will be six months from now, so he may consider using a futures contract to "sell" his crop using a specific price to hedge his risk that prices will go down later. A cereal manufacturer may want to buy corn or wheat in advance to hedge the risk of prices increasing later. Although farmers play a large role in these contracts, investors also use them to speculate on various commodities, interest rates, stock prices, and currencies.

Derivatives are often used by hedge funds, commodity traders, and complex investments. Some financial professionals and even some everyday investors use them, too, but they're uncommon for a reason. These instruments are complex. There are also derivatives called "options on futures" if you want a self-induced headache reading about them online. Over your lifetime, you're likely to stick to the other investment types mentioned within this chapter.

Overall, as you decide how to invest your money, consider intelligent risks. There's no reward without risk, so if you want big rewards, remember you may lose some or all of your investment. Luckily, there are plenty of ways you can invest with varying degrees of risk to fit your needs. Remember that diversification is important, too. While you may have multiple high-risk investments, owning many of them in different categories may lower your *overall* risk. This is why I personally own many types of investments in many different categories.

Chapter 8

Creating a Financial Plan

In this chapter:
- Why everyone needs a plan
- Six-step planning process
- Staying on course

Imagine for a moment that you'll charter a boat to cross the Atlantic Ocean. You'll leave harbor in New York as the captain of this vessel with London as your destination. The journey will take approximately one week. You prepare your boat with food, fuel, and supplies. You bring plenty of emergency equipment like medical supplies and a life raft. You know the journey will be difficult, but you're driven by thoughts of sailing through the English Channel and enjoying all that London has to offer. The day comes for you to say goodbye to dry land and set sail toward the east. As you leave harbor, you point your vessel directly toward London. Then, you focus on other things such as fishing, cleaning the boat, and gazing at the stars. Occasionally, the seas are rough, and waves crash into the hull. Some days, the fog is so thick you can't see the bow. You hope you're still headed toward London because you don't have any way of measuring your location. Eventually, you see land in the distance. As you draw closer, you see what appears to be England or possibly Ireland. Then, with the harbor in sight, you realize you're not where you thought you would be at this point of the journey. You've successfully crossed the Atlantic, but you've landed in Casablanca, Morocco, in Northern Africa, 1,124 nautical miles from where you thought you were headed. You think about how much time and money you've already spent. You wish you could go back in time and change course, but that time is now lost. How could this have happened when you were pointed *precisely* toward London when you left New York?

This analogy is how I describe financial planning. Our financial goals, whether they are buying a business, sending kids to college, or retirement, are complex and can require a significant amount of planning and measurement. Because most people don't have either the training, patience, or time to analyze their financial goals, I find many people aren't on track. These days, the average family tries to accomplish too much on a given level of income. This trend is part of the growing appetite of having more for ourselves and our families.

Let's take the example of a couple I met years ago with two kids, a daughter, age 7, and a son 10. This couple told me they wanted to pay for their children's college. The kids weren't toddlers but weren't about to graduate high school yet, either. They had set up 529 college savings plans for their kids, which was a great move. They were saving roughly $500 per month to each 529, which was $12,000 per year total between the two kids. By the time we met, they had roughly $30,000 saved for their 7-year-old daughter and $50,000 for their 10-year-old son.

I then asked about their goals for college. They hoped to pay for 100 percent of normal college costs — tuition, room and board, books, and equipment — for up to four years of college for each child. I then asked them what would happen if their daughter, who was their youngest, made it into Harvard. Would paying for 100 percent for four years still be the plan? After all, by then you would have already made the promise to your son, who is three years older and would be in college already. After some discussion, they decided to plan on covering 100 percent of four years of college, but no more than the cost of an average private university. This avoided the feeling of a blank-check promise to the kids. The average cost for a private university with all the expenses they wished to cover was about $54,000 per year at the time.

After hearing this number, it was a bit intimidating to them, but they still wanted to do it. After all, they made a comfortable living and paying for college was an important goal for them. After completing a college-planning analysis, I showed this couple how they were doing so far toward this goal. For their son, if they continued saving $500 per month, combined with the $50,000 they had already saved, they would have a shortfall of over $210,000. This even assumed that their 529 assets grew at an aggressive rate of roughly 7 percent per year until their son was 18. For their daughter, using the same assumptions and the $30,000 they had already saved, they were projected to have a shortfall of almost $230,000. Between the two kids, the shortfall would be more than $440,000. As you can imagine, they were very surprised to see the projections, especially because they already had roughly $80,000 saved for education.

Although this was one family's example, it's what I often find when discussing goals such as college. Unfortunately, I find college costs typically increase by about 5–6 percent per year. It's difficult for the human brain to project these growing costs many years into the future. Most people can complete simple math in their heads or calculate a 20 percent tip after dinner, but to consider eight years of time, compounding, inflation, additional savings, and distributions over four years requires a computer program and an understanding of the planning assumptions. Although this couple had already saved well for college and made monthly savings into 529 plans a priority, they found they weren't headed in the direction they thought they were.

While this example was only focused on college savings, imagine including other goals and complications like Social Security, portfolio income, inflation, income taxes, estate taxes, paying off debt, inheritance, health insurance, life insurance, property titling, interest rates, asset allocation, and more. Financial planning often includes a complex web of goals, assumptions, and strategies. Therefore, creating a *plan* for these goals is crucially important. Simply having an idea in your head about what you want to achieve and how you're going to get there isn't enough. It's worth repeating that statement. Having an idea of your goals in your head isn't a plan. I call that a wish. Wishes turn into plans once they're documented and analyzed. You'll likely find that your goals will include more detail than you imagined once you begin this process. Don't waste years of time before turning those wishes into goals.

Some people assume financial planning is an event, but in reality, it's a process. It's an exercise that requires an investment of time and thought at the beginning and maintenance each year to remain current. It's a bit like building a home and then maintaining that home. A financial plan that's created and then left alone without updates is what I call a relic. It's no different than calculating how you'll reach London from New York and then hoping you'll wake up on the English coast one day.

When it comes to creating a financial plan, you have two options. First, you can hire a professional to help guide you with their knowledge and experience. Second, you can create your own financial plan using the six-step process detailed in this chapter. I generally recommend hiring a professional to create financial plans. Professionals typically have advanced knowledge of various financial topics and the experience of knowing what's worked and what hasn't with other clients. This professional knowledge shouldn't be underestimated. If people often learn in life by making mistakes, learning about good financial planning may require a few potentially costly mistakes in your life. Instead, tapping into the experience of a financial planner may mean you're tapping into a collective pool of knowledge from many other people who have made plenty of mistakes and learned from them. This may save you from costly setbacks as you work on your cherished goals in life.

If you decide to search for a financial planner, I highly recommend using someone with the letters CFP® behind their name. This stands for a CERTIFIED FINANCIAL PLANNER™ professional. A CFP® has shown they have the knowledge to pass a rigorous exam created by the Certified Financial Planner Board of Standards. The CFP® Board recommends a minimum of 250 hours of preparation time for the exam and the pass rate is normally around 63 percent[24]. This means more than one-third of the candidates sitting for the exam, who are usually financial professionals of some kind already, fail the exam. As someone who took this exam many years ago, I can tell you it was very difficult. I spent nearly two years studying for it at night and on the weekends. It was the most challenging exam I've taken in my life. The topics covered in the CFP® exam include:

- Principles of financial planning
- Education planning
- Risk management and insurance planning
- Professional conduct and regulation
- Retirement savings and income planning
- Investment planning
- Estate planning
- Tax planning

Anyone can call themselves a financial planner regardless of their credentials or licensing. It's an unfortunate complication for the finance industry because the term financial planner isn't reserved for CFPs. However, only CFP® professionals can call themselves a CERTI-FIED FINANCIAL PLANNER™. These professionals may also have other licenses, degrees, or credentials in addition to the CFP®.

When looking for a CFP® to help you create a financial plan, you may learn that many charge a flat fee for their time, like a CPA or attorney. These fees vary depending on someone's experience, so it's wise to speak with a few CFP® professionals before making this decision. Ask this person what will be included in the financial plan so you understand the scope. For example, will it be a comprehensive financial plan, or will it only focus on a single goal such as college planning? Also, ask how long the CFP® will be available to help you and answer questions. You may be signing something called an engagement agreement, which officially outlines what will be included. If you pay a one-time fee for a financial plan but expect to be able to call with questions five years later, ask if that's included. Most engagement agreements have a set start and end date.

Some CFP® professionals may offer to create your financial plan for free so you can see what their firm has to offer in hopes that you'll hire them to implement the plan. The creation of a financial plan is the initial investment of time and thought, but implementing the plan is the ongoing process of working toward your goals and keeping it updated. Implementing means sailing your boat and ensuring you remain on target through changes over time. If you have zero interest in hiring a CFP® for the implementation of your plan, let them know upfront so expectations are set properly. If you aren't sure if you want to hire a CFP® for implementation, this may be a great opportunity to learn what your relationship would look like long term and how they may be able to help you. Later in this chapter, we'll cover what to look for in CFP® professionals if you're considering hiring one long term.

For those of you interested in creating your own financial plan, below is the six-step process I've created for you. I've also included stories and examples within each of these steps for improving your finances. Even if you want to work with a CFP® professional, understanding these steps may help you prepare for what may be included in a professional-grade financial plan.

1. Create a cash-flow statement
2. Establish detailed goals
3. Calculate your net worth
4. Analyze your goals
5. Implement your plan
6. Monitor your plan

Step 1 — Create a cash-flow statement

The first step in creating your financial plan is the cash-flow statement. This may resemble establishing a budget, but it's different than a budget. Creating a budget is a process people tend to avoid because it takes time and often requires them to change their spending habits. The harsh realization that someone may be overspending in certain areas is enough to make them avoid ever having a budget. Instead, the cash flow statement has one primary purpose — to calculate how much money you make and where it goes. If you already have a budget, this process will be much easier. Also, keep in mind that CFPs don't care how you spend your money. There's no judgment involved. We're interested in the numbers, not your shopping habits.

Start with your income first. Ideally, you'll want to use your pretax income, also known as gross income. This is your income before any taxes or other withholding if you work for an employer. Focus on one month's worth of income and expenses for your cash-flow statement. If your income is variable, use your best estimate on an average month. If you can't figure out your gross income, you can use your net income that's deposited in your bank account each pay period. Gross income is better because we want to include expenses such as taxes, retirement plan savings, insurance premiums, and more. If you use your net income, these expenses are already removed from your income and can't be included in your cash-flow statement. If you're an employee, you can generally find your gross income on a paystub.

Next comes your list of expenses. Write down the expense categories that typically apply to you, such as mortgage or rent payments, auto payments and maintenance, utilities, travels costs, insurance premiums, or entertainment. If you were able to find your gross income, also include income taxes, retirement savings, and any insurance premiums that may be deducted from your gross income. This will make your cash-flow statement more meaningful by including all these expenses.

If you have debt payments such as a student loan or credit card, these payments will be included in your cashflow statement. If you typically make extra payments on top of a minimum required payment, include the extra amount in your cashflow statement too. If you typically transfer money to an emergency fund or other type of account each month, include that as well. After all, a cash-flow statement is to monitor where your cash is flowing, including if you park it in special accounts each month that have a goal attached to them. For example, if you transfer $300 per month to a special savings account that's meant for your next car purchase, it may not be an expense, but it's money you're allocating to a special account that will one day be used for an expense. The same applies to money transferred to an emergency fund because it's likely you'll spend that money on an emergency at some point.

After you've recorded your income, expense, and savings amounts, you should be able to look over your cash-flow statement to see if you're spending more or less than you make in a given month. If your income represents inflows and your expenses and savings represent outflows, ideally you want these two numbers to match. If your inflows are greater than your outflows, you may have excess cash each month that can be used for goals such as paying down debt, saving more for emergencies, or increasing retirement savings. If your outflows are greater than your inflows, you may be increasing your debt.

For those of you with debt such as student loans, personal loans, or auto loans, I'm frequently asked if money should be dedicated to paying down these debts faster or if money should be used for saving and investing instead. As you learned in Chapter 2, compounding is a powerful force that can help you reach financial independence. That force can also work against you if you're the one who's paying interest to a bank instead of the other way around. If you believe you can earn 8 percent per year on average by investing in the stock market, then an auto loan at 4 percent would receive minimum payments each month to allow you to save more into the market. If you believe you could earn 8 percent in the stock market on average and your credit card balance is charging you 19 percent, pay down your credit card first. Don't mess around with high-interest credit card debt. Avoid it and pay it off immediately.

This cash-flow exercise is also a good opportunity to review your housing expenses. For many people, housing represents their largest expense. Some spend a third of their income or more on housing each month. That's a large amount of income going immediately into housing every single month, leaving the rest of your life to be funded by the difference. In the mortgage industry, lenders often use what's called the 28 percent PITI rule, which stands for principal, interest, taxes, and insurance. Lenders typically don't want to see you spending more than 28 percent of your income on a total monthly mortgage payment that includes PITI. While mortgage lenders use these types of rules to gauge if you can afford a loan, mortgage lenders may not care about your overall financial future. Sure, they may take pride in helping people buy their dream homes, but if someone isn't saving even a penny for retirement each month, it's not their concern. Their interests are focused on approving you for a mortgage and moving on to the next person.

While the mortgage industry may use the 28 percent PITI rule, I generally recommend a more conservative rule of 20 percent PITI. This means if you have a household income of $100,000, you shouldn't use more than $20,000 per year (or about $1,600 per month) on housing or rental expenses. Depending on your income and where you live, this may be a shock. You may want to challenge me on this rule. I completely understand if you do. Housing is a personal choice. However, if you rent or buy a home that barely fits your budget and you're spending nearly a third of your income each month, how are you going to have enough money to pay for your other expenses *and* save well for your future?

This reminds me of the rocks, pebbles, and sand analogy. If you place rocks into a jar all the way to the top and ask a child if the jar is full, he'll likely answer yes. If you then place smaller pebbles into the jar, shaking it and allowing the pebbles to fill empty spaces, the child may reaffirm that the jar is full. If you then place sand into the jar and allow it to take up any remaining space, the child may then understand that the jar is finally full. No space exists after the sand is poured in (although I would argue we could use water next, but that's just me). If you reverse the order that these contents are placed into the jar, with sand going in first and pebbles next, you'll find the larger rocks can't fit.

This analogy is often used to illustrate the philosophical principle of focusing on what's important in life (the rocks) before adding in the less important things. Otherwise, you won't have enough room in your life for what's most important to you. In my example, if you buy a home that requires a large portion of your income each month, you'll be leaving less room for everything else. I often find couples who buy homes they can barely afford argue about money more because they don't have much extra spending cash at the end of the month. That puts stress and strain on their relationship, which can also lead to sleep and health issues. If you live a stressful life and health issues follow, is that the future you have in mind as you work hard to become independently wealthy?

If you decide that my 20 percent PITI rule is unrealistic in your situation, possibly due to your current income, remember this rule as your income increases over time. If you buy a home and your PITI payments equal 25 percent of your income, your income may rise to a point that your PITI payments equal 20 percent or less of your income. At this point, you may be tempted to move into a larger or more expensive home. Fight this temptation, even if all your friends are doing it. If your income is growing, it's like your jar is growing and giving you more room to add rocks, pebbles, or sand. Moving into a more expensive home may feel good, but your future self may regret it one day. At the time of writing this book, my PITI payments represent 8 percent of my income. Can I afford a more expensive home? Absolutely, and I sometimes find myself looking at more expensive homes for sale online. That, however, would rob from my ability to save for college, save for retirement, start businesses, and other financial goals. This lifestyle choice also helps my wife and me live a more stress-free life, which is important to us.

On your cash-flow statement, calculate what percentage of your income you're saving for retirement. If you only save to a retirement plan at work, this should be easy because most employer retirement plans are based on a percentage of income. Overall, as you learned in Chapter 2, I recommend a rate of savings of at least 10 percent. If you're not yet saving to this level and you don't have any high-interest debt, review your expenses to determine where you may be able to make cuts to better save for your future.

Step 2 — Establish detailed goals

In this step of creating your financial plan, you'll write out your goals in as much detail as possible. This step can include retirement goals, college goals for children, starting a business, buying a second home, international travel, or anything else you want in life. I recommend categorizing your goals into one of three categories — needs, wants, and wishes. Using this categorization helps for two reasons. First, don't feel the need to hold back on writing down any goals because you can always put those that may seem far-fetched into the wish group. Second, if the analysis of your financial plan shows it may be difficult to achieve all your goals, you might decide to only focus on goals in the needs group. If someone isn't "on track" to achieve all the goals in their needs, wants, *and* wishes groups, they typically have to make changes. This could include delaying goals, such as retirement, saving more toward goals, or removing them from the list of goals altogether. If changes need to be made, it's much easier to decide where to make changes when you've identified which goals are essential and which are not.

Below are some common goals I've seen from clients in each of the following categories:

- Needs
  - Retirement and retirement income
  - Health care costs
  - Insurance premiums (life and/or long-term care)
  - Care for aging parents or special-needs children
- Wants
  - Travel
  - Vehicle purchases
  - Wedding expenses for children
  - Boat purchases
  - Starting a business
  - RVs or equipment
  - Education costs for children

- Wishes
  - Second or third homes
  - Gifts to charity
  - Gifts or inheritance to children
  - Significant travel
  - Exotic purchases (art, cars, etc.)

As you identify your goals and categorize them into each group, add as much detail as possible. For example, if you want to retire at 62, do you plan on working part-time? If so, for how long and at what expected wage? Will you pay for private health insurance until you're Medicare age or will you have a spouse who could include you on his or her health plan? If you have a goal of paying for college for children, as mentioned earlier, be as detailed as possible. If you want to pay 100 percent of your child's costs, would that still be the case at an Ivy League school? What if they want to stay for a fifth year? What if they want to earn their MBA or become a lawyer? Thinking through these goals in detail will help significantly as you work on your financial plan.

Step 3 — Calculate your net worth

Each of us can be measured in numbers, and those numbers can serve our needs. We can be measured by age, height, weight, shoe size, and blood pressure. While not as critical to your well-being as blood pressure, measuring net worth can help you plan for positive financial changes and monitor progress over time. Also, giving this information to a financial planner, insurance agent, or estate attorney can make the process of working with these professionals much easier. For example, as a financial planner, I may see someone's net-worth statement and notice immediately that specific debts can be managed differently using home equity. I may also see that someone has a large percentage of retirement money in pretax retirement accounts vs. a Roth account. An insurance agent may see areas for proper coverage; an estate attorney may see planning opportunities around the total net-worth number and types of assets owned.

To calculate your net worth, write down each of your assets and liabilities. Remember, this doesn't include bills, such as monthly utilities. Instead, write down everything you *own* and everything you *owe*. This includes retirement accounts, real estate, bank accounts, vehicles, personal property, valuable art or jewelry, boats, business interests, credit card balances, mortgages, auto loans, student loans, and any other asset or liability you may have. Once you've listed all these items, you'll total the assets. Then, you'll total the liabilities. Lastly, you'll add the total assets and the total liabilities together to arrive at your total net worth.

It's not uncommon if you're young to have more liabilities than assets due to large student loans or other debts. It's normal for people to have a negative net worth early in life. Your goal will be to pay down bad debt and grow your assets for a positive net-worth number. Then, you'll enjoy monitoring that number as it grows over time. This is an exercise I recommend updating once a year. You should also celebrate as you reach new milestones, such as moving from a negative net worth to a positive or reaching $500,000. You should definitely celebrate once you reach the $1 million net-worth level. In fact, feel free to send me a message about it. I really enjoy hearing from people who use my work to reach new heights.

Step 4 — Analyze your goals

This is the most difficult step in the financial-planning process, but also the most powerful. Analyzing your goals allows you to make calculated projections in the future to determine if you're headed in the direction you want. It's a way to make decisions today to plan for tomorrow while you still have time to make changes. If someone analyzes their retirement goals one year before they want to retire, they no longer have the benefit of time to adjust their savings levels, cash flow, or investment mix. At that point, if someone projects they won't have enough money to retire in a year, they may have to delay retirement or live a smaller lifestyle. Without the benefit of time, more drastic changes need to occur if someone isn't on track.

I highly recommend visiting with an independent CFP® for this step in the planning process. Many CFP® professionals have sophisticated software available to analyze someone's financial goals. This software may cost the CFP® thousands of dollars per year. For a professional who uses this software daily, the cost is worth it. For a do-it-yourself investor, the cost of a professional-grade program may not make sense. Plus, professional-grade planning software is complicated to use and involves a learning curve, even for professionals. It took me about a year to be highly proficient in the software I use.

If you prefer to analyze your financial goals on your own, there are a few options. First, you can build a custom spreadsheet. This option isn't ideal because it would take significant time to create a spreadsheet that produces results similar to financial planning software. Tax projections, cash flow transactions, varying rates of inflation on certain goals, and a Monte Carlo analysis are all very difficult to bring together in a spreadsheet.

Second, you can use a free online program, such as one that may be included in your employer's retirement plan website. Companies like Fidelity and Vanguard, which offer employer retirement plan services, often include basic projection tools for free. These tools are typically simple in nature, though, and don't allow for the inclusion of other goals besides retirement. These tools were built to be easy enough for anyone to use, so their features and customization options are usually limited.

Third, you can search online for software programs tailored to do-it-yourselfers. Some of these options are free, while others require a fee. As you weigh your options for which solution to use, keep in mind that I recommend updating your financial plan on an annual basis. This means you'll want to use a solution that will be around for years to come and one that has a reasonable fee for annual renewals.

As you analyze your goals, you may find you aren't on track to achieve them. While it's not always the case, it's fairly common when someone goes through this exercise for the first time. Instead of being worried about not being on track, be thankful that you discovered it now and not later because you have *time* to make changes. These changes may include spending less, saving more, changing your investment mix to be more or less aggressive, removing goals from the "wish" group, delaying goals, downsizing a home, and more. This is the power of financial planning — by bringing the future into today where you can *do* something about it. With the benefit of time, you may also find that small changes in numerous areas can make a big impact on your projections. With enough time, someone may be able to increase their savings rate from 7–10 percent and delay retirement by one year without sacrificing other goals. I've found that for most people, those two changes don't feel drastic, especially if it means keeping other goals like traveling internationally or purchasing a second home.

Below are some additional tips regardless of which option you use to analyze your goals:

- Life expectancy — According to the World Bank, life expectancy in the U.S. in 1960 was 70 as an average between men and women[25]. By 2018, life expectancy in the U.S. climbed to 79. This age was adjusted downward again in 2021, but largely due to the effects of the COVID-19 pandemic. The trend for longer life expectancy is still expected to continue, though, especially for those with wealth. If you're fortunate enough to be reading this book and you find financial success in your future, you may be expected to live longer than others. A study by the National Bureau of Economic Research in Cambridge, Mass., found that men who had reached the age of 40 and were in the top 10 percent of household incomes were expected to live to 88. Those in the bottom 10 percent of household incomes were expected to live to age 76[26]. Life expectancy has increased over time for all in the U.S., but for those fortunate enough to be financially successful, the increases have been greater. I often plan for age 92 for men and age 94 for women in my own financial planning projections, unless there are health reasons to the contrary.

- Inflation — The gradual increase in prices on goods and services is a normal part of any healthy economy. You can't ignore the effects of inflation over time in a financial projection. Therefore, remember to include an inflation adjustment that's appropriate for your specific goals. For example, average inflation on everyday expenses such as food, clothing, and other essentials might be 2–3 percent depending on market conditions. Inflation on health care might be twice that amount. This is why health care costs are typically stated separately in a retirement projection because it would be a mistake to lump them in with "everyday" expenses at a lower inflation rate. Also, if college planning is part of your projection, college cost inflation is typically higher than standard inflation rates. If you have a specific college in mind, ask the admission office what its cost increases have been the past few years. You can use that same trend to make projections on a given school into the future.

- Growth assumptions — Any financial planning projection that involves investments will include an assumed growth rate. Growth assumptions are quite subjective, but I recommend being conservative. Assuming a college plan or retirement plan will grow at an average rate of 12 percent means you're making important decisions with your precious commodity of time based on an aggressive rate of growth that may not occur. I typically use growth assumptions between 3–8 percent depending on how conservative or aggressive someone is with their investments. Regardless of which growth assumption you use, remember you may become more conservative with your assets over time. For example, a college savings plan for a 3-year-old will likely be invested much differently by age 17 when the first tuition payment is just around the corner. The same can be said for most of my clients as they grow closer to their retirement date. Most people tend to decrease their risk over time, which means growth assumptions may decrease, too. Keep this in mind as you make projections into the future.

Step 5 — Implement Your Plan

Now that you've analyzed your goals and possibly made changes to them, it's time to implement your financial plan. If you've created your own financial plan, you may notice areas where improvements can be made, such as increasing your cash flow by reducing expenses or even increasing your income. You may notice on your net-worth page that you have enough home equity in your home to open a home equity line of credit (HELOC), which could be used to pay off high-interest debt. You may need to save more to reach your retirement goals, so now it's time to work on that change.

If you find you need to be saving 12 percent of your income to reach your retirement goals, but you're currently saving half of that, this is your opportunity to plan on how you'll make this change. For some, you may have enough discretionary spending to increase your savings rate to 12 percent without changing your lifestyle much. For others, you may already feel like money is tight, so increasing your retirement savings rate to 12 percent simply isn't in the cards yet. Therefore, plan out *how* you're going to make these changes. You may decide to cut expenses immediately to make room for more savings. Then you may decide to save 100 percent of your pay raises until you reach your 12 percent savings rate. However, if saving 12 percent toward retirement seems like a pipe dream and you aren't willing to make other changes to your finances, then it's time to adjust your goals. Delaying your retirement date may mean you only need to save 10 percent instead of 12 percent because you'll have additional years to save toward this goal.

If you decide to work with a CFP® professional, this person will likely provide you with written recommendations on how to implement your financial plan. A professional may include tax-planning recommendations, such as a Roth vs. pretax savings, estate-planning recommendations, establishing certain types of trusts, insurance recommendations, how much disability insurance is needed, or business planning recommendations, such as the type of legal entity you may consider for a new business. A professional will draw upon his or her skillset and experience helping other clients to provide detailed recommendations and how to implement those recommendations.

As mentioned earlier, while working with a professional, you may have the option of using this person to implement your financial plan. This means they'll likely charge a fee to help with the time and complexity of implementation. Even with a professional, there are typically implementation steps that still require your action. Two examples are adding a payable on death agreement (POD) to your bank account or determining the cost basis (the original price paid) on a stock you purchased years ago. Whether you use a professional for implementation, for any steps that require your action, put a deadline on them. We all tend to operate better with deadlines. Otherwise, you may find yourself busy with work and family needs, causing your financial goals to suffer the consequences. This is why setting a deadline for each and every implementation step is crucial. This is also one of the benefits of working with a professional — to have someone by your side who will hold you accountable to your own goals.

Implementing your financial plan with a pro might save you significant time. While there might be a few areas where your help is needed, a professional may help you with paperwork, phone calls, research, and plenty of busywork that's easier for the professional to handle. For example, if you want to conduct backdoor Roth IRA conversions, having a professional there to take care of them for you might save quite a bit of time each year. Another example is making changes to your portfolio to be more diversified or more aggressive. If you have assets in multiple accounts, these changes may be time-consuming on your own. A professional and their team may be able to handle it for you accurately and in a fraction of the time while also keeping in mind tax considerations.

Step 6 — Monitor your plan

After you've created a cash-flow statement, a net-worth statement, established your detailed goals in writing, and taken steps to implement your financial plan after analyzing it, it's time to create a habit of updating it. Years ago, I owned a smartphone that was completely outdated. My friends would make fun of me because it was so old and didn't have the new functions their phones had. Eventually, I couldn't use my favorite apps because it was so outdated. Technology changes rapidly and so does life. If you spend the time and energy to create a financial plan, but don't update it regularly, it will become obsolete. While I still keep my smartphones longer than my friends, I update my financial plan regularly and recommend the same for others. Don't let this work collect dust. You owe it to your future to keep at it.

If you decide to work with a professional, this regular updating will likely be part of your relationship with them. I regularly meet with my clients at least once per year to update their financial plans and discuss changes. Below are some examples of how a financial plan may be updated each year:

- A child receives an unexpected scholarship for college
- Federal or state tax laws change
- Estate tax exemptions or gift tax exclusions change
- Annual limits to HSAs, IRAs, and group retirement plans change
- Investments change, such as mergers and acquisitions
- Inflation changes
- Family members need help unexpectedly
- A new child or grandchild is on the way
- Career paths change
- Unexpected bonuses or pay cuts occur
- Health changes

If you want the best chance of reaching your cherished goals in life, make it a habit of updating your financial plan at least once per year. Also, if you're married and your spouse doesn't care about financial planning, they at least need to be familiar with the plan. It's not uncommon for one spouse to be more interested in financial planning than the other, but I've found that if the less-interested spouse doesn't participate in the process, he or she will never have a vested interest in the goals. Also, if the disengaged spouse finds themself alone one day due to a tragic accident, do you think they'll be prepared to carry on financially with confidence? I've found that financially disengaged spouses often have a more difficult time coping with loss if the burden of learning about their own finance is added to the process. Find a way to bring your spouse into the fold when it comes to establishing goals, analyzing those goals, and monitoring the plan.

Chapter 9

The Compound Career Path

In this chapter:
- Salary compounding
- Finding the right employer
- Real income and growth potential

A few times throughout this book, I've mentioned the "snowball effect" and the magic of compounding. It truly is amazing to see how compounding can work over a long period of time. Benjamin Franklin once said, "Money makes money. And the money *that* money makes, makes money." This is a great explanation of how the process works.

In the Disney movie *Fantasia*, one of the most popular segments is The Sorcerer's Apprentice. Mickey Mouse stars as the apprentice of a powerful sorcerer. After practicing magic for a while, the sorcerer yawns and returns to his chambers. Mickey is left to complete his chores, including carrying buckets of water to fill a cauldron. It's hard work for the mouse. That's when Mickey decides to put on the sorcerer's hat to try some magic of his own. He commands his broomstick to come alive and carry the buckets of water for him. To his excitement, it works. After dozing off, he wakes to find the cauldron is overflowing. Without the knowledge of how to stop the spell, he decides to break the broomstick into pieces. To his disappointment, the pieces each grow into broomsticks and begin carrying buckets of water. They become an army of broomsticks, flooding the room with water. The sorcerer wakes from the commotion, cancels the spell, and saves Mickey from his mistake.

This story reminds me of the powers of compounding. You allow your money to do the work for you and grow into more money. Your job is to manage this growing army of cash so it can work for you. You can then doze off if you want, but I prefer to focus on even more work while my army is working.

You may be intimately familiar with the concept of "money value of time." A real-world example is an hourly wage. If someone makes $50 per hour, that's the monetary value of their time. Time goes into the equation and money comes out. With the magic of compounding, the concept of "time value of money" is applied. This is the money your *money* can make over time.

If you've ever paid interest on a credit card, you may know how quickly the power of compounding can work against you. A credit card with $5,000 on it at 19 percent interest can build rather quickly if not paid down. Instead, compound interest can work *for* you by growing year after year, like a snowball. This concept is like a recipe. The key ingredients to allow compounding to work for you are money, risk, and time.

As with the earlier analogy of having an army of cash working for you, compounding requires at least some level of investment in the beginning. Let's assume it's $1,000. That's the first ingredient. The next ingredient — risk — comes in the form of investing. You may decide to invest this $1,000 in a CD at your bank where you'll be paid a certain interest rate. You might also invest this money in the stock market where it can increase or decrease in value over time. A low level of risk, such as a bank CD, means your snowball may grow at a slower pace. A high level of risk, such as the stock market, means your snowball may grow (or melt) at a faster pace. The last ingredient — time — is crucial. Even with high rates of return, compounding is limited without a long period of time, such as 10 to 30 years. This is why I feel the youngest readers of this book have the greatest potential to grow wealth over time.

Here are some examples of how the magic of compounding may look based on different ingredients. The first chart assumes an amount of $1,000 is invested right away and no money is added ever again. This purely assumes your money is working for you over time and you never save another cent. Using various assumed rates of return, you can see how compounding can be a powerful force over time.

Growth of $1,000				
Years	2%	5%	8%	12%
1	$1,020	$1,050	$1,080	$1,120
5	$1,104	$1,276	$1,469	$1,762
10	$1,219	$1,629	$2,159	$3,106
15	$1,346	$2,079	$3,172	$5,474
20	$1,486	$2,653	$4,661	$9,646
25	$1,641	$3,386	$6,848	$17,000
30	$1,811	$4,322	$10,063	$29,960

Assumptions: Present value of $1,000 at the beginning of the period with no additional payments using stated time periods and hypothetical rates of return.

The next chart uses the same set of assumptions but uses an initial investment of $100,000 instead of $1,000. If the first chart didn't impress you, let's add some zeros.

Growth of $100,000				
Years	2%	5%	8%	12%
1	$102,000	$105,000	$108,000	$112,000
5	$110,408	$127,628	$146,933	$176,234
10	$121,899	$162,889	$215,892	$310,585
15	$134,587	$207,893	$317,217	$547,357
20	$148,595	$265,330	$466,096	$964,629
25	$164,061	$338,635	$684,848	$1,700,006
30	$181,136	$432,194	$1,006,266	$2,995,992

Assumptions: Present value of $100,000 at the beginning of the period with no additional payments using stated time periods and hypothetical rates of return.

Because most people don't start investing with a lump sum of $100,000, let's go back to the original investment of $1,000. This time, we'll add money to this hypothetical investment each year. In other words, we'll be using additions from your "money value of time" and allow the "time value of money" to compound these dollars like a snowball. Let's also use a hypothetical age instead of years to make this more realistic. This assumes someone makes $70,000 per year and saves 10 percent, or $7,000. This also assumes the $70,000 salary increases each year with inflation at 2 percent. Because of normal salary increases over time, the 10 percent saving amount means more dollars are being added to the portfolio too.

$1,000 investment plus 10% per year at 8% return					
Age	Start at 25	Start at 35	Start at 45	Salary	10% Savings
25	$8,640			$70,000	$7,000
26	$17,042			$71,400	$7,140
27	$26,271			$72,828	$7,283
28	$36,396			$74,285	$7,428
29	$47,490			$75,770	$7,577
30	$59,637			$77,286	$7,729
31	$72,921			$78,831	$7,883
32	$87,439			$80,408	$8,041
33	$103,292			$82,016	$8,202
34	$120,590			$83,656	$8,366
35	$139,453	$10,296		$85,330	$8,533
36	$160,009	$20,519		$87,036	$8,704
37	$182,398	$31,749		$88,777	$8,878
38	$206,769	$44,068		$90,552	$9,055
39	$233,286	$57,569		$92,364	$9,236
40	$262,124	$72,349		$94,211	$9,421
41	$293,472	$88,515		$96,095	$9,609
42	$327,535	$106,182		$98,017	$9,802

	$1,000 investment plus 10% per year at 8% return				
Age	Start at 25	Start at 35	Start at 45	Salary	10% Savings
43	$364,536	$125,475		$99,977	$9,998
44	$404,712	$146,526		$101,977	$10,198
45	$448,323	$169,482	$12,314	$104,016	$10,402
46	$495,647	$194,499	$24,757	$106,097	$10,610
47	$546,987	$221,746	$38,425	$108,219	$10,822
48	$602,667	$251,407	$53,421	$110,383	$11,038
49	$663,040	$283,680	$69,854	$112,591	$11,259
50	$728,486	$318,777	$87,846	$114,842	$11,484
51	$799,416	$356,930	$107,524	$117,139	$11,714
52	$876,273	$398,389	$129,030	$119,482	$11,948
53	$959,537	$443,422	$152,515	$121,872	$12,187
54	$1,049,726	$492,321	$178,142	$124,309	$12,431
55	$1,147,398	$545,401	$206,087	$126,795	$12,680
56	$1,253,157	$603,001	$236,541	$129,331	$12,933
57	$1,367,657	$665,488	$269,712	$131,918	$13,192
58	$1,491,602	$733,259	$305,821	$134,556	$13,456
59	$1,625,753	$806,742	$345,109	$137,247	$13,725
60	$1,770,932	$886,401	$387,837	$139,992	$13,999
61	$1,928,028	$972,734	$434,286	$142,792	$14,279
62	$2,098,000	$1,066,283	$484,759	$145,648	$14,565
63	$2,281,885	$1,167,630	$539,584	$148,561	$14,856
64	$2,480,801	$1,277,406	$599,116	$151,532	$15,153
65	$2,695,958	$1,396,292	$663,738	$154,563	$15,456

Assumptions: Present value of $1,000 at the beginning of the period with annual additions of 10 percent of salary at the beginning of the period. Hypothetical return of 8 percent per year. Salary increases of 2 percent per year.

This is where the power of compounding really shines. As I mentioned, the key ingredients to this recipe are money, risk, and time. In the previous chart, the initial investments and the rates of return are the same. The only change to the equation is time. The difference between beginning to save and invest at age 45 versus age 25 meant someone would have more than $2 million less by the age of 65. In other words, waiting 20 years to begin growing this "army of money" *cost* this person more than $2 million. Can the 45-year-old still become a millionaire one day? Yes, certainly. However, it becomes significantly more difficult when less and less time is available. I can't stress enough how important it is to use time to your advantage.

Building on the concept of compounding investments, consider the impact of the $70,000 salary in the previous chart. This assumed the salary grew by 2 percent per year. Let's use a smaller starting salary for the 25-year-old, but a growth rate on that salary of 4 percent instead of 2 percent.

$1,000 investment plus 10% per year at 8% return					
Age	Start at 25	Start at 35	Start at 45	Salary	10% Savings
25	$6,264			$48,000	$4,800
26	$12,156			$49,920	$4,992
27	$18,736			$51,917	$5,192
28	$26,066			$53,993	$5,399
29	$34,216			$56,153	$5,615
30	$43,260			$58,399	$5,840
31	$53,281			$60,735	$6,074
32	$64,365			$63,165	$6,316
33	$76,609			$65,691	$6,569
34	$90,116			$68,319	$6,832
35	$104,999	$8,754		$71,052	$7,105
36	$121,379	$17,434		$73,894	$7,389
37	$139,389	$27,129		$76,850	$7,685
38	$159,172	$37,931		$79,924	$7,992
39	$180,883	$49,942		$83,120	$8,312
40	$204,690	$63,274		$86,445	$8,645
41	$230,774	$78,045		$89,903	$8,990

	$1,000 investment plus 10% per year at 8% return				
Age	Start at 25	Start at 35	Start at 45	Salary	10% Savings
42	$259,334	$94,387		$93,499	$9,350
43	$290,583	$112,440		$97,239	$9,724
44	$324,751	$132,357		$101,129	$10,113
45	$362,090	$154,304	$12,439	$105,174	$10,517
46	$402,871	$178,462	$25,247	$109,381	$10,938
47	$447,386	$205,024	$39,552	$113,756	$11,376
48	$495,954	$234,203	$55,494	$118,306	$11,831
49	$548,918	$266,228	$73,221	$123,039	$12,304
50	$606,652	$301,346	$92,899	$127,960	$12,796
51	$669,556	$339,826	$114,703	$133,079	$13,308
52	$738,068	$381,959	$138,827	$138,402	$13,840
53	$812,659	$428,061	$165,478	$143,938	$14,394
54	$893,839	$478,473	$194,884	$149,695	$14,970
55	$982,160	$533,565	$227,288	$155,683	$15,568
56	$1,078,219	$593,736	$262,957	$161,910	$16,191
57	$1,182,662	$659,421	$302,180	$168,387	$16,839
58	$1,296,188	$731,088	$345,267	$175,122	$17,512
59	$1,419,553	$809,244	$392,559	$182,127	$18,213
60	$1,553,574	$894,441	$444,420	$189,412	$18,941
61	$1,699,134	$987,271	$501,248	$196,989	$19,699
62	$1,857,191	$1,088,378	$563,474	$204,868	$20,487
63	$2,028,777	$1,198,459	$631,562	$213,063	$21,306
64	$2,215,010	$1,318,267	$706,019	$221,586	$22,159
65	$2,417,100	$1,448,617	$787,389	$230,449	$23,045

Assumptions: Present value of $1,000 at the beginning of the period with annual additions of 10 percent of salary at the beginning of the period. Hypothetical return of 8 percent per year. Salary increases of 4 percent per year.

In this example, notice how the salary at 65 is much higher than the last example. The lower salary of $48,000 a year caught up to the higher starting salary of $70,000 a year at about age 44. Then, the lower starting salary began beating the higher starting salary because it was growing faster over time. Also, notice the amount of wealth at 65 depending on when this person began saving. The 25-year-old saver was still better off with the higher salary that grew at a slower pace, but the 35- and 45-year-old savers did better in the second example. That's because their income was growing faster than the prior example.

This illustrates two points. First, long periods of time, such as from age 25 to 65, gives significant advantage to the power of compounding. Second, it shows that *income* compounded over time at a higher rate can significantly increase wealth also. It shows having a career path that offers a higher potential for growth, especially for those who didn't save much in their early years, can offer much more wealth over time.

This is what I call the "compounding career path." Imagine your salary as the snowball for a moment. What if you could position yourself over time to grow your income at a faster rate? This may allow you to save and invest more over time. Some industries statistically have stronger wage growth over time than others. For example, according to the Federal Reserve Bank of Atlanta, between 1997 to 2020, overall wage growth for American workers was approximately 3.6 percent. The leisure and hospitality industry experienced average wage growth of approximately 2.8 percent, while the finance and business services industry experienced growth of approximately 4 percent.

Wage growth is different than industry growth, but they can be correlated. Wage growth is the change of income for a given industry over time. Industry growth is the change in the number of people working in that industry over time. If you work for an industry that's shrinking, that doesn't sound very promising as you hope for future raises. An example might be traditional printing presses since the year 2000 as more people switched from paper media to digital media. If you were in the printing industry as it slowly lost customers, how do you think that would affect your career and your salary? You want to be part of both a company *and* an industry that's growing so you can have more opportunities for advancement and wage growth.

The Bureau of Labor Statistics in the U.S. compiled labor and industry data as of 2021 and projected it to 2031[27]. The industries expected to have the most growth over this period included:

1. Event promoters, agents, and managers – 39 percent
2. Amusement parks and arcades – 38 percent
3. Performing arts companies – 35 percent
4. Individual and family services (health care) – 31%
5. Mining support activities – 31 percent
6. Spectator sports – 31 percent
7. Information services – 30 percent
8. Personal services – 28 percent
9. Travel and reservation services – 23 percent
10. Agriculture and forestry support – 23 percent

Here are the industries that are expected to have the largest decline of this time period:

1. Tobacco manufacturing – 53 percent
2. CDs and tapes manufacturing – 51 percent
3. Apparel and leather manufacturing – 36 percent
4. Printing – 26 percent
5. Coal mining - 26 percent
6. Newspaper and book publishers – 24 percent
7. Satellite and telecommunications – 22 percent
8. Cable programming – 21 percent
9. Furniture manufacturing – 20 percent
10. Engine and power transmission equipment manufacturing – 17 percent

As you think about your compound career path, you'll want to work in industries with great growth prospects. In fact, if you're in I.T., that's an industry with projected 30 percent growth itself. With certain I.T. skills, you might be able to work in health care, finance, or travel I.T.. Based on this projection, you might consider working in hospitality and leisure I.T. because the top-three growth categories on that list are all in the hospitality and leisure category.

If you're already in an industry that tends to have faster wage growth, you may be fortunate. A difference of 4 percent versus 2.8

percent can provide greater opportunities over decades, as illustrated in the previous compounding charts. If you're in an industry with slower-wage growth, it doesn't mean you need to change careers. After all, you may really enjoy your work and finding fulfillment in life can't be quantified by money alone. There may be other ways to focus on compounding your career path, however. This applies to just about any career.

One simple concept is focusing on starting early. Imagine you're a human resources professional tasked with hiring someone new for your company. You find two resumes for potential candidates that appear well-qualified. Both people have similar education, credentials, and skills. However, one candidate has six more years of experience than the other. Assuming they each have great interviews, you're likely to hire the person with more experience. Although HR professionals can't ask for someone's age without the risk of violating a few laws, in this example, it's possible that each candidate is the same age. However, one of them started focusing on their career six years *earlier*. Starting on your specific job or career as early as possible may allow your salary to snowball more than others of the same age group in the same industry.

If you're currently in school, you have the potential to start your career before graduation. During my freshman year in college, I decided to look for a job. While many of my classmates focused on working at bars, restaurants, and retail stores for income, I looked for a job in my field of study — finance. I ended up working for a subsidiary of a large financial services company that mostly sold life insurance. It was poorly paid but allowed me to gain experience and even a professional license at the age of 19. That allowed me to later secure a competitive internship with another financial services company that provided both a fair wage and great experience. I was able to work for three companies in my industry by the time I graduated. In fact, by the time I reached finals week of my last semester, I was already studying for two professional licenses to become a financial planner after graduation. Some of my classmates struggled to find jobs in their field after college, while I had years of experience on my resume by the age of 22. This gave me a big advantage as I started my career. This advantage allowed me to compound my opportunities. A bartending job would have paid more than my first internship, but the internship was the beginning of my career snowball.

A great example of starting early is Bradley Cooper. I first met Bradley after joining the board of governors for a public university. He was 19 at the time. He was the only student member for the board of governors and the first member to be appointed to the board as a freshman. He approached me and introduced himself at my first board meeting, offering a strong handshake and a confident stare as we exchanged names. As I continued getting to know Bradley, I discovered he had a clear vision of what he wanted to do in life. He was studying political science and wanted to enter the field of government relations after graduation. Not only did he have the board of governors' position on his resume already, he began his career years earlier.

At 12, Bradley was sitting in the waiting room of a doctor's office with his mother when his attention turned to the TV. The national news was on, and he saw a politician speaking in front of a large crowd. He noticed people standing behind the politician in support of him. He thought it was interesting, so he asked his mother about it. She promptly asked the staff to change the channel. Bradley went home that night and searched online for the man on the TV, reading more and more about politics, political parties, and government. You might say he was infatuated with politics after that because Bradley asked his parents, who weren't very political, if he could visit the headquarters of a local campaign. After relentlessly asking, his mother decided to take him.

Before he knew it, Bradley was volunteering for this very campaign, making phone calls and reminding people to vote on election day. He continued volunteering and made great contacts among campaign staff. Two years later, at 14, Bradley was hired by a U.S. Senate candidate. His job was to knock on doors and speak with people about the candidate. Although Bradley had the lowest ranking job for this campaign, he was making good money as a 14-year-old. That's when he realized he may be able to make a career out of it. He went on to volunteer for more campaigns and fundraisers, making more connections at each level. At just 15, he was on the paid staff for a governor's race and was involved in leadership decisions.

By the time I met Bradley on this new board, he had seven years of experience in the field of politics. He had political contacts that most 50-year-olds don't have. Not only was Bradley studying political science in college, he was living it. He even had an LLC to facilitate his consulting services to businesses, advocacy groups, political action committees, and campaign committees. Even if you aren't a political person yourself, you must admit Bradley was well ahead of his peers in the field of politics. I look forward to watching Bradley's career unfold because he learned so much at such an early age. He'll be able to use this experience to surpass others in his age group and continue advancing in the field.

While you might assume someone like Bradley must have family connections that helped him start his career so early, it was his drive and hard work. You can't teach someone hard work and determination, but you can teach them everything else. Because he started as a volunteer, he only had his work ethic to show people around him that he was capable. He could easily have been dismissed as a child if he didn't work hard. That hard work led to more opportunities, which led to more contacts, which led to more opportunities. Having rich parents or a well-connected uncle can certainly help, but anyone can leverage their hard work to advance their careers.

Don't despair if you're already well past school age and kicking yourself for not starting earlier like Bradley. I have plenty of regrets about how I should have started my career. Instead, use this information to spark ideas about the compounding career concept. Also, if you know someone who's in school now, share this knowledge with them. It's exciting to teach this concept to those in high school or college that can begin growing their snowball at an early age.

Another potential strategy for growing your income faster is seeking job changes. According to data from the Federal Reserve Bank of Atlanta, those who were categorized as "job switchers" experienced higher-wage growth on average versus "job stayers"[28]. Their definition of a job switcher is someone who changed their employer, occupation, or industry compared to the prior year. The Atlanta Fed tracks this information monthly and uses a 12-month moving average. When looking at December data, job switchers experienced faster wage growth every year from 2010 to 2022 compared to job stayers. In 2009, however, when the U.S. economy was still experiencing the effects of the Great Recession, job stayers experienced higher wage growth.

Changing jobs can involve risk. Leaving an employer that's dependable for a higher wage elsewhere means you may be stepping into an environment that's less rewarding or more stressful. Switching jobs may also make your resume appear as though you're not reliable. Switching can also put your job at risk during a recession. After all, even though you may have more experience than others in your department, if you're the "newbie," it may be easier to let you go during a recession than someone who has been in the department for 10 years. Although there are risks, those who make smart decisions on how and when to seek new job opportunities may be rewarded over time with faster wage growth.

If you do leave your employer for a meaningful increase in pay, don't burn any bridges on your way out. Most paternalistic employers will understand if you've found a higher-paying position they can't compete with. I've certainly been in that position with employees in the past. When someone approaches me with a job offer they've received elsewhere and the pay is high enough that I can't compete with it, I congratulate them. That may be an exciting opportunity for their family. When someone leaves in a respectful way, that generally leaves the door open if they want to discuss coming back one day. I've seen many people leave their employers and return months or years later, so don't burn bridges, even if you don't think you'll need to cross them again.

Ideally, you can remain with an employer that you really like and still increase your income. This can be done by pursuing a different path with the organization, seeking a promotion, or simply asking for a raise. If you decide to ask for a raise, be ready to come with value-added information. For example, if you find other employers are paying higher salaries for a position like yours and you feel you're working hard enough to be paid at that level, use the market salary info with your request for a raise. It's also smart to include a list of your accomplishments that go above and beyond your standard duties. Maybe you created a training program from scratch and it wasn't part of your job description. Maybe you discovered a new process the company could use that would save money and reduce errors. If you've exceeded expectations and have documentation to back up your request, you may have a strong chance of receiving a raise.

As you consider your compounding career path, it's worthwhile to research how the area where you live is growing. Imagine that you live in a smaller town that doesn't have many large businesses. If you're a salesperson, service representative, manager, etc., and have goals of "moving up" to give yourself or your family more opportunities, does the area where you live provide it? Do you have enough of an opportunity to grow at your place of employment or other employers in your area? The adoption of work-from-home policies have helped greatly with labor mobility, giving more people job opportunities regardless of where they live. Not all job opportunities are available remotely, though. For those career paths that wholly or partially depend on being present in a specific community, consider if that community has adequate opportunity for you to achieve your career goals over time. This doesn't mean you should pack up and leave your family and friends for a 10 percent raise. Instead, this is one component to consider if you're already contemplating a move some day. An economic region that's growing is good for local businesses and can make your opportunities more plentiful.

The U.S. Bureau of Economic Analysis (BEA) regularly publishes data on real personal income by state and metropolitan area. Within its website, you can view what's called "real personal income." The idea of "real" personal income takes into account both wages and the cost to live in certain cities or states. For example, someone making $100,000 per year in San Fransico and someone making $100,000 per year in Wichita, Kan., may be making the same wage but living quite different lifestyles. The cost to live in San Francisco is significantly higher. When accounting for the differences in costs for real estate, rent, food, taxes, etc., "real" personal income can be compared. According to the BEA, in 2019, every state in America experienced real income increases compared to the prior year. Some states, however, experienced much slower income growth than others. For example, Rhode Island, Wyoming, and Hawaii only experienced average real income growth of 0.7 percent while Utah, Washington, and Maine experienced growth of 3.8 percent, 4.0 percent, and 4.1 percent, respectively[29]. These statistics can also be broken down by areas *within* a given state. If you're considering a move, you might look into how well the area is growing and the kind of opportunities this may present for you and even your family. Remember, it's not just about how much money you make. It's about how much money you save. You may as well find a region that allows you to earn, grow, save, and enjoy your lifestyle, too.

Although the concept of a geographical focus for economic reasons may seem to prioritize those working for an hourly wage or annual salary, the same concept applies to some business owners. For example, let's assume you own a car dealership. Let's also assume there are only two car dealerships in town and yours is one of them. You might enjoy a good living and the freedoms that come with owning a business. This includes your ability to sell your business one day and transform the fruits of your labor into cash you can use to retire. But what happens if you become ill? What if you were in a position where you needed to sell your business quickly? If your competitor — the only one in town — discovered you were in distress, do you think they would pay top dollar for your business? After all, they would know they're the only other game in town. However, if you lived in a town with seven other car dealerships, you would potentially have more demand to buy your business. There would be a greater market for it.

Another concept that may help with your compounding career path is considering the size of your employer. Most businesses are structured in a hierarchy. There may be a chief executive officer, along with other C-level positions such as a chief financial officer or chief operating officer. Then, there may be vice presidents, senior managers, directors, middle managers, supervisors, and associates. At many smaller employers, there may only be a total of 10–20 employees. If you work for one of these smaller employers, you should ask yourself what your career path looks like over the next 10 years. I realize most people have never looked out that far in their smartphone calendars before, but that's what it takes to point yourself in the direction you want to go. If you're unsure what your path may look like with your employer, consider the following questions:

- Has this organization grown much in the past 5-10 years?
- Do I expect the organization to grow much over the next 5-10 years?
- Does someone need to leave or die for me to be promoted?
- Does the company offer perks, such as stock options, to long-term employees?
- Are internal promotions common or do outsiders usually fill new positions?
- If I didn't have this specific job today, would I still apply for it knowing what I know today?

If you hope to move up the ladder through hard work and dedication, but the ladder only has two rungs left, you might consider a change at some point that offers you greater opportunities. Whether you really enjoy where you work, create a career growth plan. This might include what new credentials or licenses you need to achieve to move up to the level you want. It might include conferences you need to attend to gather new ideas. It might even include a goal to have more lunches with coworkers to share ideas and brainstorm about your personal goals. Having a career growth plan allows you to go from having ideas in your head to having a plan that can be executed.

If you work in an industry that doesn't traditionally have a ladder to climb or stock options available, such as education or health care, this concept still applies to you. If you're a grade school teacher with no plans to become an administrator, your title will likely be "teacher" your entire career. Instead of climbing the corporate ladder, you'll be focused on your income and benefits. Most public school teachers have a pension plan managed at the state level. Each state pension system for public school teachers includes a formula for determining pension benefits once a teacher retires. While each formula may be different, most calculate pension benefits based on a teacher's salary and years of service. This means a teacher's pension benefit can be affected depending on their salary before they retire.

For example, Teacher 1 earned a bachelor's degree and worked for a small rural school district. Because some states pay teachers differently depending on where they live, a rural district may have lower average salaries than a metropolitan district. Teacher 1 earned an average salary of $50,000. Teacher 2 earned a bachelor's degree, just like Teacher 1, but then also worked on a master's degree over time. Many school systems have automatic pay increases for teachers with a master's degree. Teacher 2 worked in a metropolitan district that paid their teachers a higher average salary. This teacher earned an average salary of $70,000. Because these two teachers work for the same state system, they'll both use the same formula for calculating their pension benefits. Below is an example of how that may look, assuming they're the same age and worked for the same period of time.

Teacher 1

- Average three years of salary – $150,000 ($50,000 x 3)
- Years of service before retirement – 35
- Benefit factor (set by pension system) – 2.5 percent
- Monthly pension benefit – $3,645

Teacher 2

- Average three years of salary – $210,000 ($70,000 x 3)
- Years of service before retirement – 35
- Benefit factor (set by pension system) – 2.5 percent
- Monthly pension benefit – $5,104

The example formula is average monthly pay from the highest three years of salary, times years of service, times the benefit factor set by the pension. If Teacher 1 lives for 25 years in retirement, excluding increases for inflation, they would collect $1,093,500 from the pension. Teacher 2 would collect $1,531,200 over 25 years. That's a difference of more than $430,000 from the pension, not to mention the extra income teacher 2 enjoyed while working. If you're a public school teacher and want to increase your lifetime pension benefits, consider using the formula to your advantage. This might lead you to pursue a master's degree over time or to move to a different district for enough years to affect your pension. The main point here is that careers that lack a corporate ladder can still be planned out over time to maximize value.

The choice of a job or career path involves so many dynamics besides money or the cost of living in your area. As I mentioned, fulfillment can't be quantified by money alone. For most of us, if we begin working at the age of 20 and retire at the age of 65, we'll spend 45 years going to work. That's a significant number of years in a limited lifespan. While other factors are involved in the choice of a career, such as flexibility, childcare, aging parents, and personal satisfaction, your career choices will greatly affect your level of financial success. Your choices in life before 65 will determine your options in life after 65. Don't let your career path be aimlessly created for you. Create a plan for what your career path looks like and think outside the box using what you learned in this chapter.

Chapter 10

Network for Net Worth

In this chapter:
- Connections bring opportunities
- Finding motivation
- Communication skills

I n 2006, two economists, Bethany Peters and Edward Stringham, published research illustrating a surprising benefit from moderate alcohol use. You may have heard studies in the past that tout how a glass of red wine a day is good for your heart or how an occasional beer is good for the prostate. For Peters and Stringham, their research found a new possible benefit to adult beverages — the health of your paycheck. In the *Journal of Labor Research*, their study found that men who drink earn 10 percent more than nondrinkers. It also found that women who drink earn 14 percent more than nondrinkers[30]. For all the problems alcohol may cause in society, this is a surprising statistic. How can alcohol use be associated with financial benefits?

Within their research, it was found that professionals who drink responsibly are more likely to attend social events or frequent bars. As those gatherings occur, these professionals may be mixing and mingling with others, making new friends and associates. These new connections and contacts may translate into opportunities for sales, career advancement, or even business ventures. If you've heard the phrase, "It's not *what* you know, it's *who* you know," there's some truth to it.

While one could argue that alcohol use may offer more economic harm than economic advancement, the moral of the story is that networking has serious benefits. One noteworthy success story on networking comes from comedian Jimmy Fallon. Fallon began performing comedy at small venues while working on his computer science degree. His former boss from a newspaper internship shared Fallon's audition tape with a colleague. That colleague had connections with *Saturday Night Live*, which turned into two auditions. After earning a place on *SNL*, Fallon made it a point to connect with the show's creator, Lorne Michaels. Michaels eventually began inviting Fallon to afterparties, where he networked with important people in the comedy industry. His contacts eventually led to the opportunity to host the *Tonight Show* at 39. Jimmy Fallon's amazing climb through the industry is a classic example of how networking can provide countless opportunities.

If you view networking as self-centered, you're not alone. If you dread the thought of going to a traditional "networking event," you're not alone. Networking doesn't have to be a selfish pursuit. If you attend an event with the goal of walking away with three business cards, it may feel self-seeking. Others may sense it, too. It's uncommon for someone to be really excited to enter a room full of strangers, so you're not alone if this thought triggers your inner introvert. Genuine networking can come naturally by finding something you genuinely enjoy. For example, if you have a classic car, you might join a classic car club. If you enjoy reading, you might join a book club or two. If you enjoy working out, you might join a gym. When the focus is on the passion or hobby, networking becomes the natural byproduct.

As a financial planner, I often find new clients through networking. In fact, one of my favorite clients came from a networking activity that felt natural. The sales rep for my payroll provider invited me to a networking event. There would be food and drinks, which was a plus for me at 25, but I always enjoyed making new friends. At that event, I met her coworkers. One of those coworkers later introduced me to a client of theirs. That client was a chief executive looking for a financial planner, who turned in to my client. I have countless examples of how knowing networks of people has helped my career and how I've been able to help others in their careers, too. Networking and making connections don't always provide immediate benefits, but if you do so with a shared passion or approach that shows you care, it can be contagious. Whether you're in sales, I.T., publishing, or public service, making new connections can provide more and more opportunities.

Some people are naturals at making new friends and networking, while others have to dedicate more mental energy to strike up conversations. If you can relate to the latter, it's completely normal. In the same way that eating a cookie is much easier than eating a kale salad, most people would rather turn on their favorite television show at home than talk to strangers. Finding a common hobby or passion helps with this hesitation, but so does working on your communication skills. Strong communication is one of the best skills a person can have to promote financial success over time. Being a good communicator can help in the fields of business, health care, education, government, and more.

One area where strong communication skills can really support someone's career is sales. Being able to communicate with someone easily and comfortably is a great way to build trust, which is important in a sales role. Although some people seem to have a natural talent for communication, many hone their skills over time. Communication helps with sales, but sales experience helps with communication. Then, those skills can be used in other roles besides strictly sales. For example, sales professionals hone their talents through countless conversations with others. Some have leveraged this experience to advance to amazing heights in the business world.

Here are 10 CEOs who started their careers in sales[31]:

- Howard Schultz — Before he became the CEO of Starbucks, Schultz was a salesman at Xerox and an appliance salesman at Hammarplast.
- Warren Buffett — Buffett was a paperboy and also sold securities before becoming the CEO of Berkshire Hathaway.

- Mark Cuban — Before becoming a billionaire by 41, Cuban sold garbage bags. He later had a software sales job, too.
- William Weldon — Before serving as CEO of Johnson & Johnson, Weldon was a sales rep at the company.
- John Paul DeJoria — As cofounder of John Paul Mitchell Systems, DeJoria sold hair products door to-door early in his career.
- Samuel Palmisano — He worked as a sales rep at IBM before working his way to CEO.
- Nick Woodman — Woodman sold necklaces before founding his company, GoPro.
- Anne Mulcahy — Starting as a sales rep at Xerox, Mulcahy worked her way to vice president of human resources and then to CEO.
- Robert Herjavec — He worked for free for the first six months of his sales job at Logiquest before becoming a multimillionaire businessman.

As someone who once sold door to door, it greatly helped my communication skills and my confidence level. In fact, I had two different door-to-door sales jobs in college. The first was selling insurance to businesses. My job was to walk into 20 businesses a day and see if I could schedule a meeting with the owner or head of human resources. At 20, it was a difficult job full of rejection. After that role, I began selling discount automotive service cards in people's homes. That job was full of rejection, too, but that's when I began to realize that not everyone was going to buy what I'm selling. Some people may be having a bad day and don't want to speak. Some don't have enough money and others are too busy to listen. While there were days I wanted to stay home, I began to enjoy the challenge of speaking with strangers. This eventually led to public speaking, which I dreaded the first time, but grew to enjoy. That led to live television interviews, which I dreaded *the most* the first time, but aren't intimidating anymore. Now my communication skillset has been refined to the point where I feel comfortable talking to anyone, anywhere, anytime.

Communication is a skill, much like understanding computers is a skill. If you can recall your first experience with a computer, you may remember being lost among the countless buttons, icons, programs, and folders. You likely spent time learning how to use it, where to click and how to accomplish new tasks with it. Imagine your ability to communicate, especially in situations where you don't feel completely comfortable, as something you can continually improve. Have you ever been in a class, seminar, or other group where you wanted to ask a question, but didn't feel confident enough? I've known that feeling, especially if no one has asked a question yet. This feeling is completely normal. Do you know why more questions often follow after the first person asks a question? That's because most people feel the same way — they're hesitant to be the first person to raise their hand. Push yourself to be the first person to ask a question in a meeting, assuming you have one to ask. You don't need to sell door to door to improve your communication skills. It can be as easy as leaving your comfort zone from time to time.

Another way to improve your communication skills in an effort to improve your financial position is to join a Toastmasters International group. These groups are meant to help members improve their public speaking skills. They're often filled with strangers who come together with a common goal of breaking out of their shells and improving communications. I belonged to a Toastmasters group many years ago and it helped me with public speaking. The environment was non-judgmental, so when I did something wrong during a speech, no one cared! It was great experience, and I would recommend it to anyone. Public speaking doesn't just mean speaking to a room of 100 people. It can also mean presenting an idea in a group meeting of five people. You'll be hard pressed to convince me public speaking experiences won't help you in your lifetime.

Although I've discussed networking events, door-to-door sales, and public speaking, remember that networking is a broad term.

Networking can be as simple as joining a happy hour where more than your close friends will be there. If you golf and someone invites you on a golf trip where you don't know most of the group, take the trip. If someone invites you to a makeup party at their house, but you don't want to be pressured into buying something, go anyway. Just buy the cheapest lip gloss so you don't feel like a jerk and enjoy conversing with others. Networking means meeting new people and expanding your network, so look for ways to do it while also enjoying yourself. If you don't go, imagine the opportunities you might miss.

The thought of missing an opportunity often drives me to take action. Imagine some of the people in your life and how you met them. Maybe your boss is someone you met at a social function who convinced you to come work for them. Maybe your closest friend came from going to a party years ago. Maybe you met your spouse at a happy hour on a night when you would rather have stayed home and binge-watched movies. How would your life be different if you chose each time to stay in your comfort zone? When you're given the opportunity to go out and meet people or stay home, imagine a fork in a road. One path leads to sweatpants, popcorn, and movies. You know exactly what to expect if you take this path (and trust me, I love all three of these). The other path is unknown. You could go out and completely waste your time and money. You could also go out and meet someone who can change your life, just as Jimmy Fallon did. Push yourself to take the unknown path so you don't miss life-changing opportunities.

Chapter 11

The Side Hustle

In this chapter:

- Leveraging your free time
- How to increase your income
- Picking the right side hustle

When rideshare company Uber first came to market, I remember thinking how genius the idea was. Someone had discovered a way for people to monetize the unused capacity of their vehicles. After all, most vehicles have at least four seats and many times they're occupied by only one person. The same can be said of a vacation rental by owner, which helped people rent their homes when they're not being used. While many options exist today for ride-hailing apps and home rentals, the concept remains the same — monetize unused capacity.

This same principle may apply to you with unused time. We all have at least a little free time outside of work, family, and fun. Some have more free time than others, but that free time can either be monetized or wasted on watching funny cat videos. This concept of monetizing your free time is what I call the "side hustle." I wrote this book using my personal free time. It took me years, but I used plane rides, holidays, and early Saturday mornings to write this entire book. If you worry about having too little time and too many tasks, put your time into perspective. How many hours per day do you sleep? My doctor would tell you seven hours of sleep per night is the minimum amount needed for optimal health. Let's assume eight hours is ideal. How many hours per day do you work? This will obviously vary by industry, but most people average eight hours of work per day. If there are 24 hours in a day, eight of which we work and eight of which we sleep, that leaves eight hours of capacity.

Yes, showering and picking up children from school are kind of important things to do in those extra eight hours. That still leaves capacity, though. Let's assume you have three hours of free time per day during the work week and five hours per day on the weekend. That's 25 hours of free time per week and more than 1,200 hours per year. Are you filling these hours with video games or online shopping? Maybe they're filled with online poker games or sports highlights. There's nothing wrong with these activities. However, if you want to reach your goals and build wealth as quickly as possible, you might consider a side hustle instead so you can pay down debt, boost your savings, or invest long term.

You've learned in a few chapters now how impactful additional savings can be if you invest it long term. Not only can your snowball grow exponentially over time, throwing more snow on it while it's growing can compound it significantly. If you work for a company and you've already focused on maximizing your income, consider maximizing the value of your unused time.

Below are some examples of side hustles you might consider. Be sure to check with your employer before taking on any type of additional work though. Some employers don't allow second jobs due to security or ethics concerns. You wouldn't want your side hustle to sour your salary.

- **Blogging** — Do you have a passion you want to tell the world about? Do you have a skillset and the will to share helpful info about it? Writing articles and blog posts that genuinely help, motivate, or interest people may be a great way to bring in some additional income. The concept is attracting readers to a website or email list that can be used for advertisements. Money can also be made using redirected traffic to other websites. If you enjoy writing and talking about your passions, this may be an easy side hustle for you.

- Consulting — If you have experience in a niche area, individuals or organizations may be willing to pay for it. Personally, I would rather pay for a consultant to tell me how to avoid costly mistakes than to make those mistakes myself and lose precious time. If you put yourself out there as an expert who's available to consult, you may be surprised who's willing to pay for your time. Consider giving some hours away for free to build a network of clients who can introduce you to others.

- **Affiliate marketing** — If you have a favorite product, such as makeup or electronics, you may enjoy being an affiliate marketer for brands you already respect. If you find yourself telling people about a great product you love, why not make money at the same time? If you're marketing another company's products for free, you may be able to be compensated for it instead. Ask your favorite brands if they have affiliate marketing programs. You may be able to earn revenue of 5–20 percent of the sales price for referring people to these brands. It's a good practice to disclose that you're part of such a program when recommending these products, along with the fact you were a fan well before the affiliate program.

- **Virtual assistant** — Many small businesses like the idea of a part-time virtual assistant. Imagine you're the owner of a small dog grooming business and need help with scheduling appointments, data processing, and miscellaneous tasks. You may like the idea of having help from someone who isn't a full-time employee or a robot. If you're looking for a side hustle that's easy to start, being a virtual assistant is one of them.

- **Translation or teaching work** — Know a second language? You may literally have a world full of potential customers from around the globe. My kids take second language lessons from someone online located halfway around the world. Ironically, she has a day job, but enjoys teaching kids new languages in her free time.

Aside from these side hustles, you might also consider photography, pet sitting, paid surveys, handyman services, renting out extra space in your home, or becoming a tutor. There are many options available these days. If your side hustle earned you an extra $10,000 to $20,000 per year, that money could be used to pay off student loans, save for your kid's college, or invest for retirement. Saving an extra $10,000 per year for 30 years at a return of 7.5 percent would give you just over $1 million. This extra income also provides a safety net in the event of a job loss. It's what I call "income diversification." If you lose your job paying $100,000 per year, but you still have a side hustle paying $20,000 per year, you still have at least some income to meet your basic needs.

Side hustles normally aren't a way to become wealthy. They're an option for monetizing your free time so you can improve your financial situation. Some people do find their side hustle has an opportunity to become a full-time business, though. Creating significant wealth usually means creating some type of business, which we'll cover more in Chapter 13. Working a normal full-time job, plus working a side hustle and saving a decent amount of all that income can turn into hundreds of thousands or millions of dollars over time. If your ambitions are much larger than an extra $10,000 per year, you should consider a side hustle that has a chance of becoming a booming business.

In 1995, Craig Newmark created an email distribution list for people living in the San Fransisco Bay area. He used it to tell people about local events. It soon turned into an online tool where people could share information about events, items for sale, and various services. It then expanded to a few more cities throughout the U.S. Then, it expanded to most large cities throughout the U.S. Then, it went international. The side hustle Newmark created was Craigslist. The popular website that looks like it hasn't changed since the 1990s made him significant wealth. While his estimated net worth has fluctuated over the years, in April of 2020, Forbes estimated it to be $1.3 billion[32].

Before starting Craigslist, he was a computer programmer for a large corporation.

If that story doesn't resonate with you because you're not good with computers, here's one to which anyone can relate. Mike Kittredge was a teenager with no money. He wanted to give his mother a gift, so he decided to create one. After gathering old crayons, a worn shoe-string, and an empty milk carton, he melted the crayons down to create a candle. His neighbor saw the candle and convinced him to sell it to her instead. Kittredge took the money he made from selling the candle to buy wax. From this, he made two more candles, one of which he gave to his mother. He continued selling his handmade candles in his neighborhood and recruited two friends to help him. This was the start of the Yankee Candle company, which was eventually sold for $500 million to a private equity firm[33].

Most side hustles don't turn into multimillion-dollar enterprises, but I offer these examples because it's still possible. Sometimes, it involves luck, but it also depends on what you want to make of it. If your goal is to bring in some extra money to boost your bank account and you don't want the stress of running a small business, you should probably choose a side hustle with low risk, low barriers to entry, and low-to-moderate income. If your goal is to bring in extra money and plant the seeds for a larger business endeavor, make sure you're ready for it. Planting seeds means you need to tend to those seeds. A small but growing business may need more and more of your time for customer-service issues, for example. You can always decide to scale back the business, but you don't want to be in a situation where you can't deliver on your promises to customers.

Before you begin a side hustle, ask yourself the following :
1. How much time do I have available to dedicate to this? If you have newborn twins, you're taking night classes to finish your MBA, and you have a solid career that requires 40 hours a week, it may not be worth the stress. Make sure you can dedicate meaningful time to your side hustle so it has a chance of succeeding.
2. Will this hurt my career? If you work for a computer

repair company and you're thinking of repairing computers on the side, would your employer be upset by this?
The last thing you want to do is lose your 9-to-5 because
of your 5-to-9.

3.   Am I prepared if the side hustle grows? If you think your
side hustle could turn into a growing business, have a
plan for how you'll handle its growing needs without
missing your kid's talent show. If Newmark decided to
scale back Craigslist after it started taking off, he may
have invited competitors to take over. If you're considering a side hustle that's unique to the marketplace, remember that other entrepreneurs may try to replicate you.

If you worry about the stress, risk, and money involved in a side
hustle that will take more and more of your time, focus on something
that's more flexible. Money isn't worth it if you're completely stressed,
losing sleep at night, fighting with your spouse, and missing your kid's
soccer games. Find a side hustle that fits your needs and your lifestyle
so you can balance work, health, and family.

If you're like me and you would rather push your net worth to
the next level than watch football every Sunday, go for it. I still find
time to work out, spend time with my wife, see friends, attend events
with my kids, *and* work on my businesses because I cut out the activities that aren't important to me. This means I don't watch much TV,
my time on social media is minimal, I don't play video games, and I
sleep no more than eight hours a day. You may be surprised by how
much you can accomplish if you prioritize your time.

I want to reach the age of 100 and look back on my life as one
full of meaningful activity and accomplishment. I view my lifetime
as a bucket that I can fill with anything I wish. I don't think I'll regret
missing out on computer games when I'm 100 because I'll have spent
that time publishing books or playing with my kids. I don't think I'll
regret missing the hottest new TV series because I'll have spent that
time building my net worth and giving to charity. I don't think I'll
regret waking up at 5:00 a.m. every morning instead of sleeping in
because I'll have spent my time on exercising and keeping my mind

clear. The thought of not accomplishing enough in my lifetime gives me more stress than the thought of starting a business from scratch. Even if your interests and priorities are different than mine, ask yourself if you're happy with how you're currently spending your free time.

As you consider how to spend your time and whether a side hustle is right for you, don't forget to stay focused on your health. This same rule applies as we discuss business ownership in Chapter 13. There's no use in creating significant wealth if you sacrifice your body and mind along the way. Being a wealthy 60-year-old with multiple health problems due to lack of self-care probably isn't your goal. It's absolutely possible to work a busy side hustle while keeping your health in focus. As you find what works for you, remember to reinvest your extra income, either back into your business or into traditional investments, while also enjoying a little of it along the way.

Chapter 12

The Intrapreneur

In this chapter:

- Embracing your inner entrepreneur
- Growth opportunities within your employer
- Alternatives to earn equity

Having a side hustle that's meant to test the waters on a larger business idea is a great example of entrepreneurship. Entrepreneurs enjoy the autonomy, challenges, and rewards of starting and growing businesses. We'll discuss business ownership in the next chapter, but this chapter is dedicated to a different breed of entrepreneur — the intrapreneur. Intrapreneurs don't start or own businesses. They would rather work for a company and avoid the risks associated with business ownership. Investing their money into a business that may fail and take up their all their time isn't what intrapreneurs are after. Like entrepreneurs, intrapreneurs are innovative, hardworking, and ambitious. Because of these traits, intrapreneurs have the potential to make a significant impact within their organizations and benefit from it financially.

Imagine that you work for a large company and see an opportunity to improve your department. You have an idea that could potentially add millions of dollars of revenue for the company by adding a new product line for existing customers. You write up a formal proposal that lists the risks and benefits of your idea, along with how much revenue could be generated if your idea goes well. Your name is written squarely on the bottom of the front page. You bring it to your boss first. She likes the idea and shares it with her boss. It gains attention and you're asked to present it to a group of leaders in the company. They decide to test your idea, which costs you nothing because the company handles the investment, and it takes off. A year later, your idea is turning into a growing new product line for the business.

It's possible you may work for a company that would pay you a bonus for you for coming up with this idea. If not, I'm guessing your value would significantly increase and you would be able to ask for a raise or promotion with confidence. Intrapreneurs can make themselves so valuable to an organization that leaving would cause their employer harm. I don't recommend overtly leveraging your value to squeeze your employer for money. Instead, use your wit, ambition, and humility to show value while planning for your future within the organization.

A great example of an intrapreneur is Spencer Silver. Silver worked for 3M as a chemist and was tasked with creating a strong adhesive that could be used on aircrafts. He tried and tried but failed to create a strong-enough adhesive. What he did create was a weak adhesive that could be used multiple times on the same substance. It wasn't what he intended to make, but it was patented in 1972. Two years later, another employee at 3M, Arthur Fry, heard Silver speaking about his patented adhesive. Fry thought it might be helpful to add the adhesive to bookmarks because they commonly fell out of his hymnal at church. The product was launched and led to the Post-It Notes that we all know today. Fry and Silver were recognized by 3M for its innovation. Silver was named in multiple patents over his career and Fry was inducted into the National Inventors Hall of Fame.

If you've ever flown on Southwest Airlines, you may know the cabin crew often adds humor to their flight announcements. It's part of their culture. What you may not know is that it started with one of their flight attendants, Martha Cobb. If you've ever ordered a drink from Starbucks, you probably noticed your name was written on the cup. It's a nice touch to be addressed by name instead of an order number. That was started by one of their baristas before corporate headquarters adopted it for all stores.

My favorite example of an intrapreneur is Ken Kutaragi. He was an engineer at Sony in the 1990s. While working for Sony, Kutaragi was approached by Nintendo to create a new sound chip for a gaming system it was developing. At the time, Sony didn't have a video game department, but he decided to work on the chip for Nintendo in secret. Once Sony executives discovered his work with Nintendo, they weren't happy. He was allowed to keep his job and continue his project with Nintendo, though. Kutaragi then convinced others within Sony to work with Nintendo to create a Sony-branded gaming console. The deal eventually fell through, but Kutaragi had gained enough support from Sony to continue the project without Nintendo. The company called it PlayStation. The invention was obviously a huge success and became a significant driver of revenue for Sony. Kutaragi was eventually named CEO of Sony Computer Entertainment.

If an intrapreneur is in the right environment, their innovations can unleash significant value for an organization. For the intrapreneur, it doesn't require any investment or personal financial risk. They can still enjoy the security of a salary, but potentially create a rewarding environment for themselves within an organization.

If you like the sound of intrapreneurship but you're struggling with how you might show value, here are a few questions to stir ideas:

- Do you see bottlenecks or inefficiencies in your organization?
- Do you have a product idea that might do well?
- Do you have an idea for tweaking an existing product?
- Is there risk in your organization and do you have a way to reduce it?
- Could you outperform your goals if business was done differently?
- Do you see costs that could be cut from your organization without negative impact?

Networking is one area that may support your intrapreneurial goals. Just as Silver and Fry met at 3M, you may be able to meet like-minded people in your organization who work in different departments. If you work in marketing, it might be someone in product development who has an idea but lacks the confidence to market it. If you work in I.T., it might be someone in accounting that sees bottlenecks but doesn't know enough about systems or operations. Even if you work for a smaller company, the story of Kutaragi involved him bringing two different organizations together to implement his idea.

If you have ideas, it doesn't do anyone any good by keeping them a secret. If your work for an employer that doesn't value new ideas, it may be time to look for a new employer. It's possible your idea may have issues that you haven't thought about yet, but a good organization that supports intrapreneurs is willing to at least listen. If you show significant value, you may gain job security, higher pay, stock options, advancement, equity, or more.

Chapter 13

Business Ownership

In this chapter:
- Significant wealth through business ownership
- Creating a business plan
- Investing in someone's business

I f you have a goal of achieving significant wealth in your lifetime, business ownership is likely the path you need to take. You can still become a multimillionaire by working a salaried corporate job and saving well over a 40-year career. If your goal is to have an eight- or nine-figure net worth, though, business ownership can provide a path for reaching your goal. It's not for everyone, but starting your own private business can be both lucrative and rewarding. This chapter will also cover investing in someone else's private business if you don't have the time or interest in creating your own.

If you search online for the "wealthiest people in the world by source," you'll find a list of billionaires. You may recognize many of the names, especially at the top of the list. As you continue down the list, you may notice a common theme. Nearly every single person is on that list because of a business they or their family started. You'll see owners of technology companies, retail brands, luxury goods producers, logistics companies, the food industry, and more. Significant wealth comes from owning equity in a growing business. If you're more of an intrapreneur than an entrepreneur, this is why having access to stock options or some type of equity in a growing business could be lucrative for your career.

The importance of equity in a business can't be understated. Many people focus on income because that's what pays the bills and buys fancy cars, but equity in a business can be significant. Take physicians for example. According to Medscape, the average income of a physician that works for an employer is $297,332. However, the average income of a physician that's self-employed is $360,752[34]. That means self-employed physicians make over $60,000 more than employee physicians on average. That's a nice increase in income for the self-employed group. However, we're missing a significant difference between the two. Assuming a self-employed physician owns their private practice and can sell that private practice to another physician, they may have millions of dollars of *equity* as well.

If a physician's practice generates $500,000 of net profit after expenses, it may be worth three or four times that amount to a buyer. Businesses are usually valued based on something called EBITDA, but I'm keeping this simple for now. A 40-year-old physician who's tired of working for a hospital may decide to buy this practice and pay the seller over time. Based on a multiple of three- or four-times net profit, the seller may receive $1.5 to $2 million for their practice, plus they enjoyed a handsome income for operating it. While a physician's practice may be worth three- or four-times net profit, some businesses can be worth significantly higher multiples, especially in the technology industry. This is why business ownership can lead to significant wealth.

Starting a business is not for the faint of heart. It can include major financial setbacks, risks, and pitfalls. It's also an emotional rollercoaster. Take Steve Jobs, for example. The cofounder of Apple was fired by the board of directors. Think about that for a moment. He was removed by the board from a company he founded and built. This humbling experience led him to start a new computer company called NeXT. His new venture floundered for years and was eventually acquired by Apple, bringing Jobs back to his empire. Warren Buffett has had his share of failures as well. A quick search online will reveal self-professed financial mistakes that amount to billions of dollars lost. What you'll discover about true entrepreneurs is that they brush off their failures, learn from them, and try again.

Although this may sound simple, as if you can easily pick yourself up after a fall, experiencing financial failure in a business to which you've committed your heart and soul can be extremely difficult. This is why I state it's not for the faint of heart. I was once approached by someone seeking help with starting a dog-grooming business. She loved dogs and had experience in the field. At the time, she had a steady full-time job in health care and the idea of starting a business had always seemed out of reach. I showed her how to create a business plan and project revenue from her new venture. The wild card in the plan was how she would find potential customers — an aspect of any new business that's typically the most difficult. After she spent a fair amount of her savings implementing the business plan, she soon had a building, a website, insurance, and everything she needed to begin growing.

Within months, she became extremely nervous because costs were increasing and she couldn't find many customers. She had gone part time at her job to focus on her business. She began to lose sleep and feel depressed, especially as she drew money from her savings to keep the business afloat. Her nerves eventually got the best of her, and she went back to full-time work in health care. The uncertainty of the business was something she struggled with, despite being comfortable and confident with her skills. She was left with a painful experience and the memory of wasting close to $100,000 on a failed business.

Although I believe experiencing some aspect of self-employment is helpful for just about anyone, it doesn't mean everyone should quit their steady jobs to start a business. Even a part-time sales position that pays only commissions is a great way to test the waters of self-employment. Such opportunities exist in distributing wine, selling insurance, selling widgets online, or helping as a travel agent. These flavors of self-employment can be tested in tandem with full-time or part-time employment. The point is to discover if you have the stomach for creating your own wealth and taking the risks required of entrepreneurship.

If you decide to start a business that requires capital, as compared to a sales role that requires no cash at all, I recommend three strategies to increase your likelihood of success. Starting a business may seem simple on the surface, especially if you have the skills and passion. You may find you're wearing many new hats that require vastly different skillsets, such as accounting, legal, human resources, insurance, sales, and technology. If this is a goal of yours, these three steps can help you greatly increase your chances of success.

Step 1, create a thorough business plan. This is a crucial step in starting a business of any kind. It may seem cumbersome but think of it like a blueprint for a new home. Without a blueprint, you'll be taking guesses as to where the plumbing will go, where to run electrical lines, how to fit in the ventilation system, and how to keep the home structurally sound. Even professionals with vast experience in construction require a blueprint before attempting to erect a building. Your business plan will include the following, keeping in mind that it may look a bit different for each business depending on the industry:

- Vision statement
- Executive summary
- Sales plan
- Competitive analysis
- Operating budget

Because some of you may not want to start a business, I'll describe each of these areas from a high level. For those who are serious about starting and growing a business, I've included extra content and easy-to-use templates at GrowthInfo.com/business. If you're someone who may want to invest in someone's business, knowing this information will help you review investment opportunities before risking your capital.

The vision statement is meant to guide your business for years to come. It's "the why" behind your decision to start the business and where you hope to take it. Although some businesses publish their visions statements for customers to see and have made it part of their public relations strategy, for now, focus less on making it catchy and more on making it a true representation of your future vision.

The executive summary will detail "the what," how, and when of your business. Imagine writing it for someone who knows nothing about your business. It's also possible you could use your executive summary to attract investors or business partners. What type of business is it? What is the ownership structure and who controls it? What product or service are you offering and how is it different? How do you intend to grow and expand over time?

The sales plan will outline your target market. Be as detailed as possible here. For example, if you're targeting men with a new line of hair products, what is the age group? Are you targeting a certain area of the country or the entire country? What about international sales? The sales plan will also outline your strategy for selling your new product or service, such as online, through distributors, or direct sales. Will you pay for advertising? If so, what kind? This section of your business plan is crucially important. The most difficult part of starting a business is finding customers. Great businesses and products fail regularly, not because the gadget was bad or the service was poor, but because there weren't enough sales to justify the costs of continuing the business.

The competitive analysis will break down how you will compete in your industry. Even if you're coming to market with a new product or service that doesn't technically have competition, be ready for competition to develop, especially if you're successful. Include a SWOT analysis in this section — strengths, weaknesses, opportunities, and threats. Establishing the strengths and weaknesses of your business is an easy exercise. When it comes to opportunities and threats, think about the marketplace or industry you're entering. How can you tap into untapped demand? What threatens your business or product the most, such as competitors, regulations, opposition groups, or even commodity price changes? This section will help you find a place in the market so your sales plan can be focused on it.

The operating budget can be complicated, especially if you're not a "numbers person." If you're good at many things in life, but math isn't one of them, have no fear. Your goal for this section is to establish an expectation of costs for your business. This includes one-time costs for startup purposes, ongoing costs, and your best estimate of sales revenue. Here are common expenses you may need to account for:

- Rent
- Legal
- Technology
- Licensing
- Phone
- Travel
- Salaries/staff
- Advertising
- Utilities
- Office supplies
- Postage
- Website
- Inventory
- Insurance

Creating a business plan may seem unnecessary to some, but once completed, you'll feel significantly more organized and confident about making decisions in the early months and years of your new business. This first step of creating a business plan should not be skipped if you're serious about creating a successful business. Trust me when I say it will help guide your decisions.

Step 2, find help. Starting a business can be an emotional and overwhelming task, even if you've started a different business before. Let's say you're starting a restaurant and you plan to be the sole owner. You'll be met with complex decisions about equipment, insurance, food safety, lease agreements, payroll, legal documents, employee benefits, and more. Imagine hiring a consultant who ran a restaurant for 30 years before selling it and retiring. This consultant may be eager to help you and offer her experience, while earning herself money in retirement. As a new restaurant owner, you'll be able to tap into decades of experience, past mistakes, and best practices for a reasonable fee. This type of help can be well worth the cost.

It's natural for new business owners with little cash to want to do as much as they can on their own. Researching online on how to create legal documents is less expensive than hiring an attorney to do it for you. This is the wrong way of thinking. Instead of asking yourself "how" you can take on a new challenge, you should be asking yourself "who" instead. *Who* can help me create this legal document correctly so I can focus on finding new customers? *Who* can fix this website issue so I can schedule more meetings? *Who* can introduce me to retailers to sell my product so I can stop wasting my time trying on my own?

That last example is one I've seen firsthand. My wife started a skincare business years ago that specializes in spa-quality devices for home use. Once she developed her own products, she was ready to pitch them to big retailers. She was interested in calling buying agents to schedule meetings, but she didn't know where to start. She was so new to that side of the industry that she didn't even know common terms used by retailers and buying agents. Instead of spending countless hours trying to find these people, track them down, schedule meetings, and hope that she's doing it all correctly, she hired a company to do the work for her. After three months, the company found two retailers who were interested in her products. This company charged a monthly fee to my wife's business, but what took three months with a professional may have taken my wife nine months or more. It's also possible she may not have achieved the same results on her own. Again, it's not a matter of how; it's a matter of *who*.

Hiring people to handle challenging tasks can be difficult when cash is tight, but think about the cost of losing time. Imagine if someone started a business and did 95 percent of the work on their own. They created the website, they set up the legal documents, they created their own marketing materials, and they set up the online payment system. Now imagine this same business, but the owner only does 30 percent of the work, relying on experts to handle most of the setup. In the first example, this person may spend 6–12 months setting up their business. If that sounds too long, you would be surprised how much work is involved until you try it yourself. In the second example, this person may be set up and ready to begin operating in 60–90 days. Then, the business can focus on bringing in customers and revenue. While the person in the first example saved money doing everything on their own, how much potential revenue did they lose by wasting all that time? I would much rather pay extra dollars to do something correctly and quickly than to waste precious time. It's similar to the compounding concept you've already learned about. I want the snowball growing as soon as possible. I want revenue opportunities as soon as possible versus saving money and wasting time.

Another option for finding help is to bring on a business partner, especially if he or she has experience in the same industry as your new business. If you don't have the cash to pay business consultants, consider bringing on someone with business experience as a partner. Then, you would have someone with experience involved in the business who wants to see it succeed. This means you'll need to share in the profits and equity of the business over time, but if this person helps you grow, it may be well worth sharing in the spoils. Ideally, this person may also be willing to invest in the business to alleviate some of the cost and risk compared to carrying it all yourself.

Some of the best business partnerships involve two people with different skillsets. Ideally, these skillsets complement one another, such as a visionary and a manager. One of my clients started a digital advertising company years ago. He was a very creative person and had experience with advertising. He was quick to admit he didn't enjoy the business side, though. Spreadsheets and projections weren't his thing. That's why he started the company with a business partner who had advertising experience but was strong on the business side. The two of them are a great example of partners who complement one another.

Gordon Moore and Bob Noyce may not be household names in business like Steve Jobs or Bill Gates, but you likely know the business they founded. It's a little company called Intel. Before Intel had more than 100,000 employees around the world and tens of billions in revenue, it started as a small venture founded by Moore and Noyce. Both had experience with semiconductors and wanted to create new technologies that pushed beyond the traditional capabilities of their field. Noyce was a visionary who had big-picture ideas and a strong leadership skillset. Moore was a skilled scientist who helped push the envelope on new ways of thinking about computer science. The two are a prime example of business partners who leveraged their talents in a complementary way. If both had founded their own companies separately, they may not have had the same success, despite each obviously having impressive skills.

If you decide to start a business and bring on a partner, think of it like a marriage. You'll be entering into legal documents together. You'll make difficult financial decisions together. You'll be bound together in business for what may be years or decades if all goes well. With this in mind, make sure you completely trust your business partner and you have shared goals. If one person just wants to create a profitable business with no more than 20 employees because they don't want the stress of a big company, but the other wants complete industry domination across the globe, your relationship will have significant stress as the company grows. Discuss what the future looks like in an ideal situation for both of you and go through the business planning exercise from Step 1. You'll be glad you did.

Step 3, be flexible as you start your business. Ask anyone who has started a business if they changed course along the way. There's a strong chance they did. Although not a small business, take Walmart for example. Walmart was founded on the idea that customers would walk into their stores and find just about anything they need in one place. Walmart stores became larger and larger over time based on this idea. If you've shopped at Walmart, you know you can generally buy groceries, clothing, toys, makeup, furniture, school supplies, and electronics all in one place. Then, one day, retail stores with physical locations started closing because of growing popularity in online ordering and delivery. Amazon slowly became one of the largest retailers in the U.S., with virtually no physical retails locations. Rather than fight the growing trend of online ordering and delivery, Walmart embraced it. Walmart's online presence grew into a significant competitor of Amazon's. Walmart was flexible.

Another aspect of being flexible in business is removing yourself from emotions. This is much easier said than done. For example, if you start a technology business of some kind, you'll likely need to hire programmers to help your vision come to life unless you're a programmer yourself. Imagine this business is a new social media platform or online peer-to-peer payment system. You may spend months or years building the first version of your technology. Programmers can be expensive, so the costs could easily be six or seven figures in the first year. Once the first version has been created or at least near completion, what if you determine it's just not what you envisioned? What if you can now see a different path forward, helped by the experience and failures of the past year? Will you change directions and say goodbye to all of that time and money you already spent, or will you continue forward because the thought of "losing" that money is depressing? Ask any successful entrepreneur and they will tell you to change direction if you're confident in a better path forward. Remove the emotional ties of past financial commitments. Emotional ties can blind you. Keeping flexibility in mind from the onset of your business venture may help you with very difficult forks in the road that are likely to occur.

While starting a business may seem daunting, between the financial commitments, risks, and time required, it can also be easy and exciting. Some people find themselves in a position where they can quit their jobs to start businesses or do so right out of school. Quitting your job to be a full-time entrepreneur is risky, especially if you don't have family wealth or investors. It may be the best decision you make in your career, or you may come crawling back to the human resources department to ask for your job back in two years. However, there's another way to start a business besides going all-in at once. Many people start a business on the side. It's the classic side hustle concept we discussed in Chapter 11.

Two great examples of part-time businesses that grew into enterprises are Under Armour and HubSpot. In 1996, Under Armour's founder Kevin Plank decided to create an athletic shirt for himself. He was a football player at the University of Maryland and grew tired of uncomfortable shirts beneath his jersey and equipment. His "office" was his grandmother's basement in Washington, D.C. He was pleased with the results and decided there may be a market for the new garment. He then drove along the East Coast selling shirts out of the trunk of his car. His product caught on and sales began to grow to the point where he needed a real manufacturer in 1997. He began to see strong success in the early 2000s and the company went on to generate billions in annual revenue.

HubSpot began as an idea in 2004 by Brian Halligan and Dharmesh Shah. They noticed that online blogs with small budgets and free materials were generating more online traffic than companies with large marketing budgets. They coined the term "inbounding marketing" and created a free blog of their own, showcasing ideas on how businesses can develop new ways of marketing. Those visiting their blog who wanted help bringing their ideas to life could naturally hire HubSpot for the job. The company went from three customers in 2006 to thousands within five years, generating millions in annualized revenue.

When considering a side business, read through your employment contract and company policy information, if applicable. If you have a noncompete or nondisclosure agreement that you've signed, read through those as well. With the case of noncompete agreements, if you inadvertently violate this agreement, you may find yourself without a job and searching for an attorney at the same time. Be smart about your side business. There's generally a way you can do it without breaking the rules or burning bridges.

Although the idea of starting a business may sound exciting and lucrative, many new businesses don't survive. Some new businesses simply aren't profitable enough to continue running or never make a profit at all. According to the Small Business Administration, approximately half of new businesses in the U.S. survive five years and about one-third survive 10 years or longer[35]. These statistics may not be exciting to someone considering a new business, but I want you to know the reality of it. Among the common reasons new businesses fail include having a poor business plan, not putting enough capital into the business, forgoing market research, poor location, not keeping up with new trends, and expanding too quickly.

As a capitalist society, we live in an environment where taking risks allows someone to have unlimited amounts of wealth. Creating a new product or service that genuinely helps people or makes life easier can be handsomely rewarded. As you've learned in prior chapters, risks come with potential rewards and losses. Some of the wealthiest entrepreneurs in the world have experience with failed businesses but went on to start new ones. Not everyone has the money or the drive to try launching a new business after a failed one, so if you can start your business while keeping the security of a salary, it may be your best option.

Another option for accessing the growth potential of a private business is investing in one. Imagine that a friend of yours has a great idea for a new product. You listen to her idea and it excites you. You can tell she's done her research, she's knowledgeable on the subject, and her business plan is thorough. She's ready to launch this new business, but only has so much capital of her own. She needs another $500,000 to implement her business plan and asks how much you would be willing to invest, knowing this business may not survive and your cash could be completely lost. It's a difficult, yet exciting, decision to make.

If the idea of starting a business and dealing with all the complexities isn't appealing, but the potential rewards are, you might consider investing in someone else's private business. In this scenario, the risks may be just as high as starting your own business, but the road to potential reward may be much easier. Being an investor in another business means you likely don't need to be involved directly in the day-to-day operations. If you have a day job that offers you security and you don't have much free time for a side business, investing in someone else's may be the next best thing.

When it comes to investing in another business, there are generally three types of opportunities — startups, acquisitions, and private funds. Each option presents its own risks and potential rewards, but a common risk for each is liquidity. Unlike investing in a mutual fund, where you can generally redeem your shares any day the markets are trading, private businesses don't have a liquid "market" to buy and sell shares. Imagine investing in a gas station with three other investors and each person represents 25 percent ownership. One year later, a fellow investor wants out of the business because he's going through a divorce and wants to move to London to start a new life. Unless you or one of the other investors is willing and able to quickly buy out his share, he may be stuck with the liquidity risk of this gas station. He may try to sell his share to a third party, but depending on the legal documents of the business, regulatory restrictions, etc., this process could take months. Private businesses simply aren't meant to be liquid investments. This is an important factor to consider when investing in a privately held business.

With startups, you have the same risks and potential rewards discussed earlier. When it's someone else's startup business, though, you're investing in the founder or the management team just as much as the business itself. I was recently sent a packet of information from a friend who was considering investing in a startup in the golf industry. This startup was focused on a new golf technology concept. My friend was excited about the idea but had never invested in a startup. As with many startup ideas, especially involving technology, the concept was interesting. As I read through the investor pitch book the founder had created, I noticed grammatical errors and some inconsistencies. I also came away with more questions than answers from it.

I could tell this entrepreneurial founder had spent considerable time putting the pitch book together and included much of the materials I would recommend. However, it was also obvious this was his first time putting together this type of plan.

My friend acknowledged the founder was a bit new to certain aspects of this startup, but he had started a new business before with moderate success and had plenty of experience in the golf industry. The minimum investment requirement was also reasonable, so my friend was still interested, despite a few warning signs.

If you're considering investing in someone's business, here are three things to consider. First, does the person or team that will be running it have meaningful experience? If you owned a plane and needed to hire your own pilot, you would probably search for someone with at least 20 years of experience who's been through all sorts of flying conditions. That's the mentality to have when questioning someone's ability to start and run a business. You don't want someone learning on the job about legal matters, intellectual property, personnel management, and marketing. Their business plan should be thorough and reinforce that they have both the experience and the plan for a successful startup.

Second, does this business have a minimum viable product? If it's a new gadget, is the gadget already a working prototype? If it's software, does it have at least a small group of users? If it's a restaurant, can you taste the menu options and see examples of how the inside would be designed? You'll ideally want this new venture to have some kind of minimum viable product first, plus market research to determine if there's enough demand to be sustainable.

Third, you'll want to review financial projections that show what kind of return on your investment you might expect. I've seen aggressive projections for various startups, so remember that the founder may be overly optimistic. You'll still want to review these projections to gain a basic understanding of the types of costs and profits the founder is projecting. The projection should include legal costs, personnel costs, and other types of costs discussed earlier in this chapter.

Think about what might happen to these projections if revenues come in lower than expected and costs come in higher than expected.

There are plenty of other considerations before investing in a private business, such as legal agreements, how much equity you'll have, or voting rights, but these three points are key. You'll want to have your own attorney involved to review legal documents before signing them, but you might also include a financial planner with private business experience, too.

Startup investing is a bit like lighting a firework that doesn't have a label. It may fizzle out after a few sparks, it may burst into flames, or it may take off like a rocket. Startups are generally the highest-risk category when investing in someone else's private business, but that also means it may offer the highest potential reward. Think about a local company you may be familiar with that has had impressive growth. Maybe it's a new restaurant that's opening its third location or a nutrition supplement store that continues to expand. It's possible those businesses were started with a group of investors. When a business is starting from scratch and has zero revenue, zero customers, and zero name recognition, investors are taking significant risk that the business will even survive. For every successful business you see growing in your area, there are likely 10 that failed. Be prepared for high risk and limited liquidity with this type of investing.

Another way to invest in a private business is through acquisition. Unlike a startup with little to no track record, acquiring an existing business typically offers lower risk. The same risks of investing in a business exist, but with acquisitions, you can generally see a history of performance. For example, you might be able to see how many customers the business has and how long those customers have been loyal to the business. If you're wondering how someone might acquire a business, try searching online for business sale listings. In the same way you might browse online for homes that are for sale, you can browse for businesses that are for sale, too. I recommend taking a moment to do this search online. Once you do, you may notice that, unlike a real estate listing, limited information is available about the business. This is typically the case. Most businesses don't want the world to know they're up for sale because they may lose customers. Imagine if you wanted to book a wedding venue one year in advance and you discovered it was for sale. You would probably pick a different venue.

As an example, I recently found a winery for sale. Below is the information provided in the listing, available for anyone to see:

Established and profitable Winery for Sale. Great opportunity to purchase a cash flowing business for far less than what it would cost to build out new. The building is only 2 years old, sellers opened this as an investment and have too many other obligations going on to put their full time into this. Business has key management in place, which could do well for an investor, or an owner operator could come in and assume an active role and increase their compensation. This business could be expanded with a focus on the wedding business. Property with acreage is also available and gives ample opportunity for expansion. For more information, please contact the broker.

Reason for selling – Semi-retire. Have other businesses.
- *Asking price - $400,000*
- *Annual revenue - $1,422,241*
- *Net profit – Not disclosed*
- *Cash flow - $201,329*
- *Total debt – Not disclosed*
- *FF&E - $110,000*
- *Real estate - $2,800,000*
- *Year established – Not disclosed*
- *Employees – 30*

If you have experience in the restaurant or hospitality field, you may be intrigued by this listing. Maybe you have friends or family in the wedding industry that could help you expand into potentially lucrative events. There are plenty of questions to be answered still, but at first glance, cash flow of 14 percent of gross revenue is fine for the wine industry. I would want to know the net profit, which isn't disclosed at this stage. Knowing wineries in the area, 30 employees seems like a relatively high number. It could represent seasonal and part-time employees or it could mean this winery creates its own wine. Many wineries in this same area focus on importing wines from around the world for sale onsite, focusing instead on the experience of a scenic location for food and wine, plus special events. Could wine creation be scrapped in favor of lower labor costs and higher profitability?

If you were interested in this listing, you would likely be required to sign a non-disclosure agreement (NDA). This agreement assures the seller that you won't divulge private information about the business within a certain period of time. Once the NDA is signed, you would generally be able to acquire additional info about the business, such as:

- Historical profit or loss (Is the business growing?)
- Tenure of employees (Are there key employees in place?)
- Customer information (Does any single customer represent a large portion of revenue?)
- Age of equipment (Would you need to invest in new technology or equipment?)
- Existing contracts in place (Would you be taking over an existing lease?)
- Will the seller(s) be leaving the industry (Could they become a competitor?)
- Time commitment (How much time did the current owners spend on the business?)

Detailed business acquisition strategies are beyond the scope of this book, so instead, use this information as a way to envision what it takes to acquire and run a business. You can also visit GrowthInfo.com/business for more info on acquiring a business. If you plan on being directly involved in the business, will you have adequate time to dedicate to it? If you plan to invest with others, who will be responsible for certain duties? Acquiring a business means you'll be investing hard-earned money and taking on responsibility for the employees in that business. You may have enormous pressure to make the business successful, keep your business partners or investors happy, and keep employees gainfully employed.

If it were me buying this winery, I would do so as an investor, not an active owner. In other words, I would provide the cash and expertise on the business side to create more value, but I wouldn't be the person making day-to-day business decisions. I would need a key employee I could trust to run the business in my absence or another investor who could run it and co-invest with me. Plenty of people take this route when acquiring businesses.

If you consider acquiring a business, either as an investor or an active owner, think about your exit strategy before you enter the business. It may seem strange to consider an exit before you've even seen the entrance, but doing so brings clarity to how you'll approach the acquisition. If you want to build a business that you'll pass on to your two children one day, that may help you envision a business that can be expanded. It may also mean you'll retain profits in the business to invest in new technology or new products instead of taking profits out to buy yourself a vacation home. However, if you prefer to have a business that provides maximum cash flow for the next decade while you pay off debt or send three kids to college, you may consider acquiring an established business with strong cash flow.

You might also envision buying a business for the purpose of selling it withing 5–10 years. This strategy can prove valuable if you find a distressed seller that has mismanaged a business or found themselves in financial trouble to the point they're forced to sell. You may find an opportunity to turn the business around for a profit in a matter of years, exiting to potentially acquire another business. Think of it like buying a rundown house, fixing it up, and flipping it. Knowing this in advance will help you shape your strategy and the capital you'll need to make the acquisition a success. Start with the end in mind.

Starting a business, investing in a business, or acquiring a business is no simple endeavor. The risks, costs and potential time commitment are why most people never start businesses. According to the Bureau of Labor Statistics, approximately 10.1 percent of U.S. workers are self-employed, which includes those who have incorporated their businesses[36]. Most people prefer the stability and security of traditional employment over the risk and uncertainty of owning a business. If you're contemplating business ownership for the first time, be prepared for the financial and emotional ups and downs. If you succeed, however, it could prove to be a lucrative and empowering path to building wealth over time. This is why I personally focus on business ownership. My losses in business have hurt, but my gains have more than made up for them.

Chapter 14

Finding the Right Professionals

In this chapter:
- When a pro brings value
- Leveraging your time
- What to know, what to ask

Throughout my career, I've worked with families who have net worths of $1 million to more than $100 million. Those blessed with wealth, especially if they created that wealth on their own, tend to surround themselves with professionals to help them maintain what they've created. They know reducing taxes, protecting themselves from risk, and maintaining or growing their wealth requires special expertise. With few exceptions, the wealthiest people I've met in my career have had the help of attorneys, Certified Public Accountants (CPAs) and CERTIFIED FINANCIAL PLANNERS™ (CFPs). Some have also had the help of coaches, insurance experts, and business advisors. This chapter focuses on the three former professions, how to find them, and what you should know first.

As we age, our financial world becomes more complex. In our early 20s, the focus is usually on securing a good job, buying a first home, starting a family, or paying off student loans. Over time, those goals may evolve into determining if a Roth IRA conversion makes financial sense. An employer may offer stock options or restricted stock units with special tax nuances to consider. Children may require education planning for private school and college. With children also comes estate planning, such as wills with guardianship provisions. Insurance decisions must be made, such as disability insurance, life insurance, health insurance, and homeowners insurance. Some people start businesses, which propels them into myriad tax matters that generally don't apply to most people. These are just a few examples that may seem complex in and of themselves, but when combined, they become complex enough that a professional is needed. Having the right professionals around you can help you build and keep your wealth, no matter what level of wealth you may have.

If you find yourself in the middle of a major life event, such as an inheritance, death, divorce, or job layoff, it's important to seek out some of these professionals. For example, after a job layoff, I often see people use their cash in the bank to pay off debts such as auto loans or mortgages. The goal is to eliminate monthly payments because their income has been eliminated. What happens when the next job doesn't come along for months and months? You might be wishing you had that cash again. Instead, it may be better to keep as much cash around as long as possible to survive a job transition and make monthly payments as normal. With an inheritance, I often see people make financial decisions that cost them more in taxes than necessary. It might be because a friend gave them advice and didn't understand the laws, they found inaccurate information online, or they simply didn't know other options existed. Life events can be complicated, so it's important to speak with a few pros before making decisions that can't be reversed.

If you want help finding a professional, you can also go to GrowthInfo.com/pro . My team can help find financial planners, CPAs, attorneys, and other types of business professionals. This chapter includes some of the criteria we use to find qualified pros.

How to find a CFP®

The finance industry is complex. Sure, investments, tax planning, and portfolio structure are complex, but I'm talking about the industry itself. Did you know anyone can call themselves a financial planner? That's right. You can call yourself a financial planner or a financial advisor and no one will stop you. If you took a single college course in accounting and believe you can teach people about financial planning techniques, more power to you. The finance industry is highly regulated in some respects, but not in others. I often find websites of insurance professionals who sell insurance products and call themselves financial advisors. What is their solution to most financial goals? Insurance, of course. While earning licenses to legally charge a fee for financial services requires testing, ongoing education, and regulation, proclaiming you're a financial professional generally requires little more than website.

Because "financial professional" is a general term, let's first discuss the two main segments of the finance industry — brokerage firms and Registered Investment Advisors (RIAs). Both of these parts of the finance industry are regulated by different bodies. This is important because different financial professionals may follow different rules or be exempt from others.

First, brokerage firms, also known as broker-dealers, may be large or small firms that offer services like stock trading, mutual funds, annuities, tax planning, or financial planning. Brokerage firms may be discount online trading platforms, or they may be more full-service firms. Brokerage firms typically have arrangements with various investment companies, such as a mutual fund company or annuity provider. These agreements are called "selling agreements." Before the advisors of a brokerage firm can offer or recommend a certain investment product, the brokerage firm itself must approve the product to be offered to clients. Advisors who recommend financial products that aren't preapproved by its brokerage firm can find themselves in a great deal of trouble.

When a mutual fund company wants to offer its products to a brokerage firm's advisors, it generally establishes a selling agreement first. This process may also involve something called revenue sharing. Revenue sharing arrangements are when a company, such a mutual fund company, offers to share part if its revenue with the brokerage firm. In turn, the brokerage firm makes more money by receiving this additional revenue directly from the fund company. As you can see, a potential conflict of interest exists when a brokerage firm agrees to approve an investment product to be recommended by its advisors and then makes money directly from the product it approved. In other words, a brokerage firm might be incentivized to approve the sale of a product if it means they'll make more money. The brokerage firm could earn revenue-sharing dollars directly from the mutual fund company, plus revenue from the fee or commission you pay directly as a customer of the brokerage firm. It's a bit like your doctor charging you for an office visit, *plus* earning money directly from a pharmaceutical company for prescribing your medication.

Revenue sharing isn't illegal. It's actually common among brokerage firms. It's legal as long as it's disclosed. Some brokerage firms easily provide links at the bottom of their websites to find this type of information, while others make it more difficult to find. Try searching online for a popular brokerage firm and add the words, "revenue sharing." If you decide to work with a brokerage firm and your advisor recommends a financial product that's listed on the revenue sharing disclosure, ask your advisor about it.

Some brokerage firms also have what are known as "proprietary products." These types of products are produced by the brokerage firm, or an affiliate, and then sold to clients. Some brokerage firms also own insurance companies and sell their own proprietary insurance products. This means they could be paid twice. In my opinion, this represents a major conflict of interest. It's like asking your doctor for a prescription and the doctor recommending a medication he developed on his own. It's possible that a proprietary product happens to be the best for you out of all possible products in the marketplace, but the conflict itself makes me stay away from proprietary products. If I'm paying someone for unbiased advice, I don't want them recommending something that pays them more money. It may or may not be what's best for me, but I don't want the potential bias in the mix either way.

Brokerage firms are typically regulated by the Financial Industry Regulatory Authority (FINRA). FINRA is a self-regulatory organization within the federal Securities and Exchange Commission (SEC). Thanks to FINRA, you can research financial professionals for free online. Just visit brokercheck.finra.org and enter a financial professional's name. If they're licensed as a financial professional and belong to a brokerage firm, they will have a FINRA profile on this broker check website. Within the site, you can see how long an advisor has been in practice, what licenses they have, and if they've ever had any consumer complaints or regulatory issues. This means if an advisor did something wrong and broke FINRA rules, the incident may show up on their FINRA profile for all to see.

The other reason it's important to know about FINRA's broker check website is to determine if an advisor is affiliated with a brokerage firm in the first place. If you're like most people, it may be hard to know the difference between a brokerage firm and an RIA. If you visit this website and find a specific financial professional listed, this means they currently belong, or previously belonged, to a brokerage firm. Then, you can look up their firm and revenue-sharing information.

The second major segment of the finance industry is RIAs. Registered Investment Advisors may be small or large firms. RIAs offer similar services as brokerage firms, such as investments, tax planning, or portfolio construction. RIAs don't have selling agreements, though. Instead, RIAs typically recommend third-party products in the same way your doctor may recommend the medication of a third-party pharmaceutical company. While revenue-sharing arrangements may technically exist with some RIAs, I don't see them often. Sometimes an RIA may use a third-party provider for something like an employer retirement plan, and that provider has revenue-sharing arrangements with mutual fund companies. This draws the RIA into a revenue-sharing arrangement, but the RIA may rebate this revenue back to clients as a fee credit. This is especially the case with "fee-only" RIAs.

Fee-only RIAs pride themselves on only receiving compensation through transparent advisory fees, such as flat or percentage-based fees. Fee-only means an RIA does not receive compensation from the investments they recommend. You'll typically know if an RIA is fee-only because the firm will wear the term as a badge of honor on its website and marketing materials. I used to work for an independent brokerage firm early in my career before merging with a fee-only RIA and made the change with pride.

It's possible you may encounter the term "fee-based" as you speak with financial professionals. This can be a confusing term, because it's not the same as fee-only. Fee-*based* means a professional may commonly charge advisory fees for his or her services. However, whether a brokerage firm or RIA, an advisor may also receive other forms of compensation, such as commissions for selling insurance. I personally had a life insurance license early in my career and recommended insurance products. In turn, I received commissions. Nearly all my compensation came from fees, though, not commissions, so I was fee-*based*. I later relinquished my insurance license to become a fee-*only* professional. If you hear the term fee-*based*, you'll want to clarify if a professional receives any other form of compensation, even if they *also* receive advisory fee revenue. If I were looking for a CFP®, I would look for someone at a fee-only RIA.

RIAs and advisors that work within RIAs are typically regulated by the SEC. If you want to check the background of an RIA advisor, visit adviserinfo.sec.gov. Like the broker check website, you can find similar information on the SEC's website. This includes how long they've been in practice, their licenses, and possible regulatory history.

While differences exist between brokerage firms and RIAs that may be cause for concern. It doesn't mean the advisors themselves are bad people. An advisor may work on commission and sell proprietary products, but that doesn't mean the *person* is a bad advisor. Some people don't mind at all that their advisor earns a commission or sells products manufactured by their own firm. Others don't like knowing these potential conflicts of interest exist. The reason for including this information in this chapter is to help you know the basics of how this industry works and what I've learned as an insider. If you're going to invest your hard-earned dollars with a professional, you owe it to yourself to ask difficult questions and understand the nature of relationships among you, your advisor, and your advisor's firm.

While the public regulatory websites I provided may help you research an advisor, they don't cover information such as revenue-sharing arrangements, insurance commissions, or fee-only vs. fee-based. Therefore, below are questions I recommend asking as you speak with financial professionals:

- Do you or anyone at your firm accept commissions of any kind?
- Do you have an investment minimum?
- Does your firm accept revenue-sharing dollars?
- Are you regulated by FINRA?
- Do you have your CFP® marks?

The last question regarding the CFP® is an important one. As mentioned earlier, anyone can call themselves a financial planner. Obviously, if someone has a finance degree and regulatory licenses to operate as a financial professional, they're indeed a financial professional. Only those professionals who have undergone additional training and testing to become board-CERTIFIED FINANCIAL PLANNERS™ can use the marks of the CFP®. The CFP® requires 30 hours of continuing education credits every two years. If you decide to work with a financial planner who has the letters CFP® behind their name, you know you're working with someone who has proved to have the knowledge required of the CFP® program.

Overall, working with a CFP® means you'll be working with someone who may be able to help you through myriad financial decisions. These may include:

- Tax planning

- Investment management
- Estate planning
- Insurance planning
- Benefits planning
- Philanthropic gifting
- Education planning
- Overall financial planning

When you find the right financial planner, it may be a relationship you continue for years or even decades. This person may become intimately familiar with your family's goals and preferences, keeping them in mind as tax law change and important decisions must be made year after year. This is why it's important to know what to look for in a financial planner.

How to find a CPA

A CPA friend of mine told me, "We don't just count your beans, we make your beans count!" It's a great tagline for the kind of work many people find monotonous. You'll find accounting and tax work is more than just punching numbers into a calculator all day. Let's discuss what types of CPAs exist in the marketplace, when you may need one, and how to find one.

Years ago, I had recommended a Roth IRA conversion to one of my clients. As I mentioned in Chapter 5, this strategy involved converting pretax retirement dollars into after-tax Roth dollars. The downside to the strategy is that income taxes are due upon the conversion. The upside is that, if following the Roth IRA rules, no income taxes would be due again in the future. My client contacted me a few weeks later and said her "tax person" recommended against the strategy because it would increase her current-year tax liability. I then asked my client if her tax person was a CPA. She said, "yes." I was surprised by this comment from her CPA because I had already conducted an analysis estimating the long-term effects of the strategy. It was projected to increase her taxes in the short-term but reduce her taxes to a greater extent for her and her family over the long term.

After further conversation, I learned that my client did not have a CPA. She had an accountant who focused on tax preparation. This person's job was to gather tax forms, find possible tax deductions, and complete the tax return in a timely manner. This person's job was to find ways to reduce taxes each year. As an accountant focused on tax preparation with a large group of clients to finish before tax season, this person wasn't focused on long-term planning. They were focused on short-term transactions to reduce taxes as much as possible and then move on to the next client to conduct the same work. I couldn't blame the accountant for taking a stance against a Roth conversion strategy that would *increase* taxes. As someone who bills by the hour for tax-preparation work, they weren't asked to create long-term projections considering the total potential tax impact over multiple years. They were asked to reduce taxes and file the tax return in a timely manner.

While this wasn't the first time this scenario played out with one of my clients, I had just as many scenarios where a client's tax professional agreed with something like a Roth IRA conversion. This is an important lesson in working with a tax professional based on your needs. I generally categorize tax professionals into three categories:

- Tax preparers
- Transactional CPAs
- Planning-focused CPAs

Some people frankly don't need a tax professional. Some people have such simple tax situations that using an online tax preparation software is fine. For example, if you're single or married with no dependent children, you don't own a business, and your investment portfolio consists only of a retirement plan at work, using an online tax filing program is probably fine. The online program tends to be less expensive and may offer the same value. However, as life becomes more complex, such as children, college-savings plans, self-employed income, inherited assets, taxable investment accounts, or investment real estate, the experience of a knowledgeable tax expert becomes valuable.

Once your situation changes to the point where you need a professional, ask for a consultation. You don't have to make the switch right away. Conduct some research by speaking with a few pros. Some may recommend staying with your online tax program for a while longer. Others may notice tax deductions or strategies that you haven't considered yet. To help with your search, here's a general description of the three types of tax professionals mentioned earlier.

Tax Preparers — General accountants who prepare and file tax returns may be helpful if your situation is straightforward and you don't feel comfortable filing your own return online. Accountants who don't have the letters CPA behind their name may be just as intelligent as someone who passed the CPA exams. The difference is they haven't gone through the rigorous testing and education requirements to become certified. It's similar to a financial planner vs. a CFP®. While some tax preparers may be comfortable with long-term tax planning, I've found most focus on preparing and filing a tax return as quickly as possible to keep the costs reasonable for their clients. Then, they move on to the next client during the busy tax season.

Transactional CPAs — Like tax preparers, transactional CPAs tend to focus on current-year tax matters. They're more often part of smaller or midsize accounting firms. However, given the additional testing and education requirements of the CPA marks, professionals in this category tend to have more knowledge regarding advanced tax-planning matters. I've found that CPAs tend to charge higher fees than regular accountants because the market generally demands a higher fee for their knowledge and experience. If you have more complicated finances, such as rental property or self-employment income, but don't require more proactive tax planning and projections, this category of CPA may be suitable for you.

Planning-Focused CPAs — In addition to having the knowledge of a CPA, planning-focused CPAs tend to be more holistic in their craft. They consider areas such as estate planning, financial planning, and business planning in their work. This type of CPA tends to be part of a midsize to large accounting firm with greater resources and various professionals with niche backgrounds. As you may imagine, this type of knowledge and experience means planning-focused CPAs tend to cost more than the other tax professionals we've discussed. That doesn't mean planning-focused CPAs are out of the budget. It highly depends on your specific needs. As you grow your wealth, potentially start a business, or increase the complexity of your finances, this type of CPA may be best for you. The alternative is potentially missing out on tax strategies that could save you money over time. Missing out could cost you more than their fee.

If you own a business or plan on owning a business in the future, I generally recommend a planning-focused CPA with a midsize firm or larger. You may require other types of accounting work, such as payroll and bookkeeping services. You'll want to build a relationship with an accounting firm that has the capacity, experience, and services available to help you as your life becomes more complex and your business grows over time.

Regardless of the type of professional you choose, below are questions I recommend asking as you interview CPAs or accountants:

- How many clients do you have?
- Do work on an hourly rate or a flat fee?
- If I'm audited by the IRS, are you able to represent me? If so, how do your services work?
- What percentage of your clients are business entities, trusts, and individuals?
- Do you have any specialties, such as philanthropic planning, real estate, or business planning?
- Are you willing to coordinate with my CFP® and attorney?

How to find an attorney

Once upon a time, an estate attorney completed a will for an elderly client. The elderly client thanked him and asked if she could pay his $500 fee in cash. He said cash was fine. She then pulled crisp new hundred-dollar bills from her purse. She began counting them in front of him — one, two, three, four, and five. She thanked him for his work and left his office. The attorney then took the cash to his office and recounted it — one, two, three, four, five, six. The elderly woman accidentally paid him $600. The attorney then asked himself an important ethical question, "Should I split it with my partner?"

While some people view attorneys as professionals of last resort, such as hiring an attorney to defend you in court, I encourage you to view attorneys as resources to help you toward your goals. Attorneys are like doctors in that they have specialties. If you injure your knee, you will likely want to see an orthopedist, not a cardiologist. It's easy to identify the difference between an oncologist and a pulmonologist, but it's not as easy to identify an estate attorney versus a business law attorney. While it's possible you may need a traffic law attorney at some point in your life, let's focus on the more common attorneys you may need in your journey toward financial independence. These may include:

- Estate attorney
- Business law attorney
- Real estate attorney
- Employment law attorney

Estate attorneys, sometimes called elder-law attorneys, specialize in estate planning. This includes drafting estate documents such as wills, trusts, powers of attorney, and health care directives. Aside from the documents themselves, estate attorneys help with planning, such as how to structure a trust based on your marital status, net worth, state of residence, and philanthropic goals. It's important to have an estate attorney to help create an estate plan, especially if any of the following apply to your situation:

- You have minor children.
- You have a child with special needs.
- You own assets outside of your state or country of residence.
- You have a blended family.
- You own a business.

One option for creating estate documents is using an online document generator. Online legal websites may be less expensive than working directly with an attorney, but you may not receive the customized estate work your family needs. Both online websites and traditional estate attorneys use templates to create estate documents. From there, the templates can be customized to your situation. If you and your spouse were each married before and have a blended family, your wishes for how assets should be split up when you die can be complex. Some online estate document websites do a good job of customization, while others do not. Some online websites can also connect you with an attorney if you have questions. If you're worried about your family's situation, it may be best to involve an attorney who can use his or her expertise to completely customize your estate documents for your situation.

Attorneys can't specialize in every area of law. It's simply impossible. As you begin searching for an estate attorney, ask them about their areas of expertise. If you notice on their website that the same attorney handles traffic law, divorces, environmental law, real estate, *and* estate planning, go elsewhere for your estate plan. It's possible for a law firm with *numerous* attorneys to be able to handle all of these specialties, but not a single attorney. If you need estate planning, you need an estate attorney.

When it comes to business law attorneys, real estate attorneys, and employment law attorneys, your due diligence should be similar. You'll want a specialist for each area. If you find yourself needing all four, it's possible to seek out four different attorneys at four different law firms. You may enjoy finding one or two law firms to work with that have various inhouse experts to handle your needs.

When searching for an attorney, I recommend asking the following questions:

- What is your area of expertise?
- Do you have other attorneys at your firm with other specialties?
- What types of clients do you typically work with?
- Do you work by the hour or on flat fees?

- How much of this work will be done by an associate attorney or a paralegal?
- What work will be excluded from your engagement agreement that I must handle on my own?
- Are you willing to coordinate with my CPA and CFP®, as needed?

The idea of having an attorney, a CPA, and aCFP® may seem intimidating or even unnecessary at this point in your life. It greatly depends on your situation. You may even be wondering if the costs of these professionals are worth the value. As a financial professional myself, I have a CPA and two law firms who I use personally. Early in my life, I used an online tax-preparation service and didn't need much of an estate plan. As my wealth grew, children came into the picture for my wife and me, and I began owning various businesses, the value of these professionals became evident. My time is too valuable to attempt to handle everything on my own. Imagine some of the most successful businesspeople you know. Do you think they spend their precious time reading through the tax code or studying state laws for hours? Do you think they attempt to handle these complex areas on their own and risk costly mistakes? Working with a team of professionals allows you to focus on your family, your career, and your passions. Thinking and acting like a successful person is the best way to become one.

Chapter 15

The Health-Wealth Connection

In this chapter:
- Lifespan vs. health span
- The benefits of work in retirement
- Energy and health over time

There are many factors we can't control in our lives. Where we're born, who our parents are, and our genetic code are a few examples. Some of us hit the genetic jackpot at birth, being born into families that tend to live long, healthy lives. According to the World Health Organization, global life expectancy is 73 years[37]. In my family, all four of my grandparents have lived past the age of 90. The pictures I have of them holding my children — their great-grandchildren — are priceless to me. Unless my doctor tells me otherwise, I think I'm one of the lucky ones who hit the genetic jackpot at birth if my grandparents are any indication.

Living a long life doesn't necessarily mean someone will live a happy and healthy life, though. One of my personal goals in life is to live to 100. The idea of seeing scientific breakthroughs, using new technology, and meeting my future family members excites me. Not only do I have a goal of living to 100, my goal is to live to 100 *and* be relatively healthy until as close to 100 as possible. If I'm dealing with significant health issues in my early 80s, living to 100 doesn't sound appealing anymore. The difference between how long someone lives and how long they enjoy good health is lifespan versus health span. Health span is how long you can enjoy relatively good health over your lifetime. I don't just want a long lifespan, I want a long health span, too. I want to be able to travel and enjoy time with family well into my 80s and 90s. In other words, I want to enjoy my finances for a longer period of time than the average person.

If you work hard and use the strategies in this book to reach multimillionaire status, you'll have achieved a significant milestone. Most people don't create that kind of wealth in their lifetimes. However, if you sacrifice your physical and mental health along the way to reach this milestone, what will the rest of your life look like? If you sacrifice your sleep for years, how will that affect your brain and cognition in your 70s? If you eat fast food all the time because you're working 60 hours a week, how will that affect your heart when you're retired? If you never exercise because your career comes first, how many pills might you be taking later to correct high blood pressure, osteoporosis, or heart disease? Poor health habits often manifest themselves into mental and physical health problems later in life. If those poor habits are justified by your quest for significant wealth, will it be worth it?

The connection between health and wealth is multifaceted. Creating wealth often requires hard work and sacrifice. Some choose to sacrifice their health to reach their financial goals. Then, they aren't healthy enough to fully enjoy the fruits of their labor in their later years. Their life expectancy might also be shorter. On the flip side, if someone takes great care of their body and mind all their life, they may enjoy both longer lifespan and longer health span. This means they may need more money to sustain their lifestyle for a longer period of time. After all, if two different people have the same lifestyle, but one lives to 80 and the other lives to 95, the 95-year-old will have 15 more years of lifestyle expenses, thus needing more money to pay for it. This means taking good care of yourself could lead to a longer life that would require more money to pay for it. I don't know about you, but I would much rather have to worry about affording a long life than the alternative.

The solution to creating wealth over your lifetime while also taking care of yourself along the way is somewhat self-fulfilling. For example, if you prioritize your health over your working career, which means good sleep habits, healthy eating, and exercise, you may have less time for your career or your side business. That might mean less money that can compound over time. However, it may mean a healthier life, longer life span, and longer health span. Longer health span and lifespan means you may want to work longer, but in a lesser capacity, such as a part-time job, consulting, or a business. These would be roles you enjoy, but still allow you freedom as if you were partially retired. You would also be bringing in income, which puts less pressure on drawing from your nest egg to pay for your expenses. If you're blessed with decent health in your 70s, 80s, or even 90s, you would be able to enjoy your wealth more and for longer thanks to your decision to work longer and focus on good health.

While this example mentions having potentially less wealth from putting your health first over your lifetime, it doesn't mean significantly less. Over the past 10 years, if I had stopped working out and sacrificed one hour of sleep per night to work, I may have written more books or had more revenue in my businesses. However, I'm doing just fine and my long-term financial plan shows my wife and I are well on our way to reaching our financial goals. Sacrificing my health might lead to more money, but not that much more. It certainly wouldn't be worth it to me. I've also found businesses that I enjoy working in, so I suspect I'll still be working in a lesser capacity well into my 60s or 70s.

If you're able to save and invest aggressively from a relatively young age, while also focusing on career advancement, you've already learned how this can benefit your finances. If you then use your skills to begin consulting at 65 and retire from your full-time job, you may be able to have a flexible schedule while you work from anywhere with an internet connection and enjoy additional income. Assuming you enjoy the consulting work, you might continue doing it well into your

70s. This example may represent an ideal glide path from full-time work into retirement that takes pressure off your nest egg so it has a greater opportunity to last into your 90s.

If the idea of working even part-time into your 70s sounds terrible to you, no big deal. Simply make that part of your long-term financial plan. I know plenty of people who retired in their 60s, never worked another day in their lives, and are projected to be fine financially all the way to age 95. My point is that meaningful work that brings both joy and money into your life in your 70s is a great way to keep your mind engaged and take pressure off creating a mountain of wealth before your retirement party. My grandmother worked until she was nearly 90, but not because she needed the money. She worked because she enjoyed seeing people, staying engaged, and keeping her mind sharp.

While you're young, finding a balance between wealth-building activities and focusing on your health is easy. It's the same concept we discussed in Chapter 2 regarding how much to save for your future. Once you know how much money you need to save each year to reach your financial goals, you can save that amount and spend the rest of your money on whatever you want. If you focus on your health first, spend the rest of your time on whatever you want. That extra time may include your full-time job and family responsibilities but remember the extra eight-hours concept. Even if you only have two hours per day left after family, work, and health, that's still enough to have a side business. In fact, that's more than enough to write your first book. By the way, if writing a book is something you've always wanted to do, I've shared some helpful resources and lessons I've personally learned at GrowthInfo.com/book.

Creating wealth is easier the earlier you start. It's a mistake to wait until you're 50 to start taking it seriously. The same can be said for your health. It's not something to focus on once your doctor tells you there's a problem. By then, you may not be able to reverse the negative effects. In his book *Outlive,* Peter Attia discusses the importance of focusing on health for our entire lives to delay what he calls the Four

Horsemen: heart disease, cancer, neurodegenerative disease (such as Alzheimer's and Parkinson's), and metabolic dysfunction. He says, "To achieve longevity — to live longer and live better for longer —we must understand and confront these causes of slow death." The key words there are slow death. He writes about how a sedentary lifestyle, poor diet, and high stress can accumulate over time and lead to these diseases. That means the time to plan for living a long life is when you're young, just as creating wealth should begin when you're young.

Aside from the long-term benefits of living a healthy life, you may also enjoy higher energy levels in the short term. If you want to have a bustling career or run a successful company, you'll need plenty of energy. Business leaders often face high amounts of stress that drain their energy and can affect their health. Richard Branson, the billionaire founder of Virgin Group, puts fitness first in his daily routine, often waking at 5:00 a.m. to play tennis, walk, run, or bike. During an interview with Thrive Global, he said, "As long as I get my exercise in, I very rarely feel burnt out. I've always managed to get a pretty good balance in my life with things like working from home with the family and having wonderful breaks with them."[38] Imagine the energy needed to accomplish what Branson has done over his lifetime. Virgin Group has tens of thousands of employees around the globe. He's founded companies in technology, transportation, hospitality, finance, music, and more. Fitness is one way Branson can keep his energy levels high so he can focus on more and more success.

If you're wondering how exercise gives you more energy when it sounds like you would have less energy, Toni Golen and Hope Ricciotti explain it in a *Harvard Medical* article. According to them, exercise spurs your body to produce more mitochondria in your muscle cells. They call mitochondria the powerhouses of cells and when you have more of them, they can increase your body's energy supply[39]. Exercising also boosts oxygen circulation in the body, which helps the body use energy more efficiently. Lastly, the doctors say exercise can boost hormone levels that make you feel more energized. This is why successful executives and business leaders often make fitness a priority in their routines — they can do *more* with *less* time by having the energy to focus on their goals. Think of fitness as a way to invest in your financial success.

Overall, I want you to be able to live a long, healthy life and enjoy the wealth you've accumulated over time. If you focus on your health during your younger years, you may also be reaping the benefits of higher energy and focus, which is needed if you plan on pushing yourself to the next level.

Chapter 16

Conclusion

I n the foreword of this book, I mentioned everyone should be able to walk away with at least one concept that can help make positive changes to their finances. If you've made it this far, I hope you've found multiple concepts that can help you. If finding financial success was easy, everyone would do it. But it's not. It's difficult. I meet so many people who make poor decisions with their money. They're not bad people. They're not uneducated. They're not lazy. It's quite the opposite. Many of these folks are good, educated, hard-working people. When it comes to money, they simply don't have the financial knowledge or the motivation to make good financial decisions. Now that you've read this book, you have more financial knowledge than before. Use it to your advantage. I also hope you've found motivation.

The next time you have a tough financial decision and your will-power isn't kicking in, remember this book as the voice of financial reason. Too many times I find people buy more home than they can afford. As you've learned, too much home can be a financial disaster over time. It robs from your ability to save, it wastes your precious time, and can even cause financial stress in a marriage. Too many times I find people buy expensive cars and borrow money to be able to afford them. This depreciation and debt will destroy wealth. If you have a goal of owning a sports car, I hope you buy it one day, but buy it once your bad debts are gone, you can pay with cash, and you're well on track with your other financial goals. Wise financial decisions take a combination of knowledge and willpower. Many times, they simply take willpower, so be honest with yourself as these forks in the road arise.

While you may not obsess over the concepts of compounding and time as I do, I hope you'll always remember that saving, investing, growing a business, and advancing a career are all more powerful when you start early. The snowball effect can be significant over a lifetime, but you must give it as much of your lifetime as possible to work.

If you want to have financial independence, but not necessarily significant wealth, I've given you multiple strategies to consider as you create your financial plan and work toward goals. If your goals include having significant wealth, business ownership and equity are the way to do it. If you have the means to borrow from a family member or bank, don't be afraid to borrow and buy an existing business. While starting a business from scratch can lead to limitless opportunity, buying an existing business means you have a track record already from the prior owner. There can be fewer unknowns when buying an existing business with loyal customers and tenured employees. If you can then expand the business, you may enjoy both the income and the equity growth from this business over time.

Insurance planning and estate planning aren't wealth-building topics. However, they're essential to the wealth-building toolkit. Without them, you may be leaving significant holes in your financial plan. The reason I have proper insurance and an updated estate plan are so I don't have to worry about those topics. My full attention and energy should be focused on advancing closer to my goals. Address these areas so you can move on to more exciting activities and know your loved ones are taken care of in the meantime.

If investing still seems like a confusing topic, don't feel like you need to be a CFP®. My hope is you've learned enough to have at least a basic understanding of investment concepts such as asset allocation and certain financial products. If you're second-guessing yourself about whether you're making the right investment decisions, hire an independent pro. There are some great financial professionals out there. It's just a matter of finding them.

Speaking of pros, surround yourself with other professionals as complex topics arise. It's not a matter of how, it's a matter of who.

Focusing on how to do something might waste weeks or months of your time and still not be optimal. Focus instead on who. Who can help you figure out your next challenge? It may be a CPA, a business coach, an attorney, or a consultant. Professionals cost money but can save you time. You can always make more money, but you can't make more time.

Lastly, if you do well financially over time, don't forget to give back. Giving back might mean helping a younger person learn the lessons you've learned. Giving back might mean donating to charity or helping a family in need. Giving back can come in many forms and helps make the world a better place. Give your time, talents, or treasure, but give at least something if you feel fortunate.

Thank you so much for taking the time to read this book. I hope you've enjoyed it as much as I enjoyed writing it. If you have questions, comments, or commendations, feel free to reach out at GrowthInfo. com. I wish you great health and wealth.

Endnotes

Foreword

1. "List of Countries by Number of Millionaires." *Wikipedia*, Wikimedia Foundation, last edited 26 Mar. 2024, https://en.wikipedia.org/wiki/List_of_countries_by_number_of_millionaires.

Chapter 1: Your Why

2. Kahneman, Daniel, and Angus Deaton. "High Income Improves Evaluation of Life but Not Emotional Well-being." *Proceedings of the National Academy of Sciences*, vol. 107, no. 38, 21 Sept. 2010, 16489-16493. *Princeton University*, https://www.princeton.edu/~deaton/downloads/deaton_kahneman_high_income_improves_evaluation_August2010.pdf.

Chapter 2: Rethinking the Basics

3. Amadeo, Kimberly. "Components of GDP Explained: 4 Critical Drivers of America's Economy." *The Balance*, reviewed by Brian Barnier, 2021, https://www.thebalance.com/components-of-gdp-explanation-formula-and-chart-3306015.

4. "Personal Saving Rate." *Federal Reserve Economic Data*, Federal Reserve Bank of St. Louis, 29 Mar. 2024, https://fred.stlouisfed.org/series/PSAVERT.

5. "How Long Should a Car Last?" *Autolist,* 11 May 2021, https://www.autolist.com/guides/how-long-should-car-last.

6. "List of Largest Houses in the United States." *Wikipedia*, Wikimedia Foundation, last edited 6 Apr. 2024, https://en.wikipedia.org/wiki/List_of_largest_houses_in_the_United_States.

7.   Perry, Mark J. "New US Homes Today are 1,000 Square Feet Larger than in 1973 and Living Space per Person has Nearly Doubled." *American Enterprise Institute*, 5 June 2016, https://www.aei.org/carpe-diem/new-us-homes-today-are-1000-square-feet-larger-than-in-1973-and-living-space-per-person-has-nearly-doubled/.

8.   Schmall, Tyler. "Americans Would Rather Go to Jail than Figure Out a Budget." *New York Post,* 8 Jan. 2019, https://nypost.com/2019/01/08/americans-would-rather-go-to-jail-than-figure-out-a-budget/.

9.   "New Survey Shows Consumers, No Matter Their Income or Assets, Need Support with Spending, Household Budgeting." *Certified Financial Planner Board,* 23 Jan. 2019, https://www.cfp.net/news/2019/01/new-survey-shows-consumers-no-matter-their-income-or-assets-need-support-with-spending-household.

10. McCann, Adam. "Average Credit Card Debt." *WalletHub,* 15 Mar. 2024, https://wallethub.com/edu/cc/average-credit-card-debt/25533.

11. "Dow Jones – DJIA – 100 Year Historical Chart." *Macrotrends,* https://www.macrotrends.net/1319/dow-jones-100-year-historical-chart.

12. Kalbacher, JZ, and D. Deare. "Farm Population of the United States, 1985." *National Library of Medicine: National Center for Biotechnology Information,* National Institute of Health, no. 59, July 1986, pp. 1-20. *PubMed,* https://pubmed.ncbi.nlm.nih.gov/12314701/.

13. "The American Expeditionary Forces." *Stars and Stripes: The American Soldiers' Newspaper of World War I, 1918 to 1919,* Library of Congress, https://www.loc.gov/collections/stars-and-stripes/articles-and-essays/a-world-at-war/american-expeditionary-forces/.

14. Ventura, Luca. "The World's Most Indebted Companies 2023." *Global Finance,* 22 Feb. 2023, https://www.gfmag.com/global-data/economic-data/companies-largest-debt-world.

Chapter 3: Insurance

15. "Road Accidents in the United States." *Driver Knowledge*, https://www.driverknowledge.com/road-accidents-usa/. Accessed 19 Apr. 2024.

16. "Fact Sheet: Social Security." Social Security Administration, https://www.ssa.gov/news/press/factsheets/colafacts2022.pdf. Accessed 20 Apr. 2024.

Chapter 5: Tax Planning

17. Office of the Law Revision Counsel. "Current Release Point: Public Law 118-47." U.S. House of Representatives, 23 Mar. 2024, https://uscode.house.gov/download/download.shtml.

18. Sze, Ryan. "Some of the Largest Roth IRAs in Existence—and What You Can Learn from Them." *The Motley Fool,* 2 Aug. 2022, https://www.fool.com/investing/2022/08/02/some-of-the-largest-roth-iras-in-existence-and-wha/.

Chapter 6: Retirement Planning

19. O'Neill, Aaron. "Life Expectancy (from birth) in the United States, from 1860-2020." *Statista,* 2 Feb. 2024, https://www.statista.com/statistics/1040079/life-expectancy-united-states-all-time/.

20. "Pensions in the United States." *Wikipedia,* Wikimedia Foundation, last edited 18 July 2023, https://en.wikipedia.org/wiki/Pensions_in_the_United_States.

21. "Why Were 401(k) Plans Created?" *Investopedia,* reviewed by David Kindness and fact checked by Amanda Jackson, 10 Aug. 2021, https://www.investopedia.com/ask/answers/100314/why-were-401k-plans-created.asp.

Chapter 7: Investing

22. "Bill Bartmann." *Wikipedia,* Wikimedia Foundation, 28 Aug. 2023, https://en.wikipedia.org/wiki/Bill_Bartmann.

23. Statista Research Department. "Mutual Funds – Statistics & Facts." *Statista,* 10 Jan. 2024, https://www.statista.com/topics/1441/mutual-funds/.

Chapter 8: Creating a Financial Plan

24. "How Hard is the CFP® Exam?" *Kaplan Financial Education,* 26 Mar. 2021, https://www.kaplanfinancial.com/resources/getting-started/how-hard-is-the-cfp-exam.

25. "Life Expectancy Chart (United States of America)." *Data Commons,* Google, https://datacommons.org/tools/timeline#&place=country/USA&statsVar=LifeExpectancy_Person.

26. Dahl, Gordon, et al. "Linking Changes in Inequality in Life Expectancy and Mortality: Evidence from Denmark and the United States." *National Bureau of Economic Research,* July 2020, https://www.nber.org/system/files/working_papers/w27509/w27509.pdf.

Chapter 9: The Compound Career Path

27. Dubina, Kevin S., et al. "Projections Overview and Highlights, 2021-31." *Monthly Labor Review,* U.S. Bureau of Labor Statistics, 8 Nov. 2022, https://www.bls.gov/opub/mlr/2022/article/projections-overview-and-highlights-2021-31.htm.

28. "Wage Growth Tracker." *Center for Human Capital Studies,* Federal Reserve Bank of Atlanta, 10 Apr. 2024, https://www.frbatlanta.org/chcs/wage-growth-tracker?panel=1.

29. "Real Personal Income by State and Metropolitan Area, 2019." *Bureau of Economic Analysis,* U.S. Department of Commerce, 15 Dec. 2020, https://www.bea.gov/news/2020/real-personal-income-state-and-metropolitan-area-2019.

Chapter 10: Network for Net Worth

30. Peters, Bethany L., and Edward Stringham. "No Booze? You May Lose: Why Drinkers Earn More Money than Nondrinkers." *Reason Foundation,* 1 Sept. 2006, https://reason.org/policy-brief/no-booze-you-may-lose/.

31. "Top 10 CEOs Who Started as Sales Reps." *SmartWinnr,* 9 June 2018, https://www.smartwinnr.com/post/top10-ceos-who-started-as-sales-reps/.

Chapter 11: The Side Hustle

32. "Profile: Craig Newmark." *Forbes,* 7 Apr. 2020, https://www.forbes.com/profile/craig-newmark/.

33. "Yankee Candle." *Wikipedia,* Wikimedia Foundation, last edited 27 Feb. 2024, https://en.wikipedia.org/wiki/Yankee_Candle.

Chapter 13: Business Ownership

34. Najjar, Dana. "Who's Better Off: Employed or Self-Employed Physicians?" *Medscape,* 2 Sept. 2020, https://www.medscape.com/viewarticle/936731#vp_1.

35. "Frequently Asked Questions About Small Business." *Office of Advocacy*, U.S. Small Business Administration, Aug. 2018, https://advocacy.sba.gov/wp-content/uploads/2017/08/Frequently-Asked-Questions-Small-Business-2018.pdf.

36. Hippie, Steven F., and Laurel A. Hammond. "Self-Employment in the United States." U.S. Bureau of Labor Statistics, Mar. 2016, https://www.bls.gov/spotlight/2016/self-employment-in-the-united-states/pdf/self-employment-in-the-united-states.pdf.

Chapter 15: The Health-Wealth Connection

37. "GHE: Life Expectancy and Healthy Life Expectancy." *The Global Health Observatory,* World Health Organization, https://www.who.int/data/gho/data/themes/mortality-and-global-health-estimates/ghe-life-expectancy-and-healthy-life-expectancy.

38. Nguyen, Hao. "Richard Branson: Daily Routine." *Balance the Grind,* 10 July 2020, https://balancethegrind.co/daily-routines/richard-branson-daily-routine/.

39. Golen, Toni, and Hope Ricciotti. "Does exercise really boost energy levels?" *Harvard Health Publishing,* Harvard Medical School, 1 July 2021, https://www.health.harvard.edu/exercise-and-fitness/does-exercise-really-boost-energy-levels.

www.ingramcontent.com/pod-product-compliance
Lightning Source LLC
Chambersburg PA
CBHW071553210326
41597CB00019B/3222